Undergraduate Topics in Computer Science

Series Editor

Ian Mackie, University of Sussex, Brighton, UK

Advisory Editors

Samson Abramsky ⓘ, Department of Computer Science, University of Oxford, Oxford, UK

Chris Hankin ⓘ, Department of Computing, Imperial College London, London, UK

Mike Hinchey ⓘ, Lero—The Irish Software Research Centre, University of Limerick, Limerick, Ireland

Dexter C. Kozen, Department of Computer Science, Cornell University, Ithaca, USA

Hanne Riis Nielson ⓘ, Department of Applied Mathematics and Computer Science, Technical University of Denmark, Kongens Lyngby, Denmark

Steven S. Skiena, Department of Computer Science, Stony Brook University, Stony Brook, USA

Iain Stewart ⓘ, Department of Computer Science, Durham University, Durham, UK

Joseph Migga Kizza, Engineering and Computer Science, University of Tennessee at Chattanooga, Chattanooga, USA

Roy Crole, School of Computing and Mathematics Sciences, University of Leicester, Leicester, UK

Elizabeth Scott, Department of Computer Science, Royal Holloway University of London, Egham, UK

'Undergraduate Topics in Computer Science' (UTiCS) delivers high-quality instructional content for undergraduates studying in all areas of computing and information science. From core foundational and theoretical material to final-year topics and applications, UTiCS books take a fresh, concise, and modern approach and are ideal for self-study or for a one- or two-semester course. The texts are authored by established experts in their fields, reviewed by an international advisory board, and contain numerous examples and problems, many of which include fully worked solutions.

The UTiCS concept centers on high-quality, ideally and generally quite concise books in softback format. For advanced undergraduate textbooks that are likely to be longer and more expository, Springer continues to offer the highly regarded *Texts in Computer Science* series, to which we refer potential authors.

Fuchun Guo · Willy Susilo · Khoa Nguyen · Xiaofeng Chen · Zhen Zhao

Introduction to Cryptographic Definitions

A Step-by-Step Guide for Beginners

Fuchun Guo
School of Computing and Information Technology
University of Wollongong
Wollongong, NSW, Australia

Khoa Nguyen
School of Computing and Information Technology
University of Wollongong
Wollongong, NSW, Australia

Zhen Zhao
School of Cyber Engineering
Xidian University
Xi An, China

Willy Susilo
School of Computing and Information Technology
University of Wollongong
Wollongong, NSW, Australia

Xiaofeng Chen
School of Cyber Engineering
Xidian University
Xi An, China

ISSN 1863-7310   ISSN 2197-1781   (electronic)
Undergraduate Topics in Computer Science
ISBN 978-3-031-91968-8   ISBN 978-3-031-91969-5   (eBook)
https://doi.org/10.1007/978-3-031-91969-5

© The Editor(s) (if applicable) and The Author(s), under exclusive license to Springer Nature Switzerland AG 2025

This work is subject to copyright. All rights are solely and exclusively licensed by the Publisher, whether the whole or part of the material is concerned, specifically the rights of translation, reprinting, reuse of illustrations, recitation, broadcasting, reproduction on microfilms or in any other physical way, and transmission or information storage and retrieval, electronic adaptation, computer software, or by similar or dissimilar methodology now known or hereafter developed.
The use of general descriptive names, registered names, trademarks, service marks, etc. in this publication does not imply, even in the absence of a specific statement, that such names are exempt from the relevant protective laws and regulations and therefore free for general use.
The publisher, the authors and the editors are safe to assume that the advice and information in this book are believed to be true and accurate at the date of publication. Neither the publisher nor the authors or the editors give a warranty, expressed or implied, with respect to the material contained herein or for any errors or omissions that may have been made. The publisher remains neutral with regard to jurisdictional claims in published maps and institutional affiliations.

This Springer imprint is published by the registered company Springer Nature Switzerland AG
The registered company address is: Gewerbestrasse 11, 6330 Cham, Switzerland

If disposing of this product, please recycle the paper.

To

**Australian Government**
Australian Research Council

(FT220100046, FL230100033)

Preface

Definition is the first step in everything, from understanding the philosophical meaning of life to conducting scientific research. This book is written for anyone who seeks to understand (1) what a formal definition of a cryptographic primitive (e.g., encryption, digital signatures, zero-knowledge proofs, and multi-party computations) means, (2) why it is defined this way, and (3) how a definition is proposed.

Definition, construction, and security proofs are the three essential pillars of cryptologic research. Among these, definition is the foundation, and the rest of them cannot be effectively developed without a clear definition. However, formal cryptographic definitions are rather complex and abstract. Take the security definition of digital signatures as an example.

> *A digital signature scheme is (t, q, ϵ)-secure in the EUF-CMA security model if no probabilistic polynomial-time adversary can win in this security model with advantage ϵ in time t after making at most q signature queries, where ϵ is a negligible function in security parameter κ and is taken over all internal coin tosses of related algorithms.*

Beginners in cryptology should know the meaning of each word but would probably fail to understand what the whole definition says. Not to mention the difficulty in proposing well-founded definitions for new cryptographic primitives when conducting cryptographic research. It would be helpful if there were a step-by-step reference that systematically introduced cryptographic definitions.

In this book, we introduce the learning curve of formal cryptographic definitions that appear in textbooks or research papers. Specifically,

- **What:** We introduce all essential knowledge needed to understand key elements (notions, syntax, and terms) as components in cryptographic definitions. The introduction will help beginners understand the complete meaning of a cryptographic definition.
- **Why:** We explain why a cryptographic primitive is defined in this way using these elements and not others, even if they represent similar ideas.

- **How:** We explain how cryptographic definitions are developed. We hope that after reading this book, beginners will be able to validate and propose definitions for new cryptographic primitives.

To gain a comprehensive understanding of definitions, we have traced foundational knowledge all the way back to concepts like sets in mathematics. We have made an effort to fold non-essential details, progressively introducing all relevant elements from the mathematical basics to how formal definitions are structured. Along the way, we introduce several intermediate concepts (unique in this book) to ensure a smooth learning curve. Our introduction to definitions, therefore, will be beginner-friendly, focusing on an insightful overview.

How to use this book. The chapters in this book are organized as follows.

- Chapter 1 provides a brief overview on definitions, including structures and components. We encourage all readers to take a look at it.
- Chapters 2, 3, and 4 introduce concise explanations covering topics ranging from mathematics to computational complexity. You can skip these chapters if you are already familiar with these concepts.
- Chapter 5 is a transition chapter. It revisits fundamental concepts and emphasizes the key concept of "probabilistic polynomial-time algorithms". It also delivers a key principle: defining a cryptographic primitive must consider both usability for users and security against adversaries.
- Chapter 6 introduces the syntax definitions of cryptographic primitives. A correct syntax definition ensures that any proposed construction (such as a scheme or a protocol) for a cryptographic primitive meeting the syntax definition should provide usability for users.
- Chapter 7 introduces the security definitions of cryptographic primitives. A security definition ensures that any proposed construction (such as a scheme or a protocol) for a cryptographic primitive meeting the security definition should provide security against adversaries. Chapters 6 and 7 are the most important chapters of this book as they form the core of cryptographic definitions in this book.
- Chapter 8 provides other readings that do not fit neatly into the previous chapters. It mainly revisits the relationship of some concepts from different chapters.

At the end of each chapter, we have included some questions for review and exercises. Practice makes perfect, and we firmly believe in it.

Thanks & Regards,

Fuchun, Willy, Khoa, Xiaofeng, Zhen

21 March 2025

Acknowledgements

The writing of this book dates back to February 2020, during the Covid lockdown. We initially started with mathematics and complexity theory to help beginners understand the meaning of security definitions in modern cryptography but lacked a clear direction, leading to the project's suspension for more than three years. The first version, completed in August 2020, was only 110 pages long. After years of reflection and refinement, by early 2024, the direction became clear particularly in defining syntax and security, and we decided to continue and complete it. It took about two years in total to finish writing this book.

Writing a book is always time-consuming and challenging. In particular, consistency is a nightmare, and we revised it again and again until we were significantly sick of checking it. For example, changing the presentation of the syntax definition for one cryptographic primitive required changing more than 20 other syntax definitions. However, once the final version was completed, we were truly proud of it. We achieved something that had never been done in our cryptology community. Completing this book was much more exciting than solving an open problem recognized by the picky PC members of IACR conferences. We would likely do it again if another exciting book project arises.

We would like to first thank all researchers in cryptology and complexity, especially the authors whose work has been cited or mentioned in this book. Without their contributions, this book would not have been possible.

The next person we would like to thank is Yiwen Shi, who provided us with valuable feedback. She is a third-year PhD candidate at Xidian University and is currently a visiting student at the University of Wollongong. She was the only person we asked to proofread and evaluate the draft. She has identified hundreds of typos in the draft. Her personality, attitude, and professionalism demonstrate that she has the potential to be a strong co-author in the future.

We would also like to thank Wayne Wheeler, the Springer senior editor we contacted regarding the publication of this book. After the draft was nearly completed in early November 2024, we contacted Wayne, who actively and kindly provided numerous constructive comments on both the book structure and its contents. We are also grateful to the anonymous reviewers of this book. Their comments were invaluable, helping us identify important oversights in the early version. It took us over ten days to address their suggestions.

Thanks to AI, it is now much easier for non-native English speakers to write an English book compared to 2018, when *Introduction to Security Reduction* was published. We would like to express our gratitude to ChatGPT, Grok, DeepSeek, and Copilot for helping us identify grammatical issues and suggest revisions. This allowed us to focus on content and logic without worrying about silly grammatical issues.

Finally, we must thank ourselves, the five authors of this book. Without our effective collaboration, this book would not have been completed. We would also like to thank our affiliations, the University of Wollongong and Xidian University, which have provided us the freedom to do whatever we like. Special thanks from Fuchun and Willy are extended to the ARC, as acknowledged in the dedication.

We have tried our best to ensure accuracy, but some typos or poor explanations must still remain. To facilitate corrections for this book, we have provided a link (`http://documents.uow.edu.au/~fuchun/itcd.txt`). This link will remain active unless the university discontinues the service or Fuchun is unable to return to Earth.

Looking back on the entire process of writing this book, the most challenging period while completing this book was around Christmas 2024. We struggled to revise the introduction on the security modelling for a new cryptographic primitive. Despite numerous attempts, we could not come up with a convincing step-by-step modelling approach until January 10, 2025. During those days, we hardly slept well, let alone enjoyed the long holiday break. Completing this book has been a challenging journey, but it helped us realize we have strived for what we love with all our effort and pursued the ultimate, though the result is still not perfect. Through this process, we have experienced significant personal growth. Perhaps, this is the underlying motivation behind why we want to write books and also reflects our definition of the meaning of life.

Thanks & Regards,
Fuchun Guo (On Behalf of All Authors)
21 March 2025

Contents

1 Overview of Cryptographic Definitions 1
   1.1 Cryptographic Definitions in This Book 1
   1.2 Difficulties of Understanding Cryptographic Definitions 3
   1.3 Structure and Components 4
       1.3.1 From Mathematics Up to Cryptography 4
       1.3.2 Notation 5
       1.3.3 Syntax 6
       1.3.4 Term 7
   1.4 Intensional and Extensional Definitions 7
   1.5 Another Type of Definitions in Modern Cryptography 8

2 Mathematics 11
   2.1 Set and Function 11
       2.1.1 What are $a \in S$ and $F(x) = y$? 11
       2.1.2 The Meaning of "=" 12
       2.1.3 Mathematical Sets in Modern Cryptography 13
       2.1.4 Sets Defined by Functions 13
       2.1.5 Family of Sets 14
   2.2 Computing Problems 14
       2.2.1 Relation Function $R(x, y)$ 14
       2.2.2 Computing Problems: Definition 15
       2.2.3 Computing Problems: $\{(x, y) : R(x, y) = 1\}$ 16
       2.2.4 Computing Problems: Classifications.................... 16
       2.2.5 Decision Problems and Formal Languages 18
       2.2.6 How to Classify Computing Problems 19
   2.3 Event, Probability, Distribution, and Sampling 20
       2.3.1 Event and Probability: $\Pr[x_1; x_2 : A]$ 20
       2.3.2 Distribution and Sampling: $a \in_U S, b \in_D S$ 21
   2.4 Review Questions 22

3 Computing Machines ... 23
- 3.1 Solving Problems with Computing Machines ... 23
  - 3.1.1 Historical Development of Computing Machines ... 23
  - 3.1.2 From Machine to Algorithm ... 24
  - 3.1.3 Definition of Solving a Computing Problem ... 25
  - 3.1.4 Computational Result: $y \leftarrow \mathcal{A}(x)$ ... 26
  - 3.1.5 Deterministic and Probabilistic Algorithms ... 27
  - 3.1.6 Success Probability in Probabilistic Algorithms ... 27
  - 3.1.7 Why Computational Model Matters ... 28
  - 3.1.8 $\exists \mathcal{A} \in S_\mathcal{C}$ and $\forall \mathcal{A} \in S_\mathcal{C}$ ... 30
- 3.2 Computational Models: Background and Preliminaries ... 31
  - 3.2.1 Overview ... 31
  - 3.2.2 Toy Example ... 32
  - 3.2.3 Turing Machine in 1930s ... 33
  - 3.2.4 Turing Tape ... 34
  - 3.2.5 Instruction and Turing State ... 36
  - 3.2.6 Transition Function ... 37
- 3.3 Computational Models: Turing Machines ... 38
  - 3.3.1 Turing Machines ... 38
  - 3.3.2 Deterministic Turing Machines ... 39
  - 3.3.3 Probabilistic Turing Machines ... 40
  - 3.3.4 Non-Deterministic Turing Machines ... 40
  - 3.3.5 Quantum Turing Machines ... 41
  - 3.3.6 Comparisons of Different Turing Machines ... 41
- 3.4 The Church–Turing Thesis: Equivalent Capabilities ... 42
- 3.5 How to Classify Computing Problems, Revisited ... 43
- 3.6 Review Questions ... 45

4 Computational Complexity ... 47
- 4.1 Roadmap: We Are Here ... 47
- 4.2 Solving Problems: From Cost to Complexity ... 49
  - 4.2.1 Computational Cost ... 49
  - 4.2.2 Concrete Cost and General Cost ... 50
  - 4.2.3 Case Selection and Growth Rate ... 51
  - 4.2.4 Growth Class ... 52
  - 4.2.5 Growth Classes: Big O ... 54
  - 4.2.6 Growth Classes: Big Ω ... 56
  - 4.2.7 Growth Classes: Big Θ ... 57
  - 4.2.8 Growth Class: Polynomial Time $O(n^k)$ ... 58
- 4.3 Computational Models: Adding Complexity ... 59
  - 4.3.1 Polynomial-Time Turing Machines ... 59
  - 4.3.2 Polynomial-Size Circuit Family ... 60
- 4.4 Complexity Class (1): Classifying Computing Problems ... 63
  - 4.4.1 $\mathcal{P}$ and $\mathcal{NP}$ ... 63
  - 4.4.2 $\mathcal{BPP}$, $\mathcal{BQP}$, and $\mathcal{P}_{/poly}$ ... 65

Contents   xiii

	4.5	Complexity Class (2): Adding Reduction	67
		4.5.1 Reduction in Complexity Theory	67
		4.5.2 $y \leftarrow \mathcal{A}^{\mathcal{B}}(x)$	68
		4.5.3 Cook Reduction	69
		4.5.4 Karp Reduction and Levin Reduction	70
		4.5.5 $\mathcal{NP}$-Complete, $\mathcal{NP}$-Intermediate, and $\mathcal{NP}$-Hard	71
	4.6	The Extended Church–Turing Thesis: Equivalent Efficiency	72
	4.7	How to Classify Computing Problems, Summary	73
	4.8	Review Questions	74
5	**From Computational Complexity to Cryptography: Transition**		77
	5.1	Computational Complexity, Revisited	77
		5.1.1 Turing Machines ≈ Algorithms	77
		5.1.2 Algorithms and Solve	78
		5.1.3 Cost Measurement and Complexity	79
		5.1.4 Probabilistic Polynomial-Time Algorithms	81
	5.2	Cryptography and Its Algorithms	82
		5.2.1 Concepts Clarification	82
		5.2.2 Cryptography Principle: Use and Abuse	84
		5.2.3 Case Study: Key Generation Algorithm	85
		5.2.4 Guideline for Definitions	86
		5.2.5 Key Characteristic in Usability and Security: Algorithms ...	87
		5.2.6 Probabilistic Polynomial-Time Algorithms for Cryptography	88
	5.3	Summary and Roadmap	88
	5.4	Review Questions	90
6	**Cryptographic Primitives: Syntax Definitions**		91
	6.1	Role of Syntax Definition	91
	6.2	Probabilistic Polynomial-Time Algorithms for Users	92
		6.2.1 Randomized Operation, Efficiency, and Correctness	92
		6.2.2 Formulating Probability for Correctness	94
		6.2.3 Why Randomized Operations Matter	95
	6.3	Inputs and Entities of Cryptographic Algorithms	96
		6.3.1 What Can an Input Be?	96
		6.3.2 Who Can an Entity Be?	98
	6.4	Syntax Definition for a New Cryptographic Primitive	99
		6.4.1 From Scenario to Proof of Concept	100
		6.4.2 Directions of Syntax Definition	103
		6.4.3 Limitations of Syntax Definition	104
		6.4.4 Subtle Differences of Syntax Definition	105
		6.4.5 Classifications of Cryptographic Algorithms	106
	6.5	From Scenario to Proof of Concept: Examples	107
		6.5.1 Identity-Based Encryption	108
		6.5.2 Online/Offline Identity-Based Encryption	109
		6.5.3 Broadcast Identity-Based Encryption	110

		6.5.4	Fuzzy Identity-Based Encryption 111

- 6.5.4 Fuzzy Identity-Based Encryption 111
- 6.5.5 Functional Identity-Based Encryption 113
- 6.5.6 Traitor-Tracing Identity-Based Encryption 114
- 6.5.7 Revocable Identity-Based Encryption 115
- 6.5.8 Hierarchical Identity-Based Encryption 117
- 6.5.9 Server-Aided Identity-Based Encryption 118
- 6.5.10 Threshold Identity-Based Encryption 120
- 6.5.11 Key-Aggregate Identity-Based Encryption 121
- 6.5.12 Re-Encryptable Identity-Based Encryption 123
- 6.5.13 Homomorphic Identity-Based Encryption 124
- 6.5.14 Searchable Identity-Based Encryption 126
- 6.5.15 Testable Identity-Based Encryption 127
- 6.5.16 Membership Identity-Based Encryption 129
- 6.5.17 Escrow-Free Identity-Based Encryption 130
- 6.5.18 Decentralized Identity-Based Encryption 131
- 6.5.19 Accountable Identity-Based Encryption 133
- 6.5.20 Registered Identity-Based Encryption 135
- 6.6 Algorithmic Functions and Explanations 136
  - 6.6.1 Algorithms for Keying Something 137
  - 6.6.2 Algorithms for Combining Something 138
  - 6.6.3 Algorithms for Seeing Something 139
  - 6.6.4 Algorithms for Getting Something 141
- 6.7 How to Define Syntax for a New Cryptographic Primitive 142
- 6.8 Scheme or Protocol? 144
  - 6.8.1 Differences 144
  - 6.8.2 Syntax Definitions for Protocols 145
  - 6.8.3 Mixture of Scheme and Protocol 146
- 6.9 Practice Makes Perfect: Exercises 148

7 Cryptographic Primitives: Security Definitions 153
- 7.1 Role of Security Definition 153
- 7.2 Defining Security for It: In General 154
  - 7.2.1 1st Attempt at Definition: Initial 155
  - 7.2.2 2nd Attempt at Definition: PPT Adversaries 156
  - 7.2.3 3rd Attempt at Definition: Non-Negligible 157
  - 7.2.4 4th Attempt at Definition: Sampling 158
  - 7.2.5 5th Attempt at Definition: Security Model 160
  - 7.2.6 6th Attempt at Definition: Advantage 162
  - 7.2.7 PPT Adversaries, Revisited 163
- 7.3 Security Model, Revisited 164
  - 7.3.1 Role of Security Model 164
  - 7.3.2 Adversaries from Entities 165
  - 7.3.3 Input, Output, and Success Condition 166
  - 7.3.4 Characteristics of Outputs: Hidden Target or Learn Nothing 167
  - 7.3.5 Characteristics of Inputs: The Need of Oracles 168

Contents

- 7.3.6 Directions of Modelling 169
- 7.3.7 Formulating Probability for Breaking 170
- 7.3.8 Security Property and Security Notion 171
- 7.4 Defining Security for Non-Interactive Algorithms 172
  - 7.4.1 Algorithm Classifications 172
  - 7.4.2 Adversary and Security Goal 173
  - 7.4.3 Security Models for Public Keying Algorithms 174
  - 7.4.4 Security Models for Secret Keying Algorithms 174
  - 7.4.5 Security Models for Public Combining Algorithms 175
  - 7.4.6 Security Models for Secret Combining Algorithms 177
  - 7.4.7 Security Models for Public Seeing Algorithms 179
  - 7.4.8 Security Models for Secret Seeing Algorithms 181
- 7.5 Security Definition for a Cryptographic Primitive (Scheme) 182
  - 7.5.1 Challenges of Security Modelling 182
  - 7.5.2 Overview of Security Modelling 183
  - 7.5.3 Security Requirements 183
  - 7.5.4 Security Attacks 185
  - 7.5.5 Element Security 186
  - 7.5.6 Model Implication 187
  - 7.5.7 User Implication 188
  - 7.5.8 Security Modelling: First Phase 188
  - 7.5.9 Security Modelling: Second Phase 191
  - 7.5.10 Security Modelling: Third Phase 195
  - 7.5.11 Discussions on Modelling 196
  - 7.5.12 Ways of Presenting Security Models 196
- 7.6 Defining Security for Interactive Algorithms 200
  - 7.6.1 Algorithm Abstraction 200
  - 7.6.2 Adversary and Security Goal 201
  - 7.6.3 Hidden-Target Security for $Alg(x_1; x_2) \to (y, y)$ 202
  - 7.6.4 Learn-Nothing Security for $Alg(x_1; x_2) \to (y_1, y_2)$ 203
  - 7.6.5 Hidden-Target Security for $Alg(x_1; x_2) \to (y_1, y_2)$ 204
- 7.7 Security Definition for a Cryptographic Primitive (Protocol) 205
  - 7.7.1 Security Model, Revisited 205
  - 7.7.2 Important Lemma 206
  - 7.7.3 Real-Ideal World Paradigm 207
  - 7.7.4 Look-Real-but-Simulated-from-Ideal World 208
  - 7.7.5 Semi-Honest Security 209
  - 7.7.6 Malicious Security 211
  - 7.7.7 Comparison of Semi-Honest and Malicious 212
- 7.8 Practice Makes Perfect: Exercises 214

8 Other Readings ... 217
8.1 Definitions: Incomplete by Design ... 217
8.2 $\mathcal{P} = \mathcal{NP}$ and Cryptography ... 218
8.3 Clarifying Algorithmic Terms ... 219
8.4 Security Definition, Revisited ... 220
8.5 Cryptographic Definition, Revisited ... 221

References ... 223

About the Authors

Fuchun Guo received his Ph.D. degree in Computer Science from the University of Wollongong, Australia. He is an Associate Professor at the School of Computing and Information Technology at the University of Wollongong. He has been recognized as an ARC DECRA Fellow (2017–2019) and an ARC Future Fellow (2023–2026) by the Australian Research Council (ARC) for his significant contributions to cryptography. His main research interests include security proofs and research philosophy in modern cryptography. His work has been widely published, with peer-reviewed research papers appearing in international conferences and journals such as CRYPTO, EUROCRYPT, and ASIACRYPT, as well as two books: Introduction to Security Reduction (Springer) and Cryptologic Research History of Digital Signatures: From 1976 to 2020 (in Chinese). He has served as a program committee member in numerous international conferences.

Willy Susilo received his Ph.D. degree in Computer Science from University of Wollongong, Australia. He is a Distinguished Professor and the Head of School of Computing and Information Technology and the director of Institute of Cybersecurity and Cryptology (iC2) at the University of Wollongong. Recently, he was awarded an Australian Laureate Fellowship, which is the most prestigious award in Australia, due to his contribution in cloud computing security. He was previously awarded a prestigious ARC Future Fellow by the Australian Research Council (ARC) and the Researcher of the Year award in 2016 by the University of Wollongong. He is a Fellow of IEEE, Australian Computer Society (ACS), IET and AAAI. His main research interests include cybersecurity, cryptography and information security. His work has been cited more than 25,000 times in Google Scholar. He is the Editor-in-Chief of the Elsevier Computer Standards and Interfaces, SciLight Pragmatic Cybersecurity and the MDPI Information journal. He has served as a program committee member in dozens of international conferences. He is currently serving as an Associate Editors in several international journals, including IEEE Transactions in Dependable and Secure Computing. Previously, he has served in many top tier journals, such as IEEE Transactions in Information Forensics and Security. He has published more than 500 research papers in the area of cybersecurity and cryptology.

Khoa Nguyen received his Ph.D. degree in Cryptography from Nanyang Technological University, Singapore, in 2014. He is a Senior Lecturer at the Institute of Cybersecurity and Cryptology at the University of Wollongong, Australia. Previously, he held prestigious positions including Presidential Postdoctoral Fellow (2018–2020) and Senior Research Fellow (2020–2021) at Nanyang Technological University. His contributions to cryptography have been recognized through awards such as the Singapore International Graduate Award (2009–2013) and his selection as an Invited Participant at the Second Commonwealth Science Conference in 2017. His main research interests include cryptography, cybersecurity, and information security. His work has been cited over 1977 times with an h-index of 22 (Google Scholar, August 2024), and he has published more than 50 peer-reviewed papers in refereed journals and conferences, including top-tier venues such as ASIACRYPT, CRYPTO, EUROCRYPT, and PKC. Nguyen is an emerging leader in the cryptography research community, having served as Program Committee Co-chair for ProvSec 2020 and ACISP 2022, Area Chair for ASIACRYPT 2023, and Workshop Chair for AsiaCCS 2025. He has been a program committee member for over 45 international conferences, including nine IACR flagship events, and is a member of the ASIACRYPT Steering Committee.

Xiaofeng Chen received his B.S. and M.S. degrees in Mathematics from Northwest University, China, in 1998 and 2000, respectively, and his Ph.D. degree in Cryptography from Xidian University in 2003. He is currently a HUASHAN Leading Professor at Xidian University. His research interests include applied cryptography, cloud computing security, and AI security. He has published over 300 research papers in refereed international conferences and journals, with his work cited more than 18,000 times on Google Scholar. He serves on the editorial boards of several prestigious journals, including IEEE Transactions on Dependable and Secure Computing, IEEE Transactions on Knowledge and Data Engineering, and the International Journal of Foundations of Computer Science. He has also served as a program or general chair or program committee member for over 30 international conferences. He is a Fellow of IEEE and AAIA.

Zhen Zhao received her Ph.D. degree in Cryptography from Xidian University, China. She is currently an Associate Professor at the School of Cyber Engineering, Xidian University. Her research focuses on public-key cryptography, with an emphasis on security proofs, digital signatures, and encryption schemes. She has led and participated in several national research projects on public-key encryption techniques. She actively serves as a program committee member for numerous international conferences and contributes to the advancement of cryptographic research through her publications and projects. She was a joint Ph.D. student at the School of Computing and Information Technology, University of Wollongong, Australia, from July 2017 to August 2019, and later a visiting scholar there from March 2024 to March 2025.

Chapter 1
Overview of Cryptographic Definitions

Abstract A definition is a statement that explains the meaning of a term, word, concept, or idea. It serves to clarify and provide a precise understanding of the subject. In modern cryptography, cryptographic definitions are adopted to formally introduce new cryptographic concepts to the community. This chapter provides an overview of cryptographic definitions, introducing the structures and components of this kind of definitions.

1.1 Cryptographic Definitions in This Book

In cryptology, no matter it is cryptography or cryptanalysis, the subject mostly refers to an $\mathcal{X}$-secure $\mathcal{Y}$.

> **? Question**
>
> *What is $\mathcal{X}$-secure $\mathcal{Y}$?*

In this book, we refer to "$\mathcal{X}$-secure $\mathcal{Y}$" as a cryptographic concept. Here, $\mathcal{Y}$ denotes a cryptographic primitive such as digital signatures, public-key encryption, zero-knowledge proofs, or multi-party computations, while $\mathcal{X}$ denotes a security description. To formally answer this question, researchers typically use cryptographic definitions. Cryptographic definitions are precise and formal expressions of cryptographic concepts. They employ carefully defined notations, syntax, and terms within a framework of commonly accepted terminology rules. These definitions serve as the foundational language that enable clear communication and understanding in modern cryptography.

Cryptographic definitions for concepts like "$\mathcal{X}$-secure $\mathcal{Y}$" are often complex and typically presented in two segments in academic literature. The first segment defines the primitive $\mathcal{Y}$ without addressing its security, while the second segment outlines the $\mathcal{X}$-security notion for the primitive $\mathcal{Y}$. We use digital signatures as an example to explain what a cryptographic definition is in two segments as follows.

Definition 1.1.1 (Digital Signatures). *A digital signature scheme is composed of the following three probabilistic polynomial-time (PPT) algorithms fulfilling correctness.*

- KeyGen(1^κ) $\to$ (pk, sk): *The PPT key generation algorithm takes as input a security parameter κ, and returns a key pair denoted by (pk, sk), where pk denotes a public key and sk denotes a secret key.*
- Sign(sk, m) $\to \sigma_m$: *The PPT signing algorithm takes as input sk and a message $m \in \mathcal{M}$ to be signed. It returns a signature on m denoted by σ_m.*
- Verify(pk, m, σ_m) $\to$ 1/0: *The PPT verification algorithm takes as input pk and (m, σ_m). It returns 1 if σ_m is a valid signature on m signed by sk. Otherwise, it returns 0.*

The correctness of the above algorithms requires

$$\Pr[\mathsf{Verify}(pk, m, \sigma_m) = 1] = 1$$

for any key pair (pk, sk), any message m to be signed from the message space $\mathcal{M}$, and any signature $\sigma_m \leftarrow$ Sign(sk, m).

Definition 1.1.2 (EUF-CMA). *The existential unforgeability against chosen-message attacks (EUF-CMA) security model is defined as follows.*

- Setup: *The challenger takes as input a security parameter κ and generates a key pair (pk, sk) $\leftarrow$ KeyGen(1^κ). The pk is given to the adversary.*
- Query: *The adversary adaptively chooses any message m for its signature query. The challenger runs the signing algorithm and sends the output signature $\sigma_m \leftarrow$ Sign(sk, m) to the adversary.*
- Forgey: *The adversary outputs a forged signature σ_{m^*} on message m^* and wins the game if σ_{m^*} is valid and no signature query was made on m^*.*

A digital signature scheme is (t, q, ϵ)-EUF-CMA secure if no probabilistic polynomial-time adversary can win the above game with advantage ϵ in time t after making at most q signature queries, where ϵ is a negligible function in κ and is taken over all internal coin tosses of related algorithms.

We refer to Definition 1.1.1 as syntax definition and Definition 1.1.2 as security definition. The two-segment approach offers a notable advantage: it allows us to focus specifically on security definition for an existing cryptographic primitive. For beginners, it is entirely acceptable if these descriptions are not immediately clear. The above example aims to convey to beginners: "*These are the cryptographic definitions the authors will introduce in this book*". Detailed explanations will be provided in subsequent sections.

1.2 Difficulties of Understanding Cryptographic Definitions

Understanding cryptographic definitions can be challenging for beginners. While beginners may understand individual words or symbols, the combination of these elements in definitions can remain unclear or confusing. These elements include notations, syntax, and terms, and their complexity stems from two distinct reasons.

- First, cryptographic definitions consist of notations, syntax, and terms. Each element must be learned separately, but some are interconnected and difficult to learn in isolation. Additionally, many elements originate from foundational disciplines like mathematics and computational complexity. Without sufficient background knowledge, it can be challenging to understand why these elements are used in cryptographic definitions.
- Second, beginners may not understand the principles guiding the definition of cryptography. A cryptographic concept can be defined using many similar but distinct elements, and the principles of cryptography guide the selection of the right elements. For example, we have similar term "probabilistic algorithms" and term "deterministic algorithms" in computational complexity but cryptographic definitions typically use only "probabilistic algorithms".

Continuing digital signatures as an example, we have collected a set of questions commonly asked by beginners, as depicted in Figure 1.1. Without a comprehensive understanding of these elements, grasping the core essence of cryptographic definitions is challenging.

---

1. What do notations "$1^\kappa, \rightarrow, 1/0,$ and $\Pr[\text{Verify}(pk, m, \sigma_m) = 1]$" represent?
2. What do terms PPT, security parameter, advantage, and negligible function refer to?
3. Why is the definition based on three algorithms not four or five algorithms?
4. Why are these objects included in input and output of algorithms?
5. Why is there a correctness description?
6. Who is the challenger?
7. Why is it "adaptively chooses" and not "randomly given"?
8. Why is it "no probabilistic polynomial-time adversary"?

Fig. 1.1 Examples of questions related to notations, syntax, and terms in digital signatures

A lack of deep understanding of fundamental elements and principles for cryptography can lead to difficulties for beginners when formulating new cryptographic definitions in their research. For example, beginners may emulate existing definitions when defining a new cryptographic primitive, potentially leading to misconceptions or inaccuracies in their work.

1.3 Structure and Components

To help beginners comprehensively understand the elements of cryptographic definitions, we will first categorize all elements into different disciplines, allowing beginners to acquire knowledge progressively. Next, we will explain the meanings and distinctions of notations, syntax, and terms. In the following chapters, before entering cryptography, we will focus on introducing and explaining notations, syntax, and terms within each discipline.

1.3.1 From Mathematics Up to Cryptography

We categorize all elements into distinct disciplines, as shown in Figure 1.2. These disciplines, progressing from foundational to advanced levels, include mathematics, computing machines, computational complexity, cryptographic principles, syntax definitions, and security definitions. Mathematics is the most fundamental one, followed by computing machines. Security definitions are the most advanced, building on the others. The arrows illustrate how elements from one discipline are adopted in another discipline.

These disciplines also contain elements that are tightly interconnected. Here is our understanding of their relations and interconnections.

- **Mathematics:** This category focuses on the existence of solutions for specific computing problems. Key elements in this discipline related to cryptographic definitions include computing problems, their characteristics for classification, and probability theory.
- **Computing machines:** This area focuses on whether solutions to a computing problem can be automatically generated using computing machines. Central elements in this domain for cryptographic definitions include the interpretation of "automatically" and an understanding of computing machines.
- **Computational complexity:** This discipline focuses on whether solutions to a computing problem can be efficiently generated using computing machines. Core elements in this context revolve around the definitions of "efficiency" and "inefficiency".
- **Syntax definitions:** This category focuses on explaining which algorithms in a cryptographic primitive users can effectively execute using computing machines. Key elements include cryptographic algorithms and their related concepts for users.
- **Security definitions:** This discipline focuses on defining what adversaries cannot efficiently accomplish using computing machines. Key elements include the computational capabilities of adversaries and the specific actions they aim to perform within security models.

1.3 Structure and Components

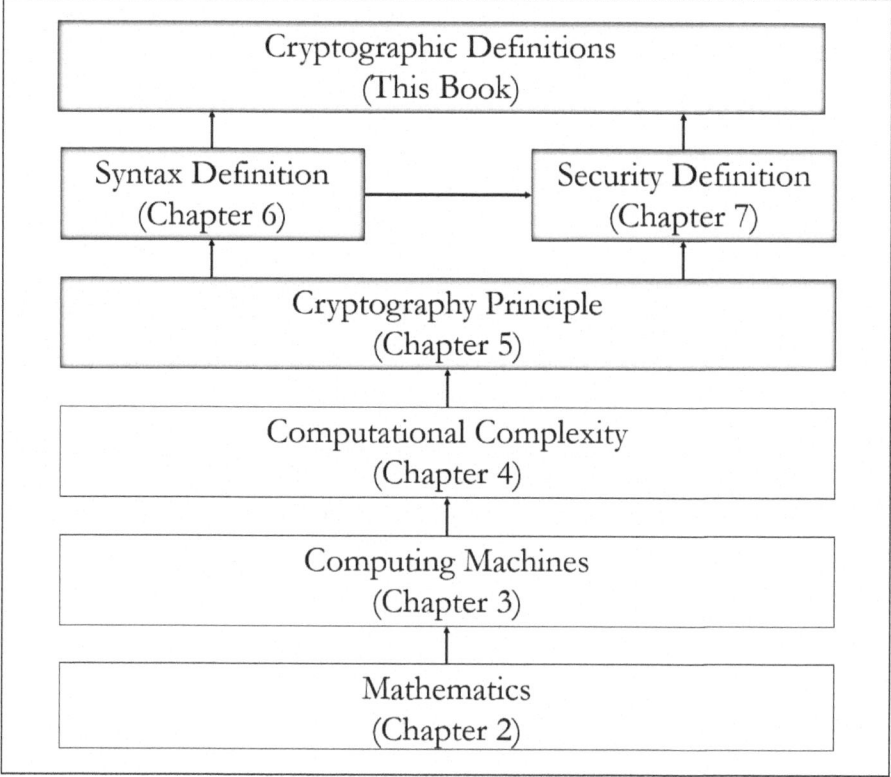

Fig. 1.2 Elements (notations, syntax, and terms) in cryptographic definitions from different disciplines. This picture also shows the role of cryptography principle in definitions, focusing on usability and security when using cryptography.

The above classification offers a structured approach, helping beginners gradually understand the complex landscape of cryptographic definitions. We observe that each discipline includes notations, syntax, and terms. To prepare for the detailed explanations in the later chapters, we first clarify the distinctions among notations, syntax, and terms.

1.3.2 Notation

Notation is a systematic way of using symbols to create meaningful expressions or representations within a specific context or domain. For example, the probability formula $\Pr[A(x) = y]$ is a notation that quantifies the likelihood of the event "the output of $A(x)$ being equal to y".

Consider X and Y as notations. The following commonly accepted language has been adopted to present the meanings of notations.

- X is ...
- X represents ...
- We denote ... by X.
- We use X to denote ...
- We write X to represent
- Let X denote ...
- For X, $X(Y)$ denotes ...
- For X, let $X(Y)$ be ...

For example, let $(\mathbb{G}, g, p)$ denote a cyclic group, where $\mathbb{G}$ is the set of group elements, g is the group generator, and p is the group order.

> **! Attention**
>
> The above notation presentation can be viewed as an informal definition of a notation. In this book, we will formally define objects that are important or complex. The first formal definition introduced in this book for beginners will be Turing machines.

1.3.3 Syntax

> **Overview**
>
> $$\text{Syntax has been applied for defining} = \begin{cases} \text{Function} \\ \text{Algorithm} \\ \text{Sampling} \\ \text{Cryptographic Primitive} \end{cases}$$

Syntax is based on notations and the rules that govern their arrangement. In cryptographic definitions, syntax describes the connections between notations through inputs and outputs.

Firstly, syntax can be used to define functions and algorithms. For example, $F_k(x) \rightarrow y$ is a syntax defining a function with (k, x) as the input; $Sign(sk, m) \rightarrow \sigma_m$ is a syntax defining the signing algorithm whose input is (sk, m) and the output is σ_m. We note that function and algorithm are not the same although both have the mapping operation and they look identical from the syntax. While functions describe relationships between inputs and outputs through mathematical expressions, algorithms provide a step-by-step procedure to compute outputs from inputs.

1.4 Intensional and Extensional Definitions

The third application of syntax is to define sampling, which is relevant to both functions and algorithms. For example $x \leftarrow_D X$ denotes sampling a value for the variable x from the distribution D defined over the set X. This notation captures the randomness inherent in cryptographic processes, such as selecting a random string as a secret key, and helps clarify probabilistic elements in cryptographic definitions.

Finally, syntax is also crucial for defining cryptographic primitives. When we say the syntax of digital signatures, "syntax" includes all the defined algorithms ($KeyGen$, $Sign$, $Verify$). Specifically, the syntax of a cryptographic primitive defines the input and output of each algorithm. This kind of syntax offers a structured framework for understanding the functionality and interactions of a cryptographic primitive.

1.3.4 Term

Overview

$$\text{Term can denote} = \begin{cases} \text{Entity, such as polynomial-time adversaries} \\ \text{Object, such as group generator and group order} \\ \text{Operation, such as adaptively choose messages} \\ \text{Property, such as indistinguishable and malicious} \end{cases}$$

A term denotes a particular entity, object, operation, or property within the cryptographic language. This representation may or may not explicitly involve notations, emphasizing its role as a fundamental unit conveying meaning within the cryptographic framework. The most often words that are used to denote a term are nouns such as "challenger" or an adjective such as "indistinguishable". These two kinds of words can be combined to describe more complex terms like "probabilistic polynomial-time adversaries".

We note that concepts, such as cryptographic concepts "$\mathcal{X}$-secure $\mathcal{Y}$", have a broader scope. They capture the larger picture or framework that ties together various notations, syntax, terms, and ideas.

1.4 Intensional and Extensional Definitions

Intensional and extensional definitions are two ways that terms and cryptographic concepts can be formally defined especially when they are complex and hard to understand.

- **Intensional definitions** specify the properties or characteristics that define a concept or term. It focuses on the internal aspects or attributes that make something what it is. For example, "*Symmetric-key encryption algorithms are cryptographic encryption algorithms for confidentiality where the same key is used for both encryption and decryption*".
- **Extensional definitions** specify instances or examples of a concept. It provides a list of objects or situations that fall under the defined concept without specifying their defining characteristics. For example, "*Symmetric-key encryption algorithms are the cryptographic algorithms such as DES, AES, and RC4*".

In the cryptology community, it is common to use intensional definitions to formally define terms or concepts. These intensional definitions typically start with an established yet expansive term or concept, subsequently depicting the precise properties or characteristics that the newly introduced term or concept should include. In essence, the formula guiding this process can be expressed as the following tips.

Tips

New term (concept) = Established term (concept) with specific properties

Intensional definition allows for a systematic exploration and refinement of cryptographic terminology, enabling a more targeted understanding of the evolving landscape within the field. Take "probabilistic polynomial-time (PPT) algorithms" as an example, we can use three steps starting from the term "Procedure" to define PPT algorithms as depicted in Figure 1.3. That is, definition is given on the assumption that the readers have already known what procedure is.

We observe that the earlier definitions for digital signatures and EUF-CMA are also intensional but less structured compared to the definition framework in Figure 1.3. Upon closer examination, it becomes apparent that digital signatures are defined as cryptographic algorithms with specific procedures, while EUF-CMA represents a security model between a challenger and an adversary, featuring specific rules in engagement.

1.5 Another Type of Definitions in Modern Cryptography

Overview

$$\text{Definitions in Modern Cryptography} = \begin{cases} \text{Cryptographic Definitions} \\ \text{Building-Block Definitions} \end{cases}$$

1.5 Another Type of Definitions in Modern Cryptography

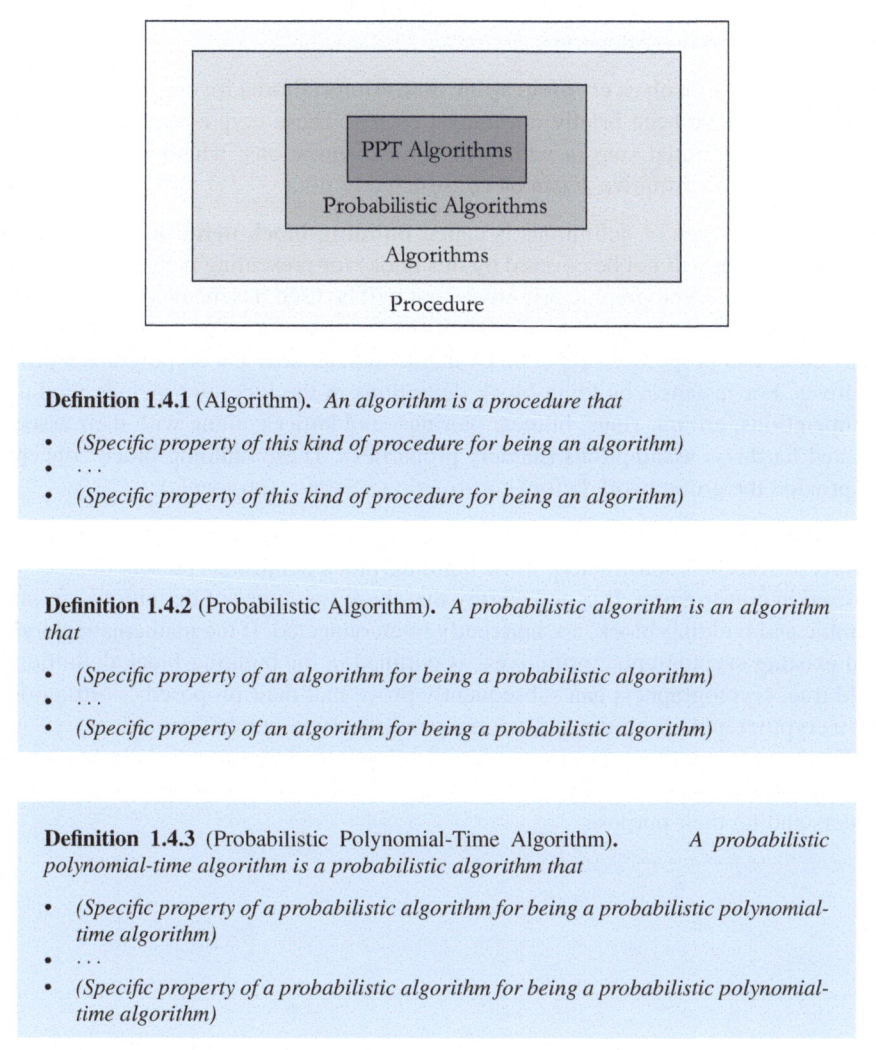

Fig. 1.3 Terms and definitions from procedure down to PPT algorithms.

In the realm of modern cryptography, definition, construction, and security proof are the three essential pillars. Among them, definition serves as the foundation not only for specifying a cryptographic primitive to be constructed but also for defining the building blocks that enable such constructions. Informally, a construction is a process that transforms "A" into "B", where building blocks (A) are utilized to design/implement a cryptographic primitive (B). Clear definitions of these building blocks are essential for understanding and implementing constructions effectively.

Consequently, the definitions found in textbooks or research papers can broadly be classified into two categories:

- The first type involves **cryptographic definitions** tailored for cryptographic concepts that have been briefly introduced earlier. These cryptographic definitions serve as the initial step in addressing crucial questions: whether an $\mathcal{X}$-secure cryptographic primitive $\mathcal{Y}$ can be constructed or not.

- The second type of definitions is called **building-block definitions** (named by this book but will not be covered by this book) for presenting mathematical tools and existing cryptographic primitives that will be used in scheme (protocol) constructions. These building-block definitions focus on formally presenting the operations and properties supported by mathematical tools and cryptographic primitives. For instance, building-block definitions in the literature include modular operations, groups, rings, bilinear pairings, and lattices, along with their associated hardness assumptions (namely properties). These building-block concepts provide the groundwork before constructing schemes (protocols).

Cryptographic definitions formally present the cryptographic primitive to be studied/researched/constructed, while building-block definitions present the tools to be used in construction. It is noteworthy that these two types of definitions, cryptographic and building-block, are inherently interconnected. If the mathematical tools and existing cryptographic primitives, as outlined in the building-block definitions, hold true, cryptographers can subsequently prove that their proposed constructions for a cryptographic primitive meet corresponding cryptographic definitions.

We have highlighted these two classifications of definitions to help beginners avoid confusion and difficulty when reading definitions in academic papers without understanding their purpose

Chapter 2
Mathematics

Abstract This chapter introduces what set and function are, what computing problem is, how to represent computing problems, concepts in probability theory, and how to classify computing problems.

2.1 Set and Function

In mathematics, the concept of a set came earlier than the concept of a function. This section briefly introduces what they are, how they are related, and how they are mixed and used together for defining computing problems later.

2.1.1 What are $a \in S$ and $F(x) = y$?

In mathematics, a set, denoted as "S", is a well-defined collection of distinct objects. The individual items within a set are referred to as its elements. We use $a \in S$ to denote that a is a specific element belonging to the set S.

In the context of set theory, a function, denoted as "F", establishes a relation between a set of inputs X (called domain) and a set of possible outputs Y (called codomain), ensuring that each input is associated with exactly one output. The symbolic representation of a function is typically denoted as

$$F : X \to Y.$$

We use $F(x) = y$ to denote that the element x in the domain X is mapped to the element y in the codomain Y by the function F. When X and Y are well-defined sets, the function F could be expressed using a mathematical formula that links any input x to its corresponding output y.

Overview

$$x = \begin{cases} \text{Value, a specific value such as 3} \\ \text{Variable, holding a value chosen from a set such as } \{9,5,2,7\} \end{cases}$$

In mathematics and cryptography, when the symbol x is employed to represent a number for operation, it generally means a variable from a well-defined set rather than denoting a specific value. For instance, a specific value could be an integer like 3, while a variable could range from a set such as $\{9, 5, 2, 7\}$. The variable x takes on a specific value when assigned. Suppose $a \in \mathbb{Z}$. Then, $x = a$ denotes that the variable x now assumes the value of a. Once more, it is crucial to emphasize that x serves as a variable, a key concept essential for comprehending cryptographic definitions within this book.

2.1.2 The Meaning of "="

It might seem odd to explore the meaning of the symbol "=" given its apparent simplicity and our early exposure to it, often since preschool. However, in the process of looking into this for the creation of this book, we found that explaining its significance can be particularly helpful, especially for beginners trying to quickly understand the meaning of various descriptions.

The symbol "=" serves three distinct purposes:

- **Comparison:** In expressions like $a = b$, the symbol "=" means checking if the value of a is the same as the value of b. Here, a, b are not variables.
- **Relationship:** Additionally, the symbol "=" is used to show the connection between the input and output of a function. For instance, "*let $f(x) = y$*" shows the definition of a function and the relation between x and y.
- **Assignment:** In statements like $x = a$, the symbol "=" also shows an assignment, where the variable x is set to the value of a. For example, "*compute $x = f(a)$*" or "*let $x = f(a)$*" involves giving the value of the function $f(a)$ to the variable x. In comparison with the first purpose for comparing two values "$a = b$", the assignment purpose is to bind one variable to one value.

All three of these uses are seen in cryptography, but the symbol is mainly used to show relationships or assignments in cryptographic definitions. The symbol for comparison purpose is quite common in scheme or protocol construction. We notice that most references do not explicitly introduce the meaning of "=" when using it and this has increased the reading difficulty especially for beginners. For assignment purpose, we note that some authors prefer "$x := a$" instead of "$x = a$".

2.1.3 Mathematical Sets in Modern Cryptography

In the first chapter, we classified definitions in modern cryptography into: (1) cryptographic definitions for formally defining cryptographic concepts, and (2) building-block definitions for defining tools for scheme/protocol constructions. Both types of definitions utilize mathematical sets, but they are slightly different.

- In cryptographic definitions, sets are abstracted to capture all potential constructions. For example, let $\mathcal{M}$ be the message space to be signed in digital signature schemes without specifying what are elements in $\mathcal{M}$. An exception is the use of bit strings, as in $\{0, 1\}^n$, defining the set containing all n-bit strings. Here, n is not a value but a variable called security parameter to be introduced. Similarly, $\{0, 1\}^*$ represents the set containing all bit strings of arbitrary length.
- In building-block definitions, sets are defined in relation to specific operations and their outputs. For example, $\mathbb{G}$ denotes the set of group elements, $\mathbb{Z}$ denotes the set of all integers, and $\mathbb{Z}_p$ denotes the set of integers in $\{0, 1, 2, \ldots, p-1\}$. Similarly, $\mathbb{R}$ denotes the set of real numbers, $[n]$ denotes the range of integers from 1 to n, and $[a, b]$ denotes the range of integers from a to b, commonly used for loop operations.

While sets in cryptographic definitions are generally abstracted, set definitions can be complex for beginners (see the next subsection). In this book, we will introduce the applications of sets in many fields in the following chapters.

2.1.4 Sets Defined by Functions

Recall that a set refers to a well-defined collection of distinct objects or elements. In mathematics and cryptology, elements in sets often follow patterns (shared characteristics) formalized using functions. Let F be a function and S be a set. Here are three common examples:

- In the first example, $\{x : \forall x \in \{0, 1\}^* \text{ s.t. } F(x) = 1\}$, this set contains any element x if x satisfies $F(x) = 1$. Therefore, this is a subset of the domain of the function F.
- In the second example, $\{F(x) : x \in S\}$, this set contains the function outputs generated using inputs from the set S. This example is a subset of the codomain depending on S.
- In the third example, $\{y : \exists x \in \{0, 1\}^* \text{ s.t. } F(x) = y\}$, this set contains function outputs y for which there exists an input $x \in S$ such that $F(x) = y$. It encompasses the entire codomain of the function F.

In the above definitions, the right part of the colon (":") states the conditions when an element should be included. When more than one condition is stated, a comma (",") will be used to separate them. While the variable to the left of the colon denotes all elements in the set.

2.1.5 Family of Sets

Consider the set $S_F = \{x : \forall x \in \{0,1\}^* \ s.t. \ F(x) = 1\}$ defined in the previous subsection. In mathematics and cryptography, a set can be further broken down into a series of subsets with more common characteristics. For example, we can divide the set S_F into subsets, each containing elements with the same length, namely

$$S_F = S_F[1] \cup S_F[2] \cup S_F[3] \cup \cdots \cup S_F[i] \cup \cdots = \bigcup_{i \geq 1} S_F[i],$$

where $S_F[i]$ is a set defined as

$$\begin{aligned} S_F[i] &= \{x : \forall x \in \{0,1\}^* \ s.t. \ F(x) = 1, |x| = i\} \\ &= \{x : \forall x \in \{0,1\}^i \ s.t. \ F(x) = 1\}. \end{aligned}$$

Roughly speaking, a family of sets, namely $S_F[i], i \in \{1, 2, 3, \cdots\}$, refers to a collection of multiple sets with common properties or characteristics. These distinct sets are distinguished with indexes that determine the structure of the family. From a single set to a family of sets, the motivation is to study the distinct features of each set in the family. For example, in the next section, S_F can be seen as a set representing a computing problem, and solving those instances/elements in $S_F[i]$ will have different levels of difficulty related to i. Without dividing into families of sets, it would be challenging to evaluate the difficulties of solving instances. The need for evaluating distinct characteristics motivates the subdivision into families rather than treating the entire set as a whole.

2.2 Computing Problems

After explaining the concepts of sets and functions, we are prepared to introduce computing problems, which can be regarded as the initial step in comprehending cryptographic definitions. We start with a term called relation function which plays an important role in defining computing problems.

2.2.1 Relation Function $R(x, y)$

A relation function is a generalized function and defined as

$$R : X \times Y \to \{0, 1\}.$$

The domain is a pair of elements (x, y) from the set X and Y, respectively. The codomain is $\{0, 1\}$ having two answers only. Further, if $R(x, y) = 1$, we say (x, y)

2.2 Computing Problems

is in relation and a true pair. Otherwise, $R(x,y) = 0$ meaning that (x,y) is a false pair.

Given a function $f(x)$, there is a relation function $R(x,y)$ reflecting $f(x)$. In particular, we have

$$R(x,y) = \begin{cases} 1 \text{ if } y = f(x) \\ 0 \text{ if } y \neq f(x) \end{cases}$$

Therefore, a relation function is at least as powerful as a function. On the other side, given a relation function $R(x,y)$, we might not be able to find a proper function to define it. For example, a relation function allows the existence of two pairs (x,y) and (x,y') with same x satisfying $R(x,y) = R(x,y') = 1$, but we cannot find the corresponding function. This is because a function only allows exactly one output for each input x. Therefore, a relation function is more powerful than a general function in linking two elements.

2.2.2 Computing Problems: Definition

Now, we can informally define what computing problem is.

Overview

A computing problem P, defined over a relation function R, involves computing y given x such that $R(x,y) = 1$.

In the above informal definition, x represents the problem instance, and y denotes the corresponding solution. The nature of y is determined by both the specific problem instance x and the underlying rule by the relation function R. Informally speaking, solving the computing problem P means that the problem solution y can be successfully found for the input problem instance x. In this book, for simplicity, a computing problem P is equivalent to a relation function R.

The computing problem P here is a mathematical problem. We say a computing problem P is non-trivial if:

- There is an infinite number of problem instances, and
- The problem solutions to all instances are not identical.

In the following sections of this book, computing problems refer to those non-trivial computing problems. It is important to note that the term "computing problems" in this book is equivalent to "computational problems" in other references, as defined in computational theory and computational complexity literature. This distinction is made to avoid confusion with the term "computational problems" as used in modern cryptography.

2.2.3 Computing Problems: $\{(x, y) : R(x, y) = 1\}$

Computing problems in the previous subsections are defined over relation functions. However, this kind of representation is not straightforward enough to clearly convey the complexity and efficiency of solving problems. Therefore, mathematical sets are used to clarify the definition of computing problems.

Given a computing problem P represented as the relation function R, all pairs of instances and solutions for this computing problem can be collected together as a set, which is defined as:

$$S_P = \Big\{(x, y) : \forall x, y \in \{0, 1\}^* \ s.t.\ R(x, y) = 1\Big\}.$$

Besides using a relation function, the set S_P is another way of representing the computing problem P. We can further break down the set S_P into subsets according to the instance length as:

$$S_P = \bigcup_{i \geq 1} S_P[i], \quad S_P[i] = \{(x, y) : \forall x, y \in \{0, 1\}^* \ s.t.\ R(x, y) = 1, |x| = i\}.$$

Each subset $S_P[i]$ captures instances of a specific length, providing insight into the complexity or efficiency of solving the computing problem P which is related to the instance length. This representation using sets aids in understanding the common characteristics within each subset $S_P[i]$, motivating its use in analyzing computing problems.

2.2.4 Computing Problems: Classifications

Overview

$$\text{Two problem categories} = \begin{cases} \text{Decision Problems} \\ \text{Search (Computational) Problems} \end{cases}$$

Let $S_\mathbb{P}$ be the set of all computing problems represented using sets as

$$S_\mathbb{P} = \{S_{P_1}, S_{P_2}, S_{P_3}, \cdots\}.$$

Computational theory and computational complexity primarily study two subsets of computing problems within $S_\mathbb{P}$ which are related to cryptography. They are decision problems and search problems. Decision problems are the most crucial for studying

2.2 Computing Problems

computational complexity. In the cryptology community, search problems are also referred to as computational problems.

Decision Problem. A decision problem is defined by a relation function

$$R : X \times \{0, 1\} \to \{0, 1\},$$

where X in the domain represents the instance space and $\{0, 1\}$ in the domain represents the solution space. Hence, the solution space has only two possible answers: 0 (false) and 1 (true), indicating whether a problem instance is false or true.

For instance, consider the Decisional Diffie-Hellman (DDH) problem defined over the group $(\mathbb{G}, g, p)$. Let $a, b, c, d \in \mathbb{Z}_p$ be random integers satisfying $c \neq ab$ mod p and $d = ab$ mod p. Suppose there are two instances:

$$x_1 = (g, g^a, g^b, g^d), \quad x_2 = (g, g^a, g^b, g^c).$$

In the DDH problem definition, x_1 is a true problem instance ($d = ab$ mod p) while x_2 is false ($c \neq ab$ mod p). Thus, with the description of the relation function, the DDH problem can be defined using the relation function as:

$$R(x, y) = \begin{cases} R(x_1, 0) = 0 \\ R(x_1, 1) = 1 \\ R(x_2, 0) = 1 \\ R(x_2, 1) = 0 \end{cases}$$

Therefore, $(x_1, 1)$ and $(x_2, 0)$ are two instance-solution pairs of the DDH problem, while $(x_1, 0)$ and $(x_2, 1)$ are not.

Search Problem. A search problem is defined by a relation function

$$R : X \times \{0, 1\}^* \to \{0, 1\}.$$

In general, the problem solution for a given problem instance $x \in X$ can be any bit string in $\{0, 1\}^*$. The objective of a search problem is to find a bit string y as the problem solution for a given bit string x as the problem instance, satisfying $R(x, y) = 1$.

For example, consider the Computational Diffie-Hellman (CDH) problem defined over the group $(\mathbb{G}, g, p)$. Let $a, b \in \mathbb{Z}_p$ be random integers satisfying $c \neq ab$ mod p. Suppose there is one instance:

$$x = (g, g^a, g^b).$$

In the CDH problem definition, the objective is to compute the problem solution g^{ab} for the given problem instance x. Therefore, with the description of the relation function, the CDH problem can be defined using the relation function as:

$$R(x,y) = \begin{cases} R(x, g^{ab}) = 1 \\ R(x, g^c) = 0 \end{cases}$$

Thus, (x, g^{ab}) is an instance-solution pair of the CDH problem, while (x, g^c) for any $c \neq ab \mod p$ are not.

A variant of search problem is called optimization problem. As we have introduced before, the number of solutions to x can be more than one. Optimization problem aims to find a specific solution y from all potential solutions, based on certain criteria definitions within the problem. More precisely, if $\{y_1, y_2, \cdots, y_K\}$ represents all solutions to x, the optimization problem seeks to identify the "best" solution according to predefined criteria. For instance, given an input x, an optimization problem may involve finding a solution y to x in the search problem abstracted as R such that $R(x, y) = 1$, and y contains the maximum number of bit-1s among all solutions to the instance x. Another example related to cryptography is the Shortest Vector Problem (SVP) in lattices. It involves finding the shortest non-zero vector in a given lattice, typically measured using the Euclidean norm.

2.2.5 Decision Problems and Formal Languages

Another term related to decision problems is known as formal language. This term plays a crucial role in computational complexity for defining complexity classes. However, it is not commonly adopted in the cryptology community due to its limitations in decision problems only.

A formal language is a set of words whose letters are drawn from an alphabet Σ. Each word in this set must adhere to a set of rules defined within the formal language. Since all objects can be encoded into bit strings, a formal language can also be viewed as a subset of $\{0, 1\}^*$.

Now, let's consider a special formal language based on a decision problem. Given a decision problem represented with a relation function R, we categorize all instance-solution pairs in

$$S_P[i] = \{(x, y) : \forall x \in \{0, 1\}^i, y \in \{0, 1\} \text{ s.t. } R(x, y) = 1\}$$

into two subsets $S_P^T[i]$ and $S_P^F[i]$, defined as

$$S_P^T[i] = \{(x, y) : \forall x \in \{0, 1\}^i \text{ s.t. } R(x, 1) = 1\},$$

$$S_P^F[i] = \{(x, y) : \forall x \in \{0, 1\}^i \text{ s.t. } R(x, 0) = 1\}.$$

In other words, all instances in $S_P^T[i]$ are true instances, while all instances in $S_P^F[i]$ are false instances of the same length i. Then, the entire set S_P can be partitioned into a subset of true instances and a subset of false instances as follows:

Overview

$$S_P = \bigcup_{i \geq 1} S_P[i]$$

$$S_P^T = \bigcup_{i \geq 1} S_P^T[i] \qquad\qquad S_P^F = \bigcup_{i \geq 1} S_P^F[i]$$

In these two subsets, each element represents a pair of instance and solution. Let L be the set consisting of all true instances x (excluding their solutions), defined as

$$L = \{x : \forall x \in \{0,1\}^* \text{ s.t. } (x,1) \in S_P^T\}.$$

Then, the set L forms a formal language, where the rule is based on the computing problem P and its relation function R. With this term, a decision problem described using a formal language aims to determine whether $x \in L$ for a given $x \in \{0,1\}^*$, indicating whether the input is a true instance or false. This variant is also known as a membership problem in the literature.

2.2.6 How to Classify Computing Problems

Let $S_\mathbb{P}$ be the set of all computing problems represented using sets:

$$S_\mathbb{P} = \{S_{P_1}, S_{P_2}, S_{P_3}, \cdots\},$$

where S_{P_i} is the set representation for the computing problem P_i under relation function R_i:

$$S_{P_i} = \{(x,y) : \forall x, y \in \{0,1\}^* \text{ s.t. } R_i(x,y) = 1\}.$$

This chapter has introduced the following ways of classifications:

- **Solution Structure.** The whole set of computing problems $S_\mathbb{P}$ can be divided into subsets with similar structures of problem solutions, such as decision problems and search problems. One subset contains all decision problems, while another contains all search problems.
- **Instance Length.** Each computing problem S_{P_i} can be broken down into subsets with the same instance length (as shared characteristic):

$$S_P = \bigcup_{i \geq 1} S_P[i], \quad S_P[i] = \{(x,y) : \forall x, y \in \{0,1\}^* \text{ s.t. } R(x,y) = 1, |x| = i\}.$$

This classification is important as the complexity and efficiency of solving problems are related to instance length.

So far, we have defined what a computing problem is and provided a preliminary classification based on solution structure and instance length. However, this classification is not complete and will be further classified in the next two chapters.

2.3 Event, Probability, Distribution, and Sampling

Besides sets and functions, the mathematical terms such as events, probability, distributions, and sampling will also be crucial in certain aspects of computational complexity and security definitions in cryptography.

2.3.1 Event and Probability: $\Pr[x_1; x_2 : A]$

In probability theory, an experiment is a process or action that produces a set of outcomes. For example:

- **Experiment:** rolling a six-sided dice.

An event is a subset of outcomes that are of interest in a given experiment. Let S_O be the set representing all possible outcomes. A specific event focuses on those particular and well-defined outcomes in an experiment, which forms a subset of S_O. Events are often associated with real-world experiments. For example:

- **Event A:** Rolling the number 2.
- **Event B:** Rolling an even number (this event consists of the outcomes $\{2, 4, 6\}$).
- **Event C:** Rolling a prime number (this event consists of the outcomes $\{2, 3, 5\}$).

When an experiment is repeated numerous times, the likelihood of events occurring can be observed. For example:

- The event A will occur with chance close to $\frac{1}{6}$.
- The event B will occur with chance close to $\frac{1}{2}$.
- The event C will occur with chance close to $\frac{1}{2}$.

Probability measures the likelihood of specific outcomes or events occurring based on experimental data. It ranges from 0 to 1, where 0 indicates impossibility and 1 indicates certainty. For example, let RSSD represent the experiment of rolling a six-sided dice. The syntax $a \leftarrow$ RSSD represents that the experiment returns a (variable) as the outcome. The following notation

$$\Pr[a \leftarrow \mathsf{RSSD} : a = 2] \text{ or } \Pr[\mathsf{RSSD} : A]$$

represents the probability of event A (rolling the number 2) occurring in the experiment of rolling a six-sided dice. A generalized probability is written as

$$\Pr[x_1; x_2; x_3; \cdots ; x_n : A],$$

2.3 Event, Probability, Distribution, and Sampling

representing the occurrence of event A after conducting a complicated experiment composed of a series of steps from x_1 to x_n, namely $\mathsf{Exp} = (x_1, x_2, \cdots, x_n)$. We also note that the probability could be presented in a different format using the symbol "|" such as $\Pr[A|x_1; x_2; x_3; \cdots; x_n]$. Both formats are acceptable but the former one seems more commonly used in cryptography.

2.3.2 Distribution and Sampling: $a \in_U S, b \in_D S$

Given an experiment and all possible outcomes from this experiment, there are two related mathematical terms.

- The first term is distribution which refers to the set of all possible outcomes and their associated probabilities in a given experiment. For example, the distribution in the experiment RSSD should be:

Outcome	1	2	3	4	5	6
Probability	$\frac{1}{6}$	$\frac{1}{6}$	$\frac{1}{6}$	$\frac{1}{6}$	$\frac{1}{6}$	$\frac{1}{6}$

- The second term is sampling which refers to the process of selecting outcomes from an outcome space in a given experiment according to a predefined distribution. The term sampling was developed to mathematically model experiments in the physical world.

Informally speaking, experiments and events will be mathematically and formally studied using distribution and sampling to understand their patterns and characteristics.

There are two types of sampling as stated in the subsection title. Both are crucial in cryptography, both presenting sampling an element from a set S and assigning it to a variable.

- $a \in_U S$: This represents sampling based on a uniform distribution described as U, where each element in the set S is chosen with equal probability and the total probability for all outcomes is 1. It also means that a is randomly chosen from the set S.
- $b \in_D S$: This represents sampling based on a general distribution described as D, where each element may be selected with different probability which have been clearly defined in the distribution D.

To help beginners further understand distribution and sampling, we provide two examples. In the first example, $a \in_U \{0, 1\}^n$ represents choosing a random n-bit string. This is straightforward. In the second example, let p be a prime number less than 2^n. Suppose that b is computed as follows by using a random $a \in_U \{0, 1\}^n$ defined as:
$$b = f(a) = 9a^3 + 5a^2 + 2a + 7 \mod p.$$

Computing b can be viewed as a mathematical experiment. Then, after encoding b into a bit string, it can be considered as sampled from the set $S = \{0,1\}^n$ following a distribution D (not uniform). We will introduce more about this kind of sampling in the later chapters (Section 7.2.4) which is crucial in security definition.

2.4 Review Questions

? Question 1

Let $F : \mathbb{Z} \to \mathbb{Z}$ be a function. Justify the meaning of the following set including elements and shared characteristics

$$\{(x, y) : \forall x, y \in \mathbb{Z} \text{ s.t. } F(x) + y \geq 1\}.$$

? Question 2

Let S be a set associated with a computing problem. What kinds of elements can this set contain? How many shared characteristics can you use to divide S into subsets?

? Question 3

Let S be a set associated with an experiment or a probability distribution. What kinds of elements can be represented within this set? How can you create subsets of S with other shared characteristics?

? Question 4

Let x be randomly chosen from the set $\{0, 1, 2, 3, 4, 5, 6, 7, 8\}$. Let $f(x) = 2^x$ mod 5 be a distribution and its outcomes include $\{0, 1, 2, 3, 4\}$. What is the probability of each outcome?

Chapter 3
Computing Machines

Abstract In the course of history, computing machines (denoted by $\mathcal{M}$) were invented with the purpose of employing machinery instead of the human brain for the execution of automata operations, particularly in the realm of solving computing problems. In this chapter, we begin introducing what solving computing problems using computing machines entails and the related knowledge.

3.1 Solving Problems with Computing Machines

We noticed that other reference books preferred the term "machines" without the qualifier "computing", but we chose to use the term "computing machines" to highlight the role of machines in computing.

3.1.1 Historical Development of Computing Machines

A succinct way to summarize the historical development of computing machines and related knowledge is described as follows.

- **Specific-Purpose Machines:** Early computing machines (devices) were purpose-built for specific tasks or mathematical challenges. Examples include the abacus, utilized for arithmetic calculations as early as 2700-2300 BC; the slide rule, employed for various mathematical computations since the 1620s; and the Bombe, designed in 1939 to decipher messages encoded by the Enigma machine for encryption and decryption.
- **Computational Models:** A computational model is an abstract representation or conceptual framework that describes the process of computation. It provides a theoretical basis for understanding how computations can be performed and

establishes the boundaries of computing capabilities. The most famous computational model is the Turing machine, proposed by Alan Turing in the 1930s.
- **General-Purpose Machines:** A general-purpose machine, also known as a universal machine, refers to a computing device that is designed to perform a wide range of tasks or computations. Unlike specific-purpose machines that are tailored for particular applications, a general-purpose machine is versatile and can be programmed to execute different operations. For example, the digital computers we use today, developed in the mid-20th century, are general-purpose computing machines.

If we seek to distinguish between computing machines and computational models, it is crucial to note that the former primarily focuses on operations, while the latter is concerned with defining the boundaries of computing capabilities. That is, computational model studies how powerful computing machines are within a computational model.

3.1.2 From Machine to Algorithm

Overview

"The computing machine $\mathcal{M}$ can solve computing problem P"

$\approx$

"The algorithm $\mathcal{A}$ can solve computing problem P"

Computing machines were initially invented to address computing problems, yet a comprehensive explanation of what it means to "solve computing problems" remains to be fully explained later. Here, we begin by outlining the high-level distinctions between solving computing problems with specific-purpose machines and general-purpose machines.

- **Solving computing problems using specific-purpose machines:** In this method, we input the description of a computing problem into a specific-purpose machine, which then outputs the solution to that problem.
- **Solving computing problems using general-purpose machines:** In this method, two distinct inputs are required for general-purpose machines. The first input is the description of the computing problem, and the second input is the description of a specific-purpose machine capable of solving the given computing problem. With these two inputs, the general-purpose machine processes the information and outputs the solution.

3.1 Solving Problems with Computing Machines

These differences stem from the fact that general-purpose machines only understand basic operations, and we must instruct them how to combine basic operations into specific ones to execute, similar to how specific-purpose machines produce solutions.

Based on the above introduction, we refer to the description of a specific-purpose machine running on a general-purpose machine as an algorithm. In essence, an algorithm is a step-by-step procedure or set of rules for addressing a specific problem or performing a computation. In the realm of cryptographic definitions, the statements "A (specific-purpose) computing machine $\mathcal{M}$ can solve computing problem P" and "An algorithm, denoted by $\mathcal{A}$, can solve computing problem P" convey a similar idea: we can employ a computing machine, whether specific or general-purpose, to solve computing problem P.

3.1.3 Definition of Solving a Computing Problem

Recalling that a computing problem P can be represented as the following set

$$S_P = \Big\{(x, y) : \forall x, y \in \{0,1\}^* \ \ s.t. \ \ R(x,y) = 1\Big\}.$$

This set should contain an infinite number of instance. Roughly speaking, the meaning of "solving a computing problem" is to ask the following question:

> **? Question**
>
> *Is computing problem P solvable?*

The key to answering this question is understanding the conditions under which we can say "YES". Notice that a computing problem involves finding a problem solution y for a problem instance x satisfying $R(x, y) = 1$. Intuitively, if a computing machine can solve the problem P, it means that on input x, the computing machine should return an output that is a problem solution denoted as y.

However, the meaning of the above question can be interpreted in multiple ways. We expand its meaning progressively in three steps.

- **Step 1 (problem instance and computing machine are both given):** Given a specific problem instance, for example x_1, from S_P and a specific-purpose computing machine $\mathcal{M}$ (or a specific algorithm $\mathcal{A}$), we say the problem can be solved if the machine can return y_1 satisfying $R(x_1, y_1) = 1$. Here, x_1 represents a specific instance, rather than a variable.
- **Step 2 (problem instance is given but need to find a computing machine):** Given a specific problem instance, for example x_1, from S_P and a set of specific-purpose computing machines $S_\mathcal{M}$ (or a set of algorithms), we say the problem

can be solved if there exists a machine $\mathcal{M} \in S_\mathcal{M}$ that can return y_1 satisfying $R(x_1, y_1) = 1$. Compared to Step 1, the problem is solvable as long as one machine can work correctly and can be identified.

- **Step 3 (need to find a computing machine for any problem instance):** Given a variable problem instance from S_P and a set of specific-purpose computing machines $S_\mathcal{M}$ (or a set of algorithms), we say the problem can be solved if there exists a machine $\mathcal{M} \in S_\mathcal{M}$ that on input any (variable) instance $x \in S_P$, it returns y such that $R(x, y) = 1$. Compared to Step 2, the machine should be able to find problem solutions to any instance.

The definition in Step 3 is the closest to the definition to be used in computational complexity and cryptography. In summary, the difficulty of solving a computing problem using computing machines is not dominated by running machines but finding machines especially when the set of computing machines is huge. To show that we can solve a computing problem, we should be able to finding a proper computing machine from the given set $S_\mathcal{M}$, and this computing machine can return problem solutions to any input problem instances from a set having an infinite number of instances.

3.1.4 Computational Result: $y \leftarrow \mathcal{A}(x)$

From the previous introduction, the task of solving a computing problem involves finding a solution by executing an algorithm or a specific-purpose computing machine on an input instance. Let $\mathcal{A}$ be an algorithm, and (x, y) be a pair of problem instance and problem solution. The syntax

$$y \leftarrow \mathcal{A}(x)$$

conveys the idea of executing the algorithm $\mathcal{A}$ on input x and assigning the output to the variable y.

We note that some researchers may use $y = \mathcal{A}(x)$ to denote the same meaning for simplicity. We recommend beginners use the syntax $y \leftarrow \mathcal{A}(x)$, as this syntax is more commonly used for all algorithms, including probabilistic algorithms to be introduced later. In particular, when the same instance x is inputted to a probabilistic algorithm, the output could vary, and using the symbol "=" might not be appropriate in this context.

Another reason that we suggest the syntax $y \leftarrow \mathcal{A}(x)$ is consistency with the probability theory. The algorithm $\mathcal{A}(x)$ with x as input can be treated as an experiment and $y \leftarrow \mathcal{A}(x)$ is the outcome from this experiment. This syntax becomes more crucial when we need to analyze how well a probabilistic algorithm solves a computing problem and returns a correct y.

3.1.5 Deterministic and Probabilistic Algorithms

All algorithms can be classified into two types: deterministic algorithms and probabilistic algorithms. We explain the difference by treating algorithms as experiments:

$$y \leftarrow \mathcal{A}(x).$$

Let $\mathcal{A}(x)$ be the experiment and y be its outcome.

- **Deterministic:** The outcome space of the experiment contains only one possible outcome. That is, repeating the experiment always produces the same outcome.
- **Probabilistic:** The outcome space of the experiment has more than one outcome. That is, repeating the experiment multiple times may yield different outcomes.

A deterministic algorithm can be viewed as a special probabilistic algorithm, where the outcome space contains only one possible outcome for each input instance. In the literature, probabilistic algorithms are also referred to as randomized algorithms.

A probabilistic algorithm may produce different outcomes because random numbers are chosen and used in its operations. That is, given the same instance x as the input, when running a probabilistic algorithm to solve it, a random number (or different numbers across executions) is chosen during computation. In general, probabilistic algorithms are more powerful than deterministic ones in solving computing problems. It is important to note that probabilistic algorithms are not merely used to speed up computations but randomize operations, which will be introduced in cryptography section of this book.

Due to the above syntax $y \leftarrow \mathcal{A}(x)$ for probabilistic algorithms, to denote choosing a random element or instance x from the set X, the syntax $x \in_U X$ has been replaced with $x \leftarrow_U X$, which is quite common in the cryptology community. We can imagine that a probabilistic algorithm is used to randomly choose x from X.

3.1.6 Success Probability in Probabilistic Algorithms

When running probabilistic algorithms for solving a computing problem, it may be the case that only one of the outcomes is a valid problem solution. As a consequence, we are concerned with the probability of returning a valid problem solution. For beginners, we note that it becomes very complex when delving deeper into the discussion of probability. We introduce essential probability concepts based on the following statement.

Statement

The computing problem P can be solved by algorithm $\mathcal{A}$ with probability $\frac{2}{3}$.

Recalling that a computing problem is composed of an infinite number of instance-solution pairs.

$$\mathbb{S}_P = \Big\{(x,y) : \forall x, y \in \{0,1\}^* \text{ s.t. } R(x,y) = 1\Big\}.$$

There are two different ways for measuring probability $\frac{2}{3}$ in the above statement.

- In the first way, the probability $\frac{2}{3}$ refers to *every* instance $x \in \mathbb{S}_P$. Let r be a random number chosen from space $\mathbf{R} = \{r_1, r_2, r_3, \cdots\}$ by the probabilistic algorithm $\mathcal{A}$ in finding problem solutions. More precisely, the probability is defined as

$$\forall x \in \mathbb{S}_P, \Pr[y' \leftarrow \mathcal{A}(x) : R(x, y') = 1] = \sum_{r \leftarrow_U \mathbf{R}} \Pr[r = r_i \wedge \mathcal{A}(x, r_i) = y] \geq \frac{2}{3}.$$

This probability is equivalent to calculate the probability of sampling those right random numbers which help $\mathcal{A}$ find a correct solution denoted by y.

- In the second way, the probability $\frac{2}{3}$ refers to all instances of *every* same length on average. Let the space of length-i instances be $\mathbb{S}_P[i] = \{x_1, x_2, x_3, \cdots\}$. More precisely, the probability is defined as

$$\forall i \in \mathbb{N}, \sum_{x \in \mathbb{S}_P[i]} \Pr[x = x_i] \Pr[x = x_i, y'_i \leftarrow \mathcal{A}(x_i) : R(x_i, y'_i) = 1] \geq \frac{2}{3}.$$

This probability definition says that for some instance the probabilistic algorithm might solve it successfully with probability less than $\frac{2}{3}$ while the probability is at least $\frac{2}{3}$ on average for all instances of the same length.

Therefore, the above probability statement is unclear and needs contexts to further understand how probability is measured. It is important to note that probability can be calculated in a third way, distinct from the above two measurements. We highlight these two methods because the first method is used in complexity theory for defining complexity classes such as $\mathcal{BPP}$ and the second method (after modification) is used in cryptography for security definitions. Both will be introduced in later chapters.

3.1.7 Why Computational Model Matters

Let P be a computing problem to be solved and the meaning of "solve" is clear. An inherent question is given as follows.

3.1 Solving Problems with Computing Machines

> **? Question**
>
> *Is computing problem P solvable by an algorithm?*

The answer to the above question can be either YES and NO, depending on the proposed algorithm and the computational power of general-purpose computing machines. In other words, this question cannot be answered until a clear definition is provided.

To clarify, consider the following example. Suppose the computing problem P is to determine which of two given integers, a and b, is larger.

- In a general-purpose computing machine like our digital computers, it is evident that many algorithms exist for solving this computing problem. Thus, the answer to the above question is YES.

- Consider another general-purpose computing machine that only knows how to add or multiply two positive integers. In this case, regardless of how algorithms are designed for this machine, it cannot return the comparison result for input (a, b). So, the answer to the above question is NO.

The above question has no definitive answer because the set of operations available to the algorithms we can design is not specified. A computational model, denoted by $\mathcal{C}$, can be viewed as well-defined operational rules that explicitly constrain proposed algorithms. Informally, we say that an algorithm is within a computational model if all operations inside this algorithm can be captured/supported by this computational model.

Suppose that a computational model $\mathcal{C}$ is given. Let $S_\mathcal{C}$ be the set of all algorithms that we can propose within this computational model. A revised question is described as follows:

> **? Question**
>
> *Is computing problem P solvable by an algorithm from $S_\mathcal{C}$?*

In short, computational models constrain the range of possible algorithm choices. Intuitively, this revised question should have a definitive answer, either YES or NO, when the computational model $\mathcal{C}$ is clearly defined. This is because we could, in principle, test all algorithms in this set one by one.

However, it is not easy to answer this question. There are two reasons. First, a general-purpose computing machine such as a digital computer can run an infinite number of distinct algorithms. Therefore, $S_\mathcal{C}$ contains an infinite number of algorithms within a computational model. It is not feasible to exhaustively test algorithms one by one in this set to answer the question. Second, even if the answer to the above question is YES within a given computational model, it does not mean that the computing problem can be solved in our physical world. The key factor is whether or not we can implement the corresponding general-purpose computing machine to execute the algorithm. An example is the algorithm designed by Peter Shor to find the prime factors of an integer. Specifically, given an integer $N = p \cdot q$, the algorithm can find and return p and q. The operations in such an algorithm are incompatible with existing general-purpose computing machines, such as digital computers, requiring instead quantum computers. However, quantum computers are still being developed in laboratories by scientists and are far from practical use, as they are currently limited to factorizing very small values of N.

3.1.8 $\exists \mathcal{A} \in S_\mathcal{C}$ and $\forall \mathcal{A} \in S_\mathcal{C}$

Let $S_\mathcal{C}$ be the set of algorithms (or specific-purpose computing machines) associated with the computational model $\mathcal{C}$. Let $\mathcal{A} \in S_\mathcal{C}$ be an algorithm and P be a computing problem. The answers to the previous question (YES or NO) have mathematical representations. Two notations are commonly used to express these answers.

- **YES:** If there exists an algorithm in $S_\mathcal{C}$ that can solve this problem, we say

    "$\exists \mathcal{A} \in S_\mathcal{C}$, the algorithm $\mathcal{A}$ can solve the problem P".

    In modern cryptography, this notation is used to indicate that a computation can be performed using an algorithm $\mathcal{A}$ that exists in $S_\mathcal{C}$. The definition of a cryptographic primitive is based on the existence of certain algorithms. In scheme or protocol construction, the existence of this algorithm must be demonstrated by explicitly constructing it.

- **NO:** If there exists no algorithm in $S_\mathcal{C}$ that can solve this problem, we say

    "$\forall \mathcal{A} \in S_\mathcal{C}$, the algorithm $\mathcal{A}$ cannot solve the problem P".

    In other words, there exists no algorithm in $S_\mathcal{C}$ that can solve the problem P. In modern cryptography, when defining a computing problem or a cryptographic scheme that cannot be solved or broken, this notation is used to indicate that no adversary in the set $S_\mathcal{C}$ can solve the computing problem or break the cryptographic scheme.

Informally, the symbol "$\exists$" is primarily used in syntax definitions for cryptographic primitives, while the symbol "$\forall$" is mostly used in security definitions for cryptographic primitives. We note that the symbol "$\forall$" is also used in syntax definitions to define the correctness of a cryptographic primitive (see Section 1.1.1).

We have completed our introduction to the concept of solving computing problems using computing machines. The key aspect is the definition of computational model $\mathcal{C}$ which determines the set of algorithms $S_\mathcal{C}$. In the next sections of this chapter, we will introduce computational models.

3.2 Computational Models: Background and Preliminaries

This section introduces the knowledge towards understanding Turing Machine, which is the most well-known computational model.

3.2.1 Overview

A computational model is a mathematical representation of computations. There are two key components in modelling: fundamental operations and computational flow.

- **Fundamental Operations:** These are the basic operations upon which all algorithmic steps (executions) must be directly or indirectly based. For example, in digital computers, logical operations (AND, OR, NOT) and shift operations are fundamental. The addition algorithm directly uses these operations, while the multiplication algorithm indirectly relies on them by invoking the addition algorithm.
- **Computational Flow:** It defines the order in which operations are executed. There are two types of computational flows: sequential and parallel. Sequential computing, also referred to as serial computing, processes instructions one at a time in a linear sequence. Each instruction executes only after the previous one has completed. Parallel computing enables the simultaneous execution of multiple tasks or instructions. It is worth noting that continuous parallel computing can lead to an exponential impact. For instance, if one operation initiates the process, but the output undergoes two different operations in parallel, by the i-th step, up to 2^i operations may be executed simultaneously (Figure 3.1).

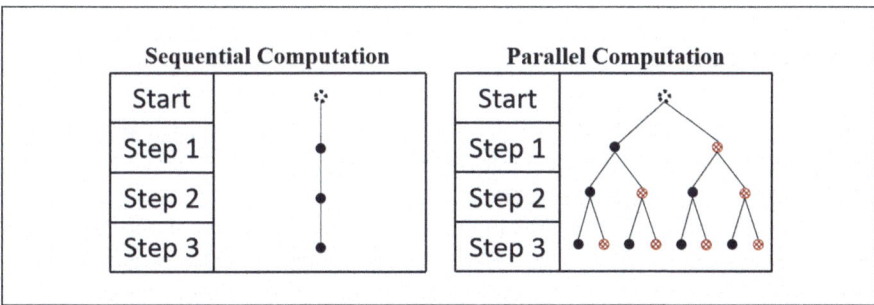

Fig. 3.1 Computational flows in sequential computation and parallel computation

We can define many different computational models. After modelling, suppose a computational model is clearly defined. Beginners should pay attention to the following three questions:

1. **Is this computational model powerful enough?** This question focuses on assessing the overall capability and versatility of the computational model. A computational model can be viewed as a set of algorithms. This question prompts an evaluation of whether the computational model can solve a broad range of computing problems and tasks. The goal is to understand the scope and limitations of the computational model in handling various computational scenarios. For example, if a human can solve a computing problem using pen and paper, but no algorithm in this computational model (i.e., its set of algorithms) can solve it, then this suggests that the computational model is not powerful enough.

2. **Is there another computational model more powerful than this model?** This question investigates the relative strength and capabilities of the computational model compared to alternative models. It prompts a comparative analysis to determine whether other computational models offer greater computational power or extend the capabilities of the given model.

3. **Can we design a real computing device fulfilling this computational model?** This question explores the practical feasibility of implementing the computational model as a physical or electronic computing device. It addresses considerations related to hardware design and architecture. The goal is to determine whether a real-world computing device can be built to adhere to the principles and specifications of the computational model.

These three questions are closely tied to the principles of cryptography. Security definitions in cryptography rely on the answers to these three questions, and only appropriate computational models should be selected for defining security. Otherwise, a cryptographic scheme that is secure in the physical world may be deemed insecure according to the security definition, or a scheme that is insecure in the physical world may be considered secure under an incorrect security definition.

3.2.2 Toy Example

To help beginners understand what a computational model is and what algorithms it can include, we provide a toy example that is somewhat simpler than real computational models, such as Turing machines.

In this toy example, the fundamental operations are composed of two functional operations denoted by $f_0, f_1 : X \to X$, and the computational flow is sequential computation. The computational model can represent all algorithms that execute in N steps, where N is a positive integer, as described below:

3.2 Computational Models: Background and Preliminaries

Computational Model (Example)

Input: x
Step 1: $f_{B_1}(x_1) = y_1$ where $B_1 \in \{0, 1\}$ and $x_1 \in \{x\}$.
Step 2: $f_{B_2}(x_2) = y_2$ where $B_2 \in \{0, 1\}$ and $x_2 \in \{x, y_1\}$.
Step 3: $f_{B_3}(x_3) = y_3$ where $B_3 \in \{0, 1\}$ and $x_3 \in \{x, y_1, y_2\}$.
Step 4: $f_{B_4}(x_4) = y_4$ where $B_4 \in \{0, 1\}$ and $x_4 \in \{x, y_1, y_2, y_3\}$.
$\vdots$ $\vdots$
Step N: $f_{B_N}(x_N) = y_N$ where $B_N \in \{0, 1\}$ and $x_N \in \{x, y_1, \cdots, y_{N-1}\}$.

Output: y_N (result after Step N)

In this computational model, at each step, the operation consists of calling either the function f_0 or f_1, where the input to this function can be either the initial input x or any previously generated output from the two functions.

The set of algorithms captured by this computational model is

$$S_{\mathcal{C}} = \left\{ (N, B_1, j_1, B_2, j_2, \cdots, B_N, j_N) : N \in \mathbb{Z}^+, B_i \in \{0, 1\}, j_i \in \mathbb{Z}^+ \right\},$$

where j_i indicates the index of value to be assigned to x_{j_i}. Each algorithm is described in a tuple $(N, B_1, j_1, B_2, j_2, \cdots, B_N, j_N)$ with specific parameters for choices, and this set contains an infinite number of algorithms. This toy example also illustrates that validating the existence of an algorithm in this set for solving a computing problem is non-trivial, as we cannot test an infinite number of algorithms one by one.

In the above toy example, there are two fundamental operations. Suppose computing $f_1(x)$ for any input x can be simulated and computed with the other function f_0 in a finite number of steps. Then f_1 does not need to be explicitly defined, and the computational model can be described solely using the fundamental operation f_0. Therefore, in a computational model, if it includes more than one fundamental operation, these operations must not be computable from one another.

3.2.3 Turing Machine in 1930s

Overview

1936   1946   1965
Turing Machine $\rightarrow$ Digital Computer $\rightarrow$ Computational Complexity

The most well-known computational model is the Turing machine. The Turing machine was proposed in 1936, preceding the invention of the first digital computer in 1946 and the emergence of computational complexity in 1965.

Before the Turing machine was proposed, the study of solving computing problems using computational machinery was an active research topic. The concept of computation was not well defined, nor was the formalization of algorithms written on paper for problem-solving. In 1936, Alan Turing introduced the a-machine (where a stands for automatic), which was later named the Turing machine by Alonzo Church.

Alan Turing did not invent the Turing machine with the goal of building a computer but rather to challenge a prominent mathematician's perspective on mathematics. The proposed Turing machine exhibits two properties:

- **Capability:** All algorithms that can be executed using paper and pencil to solve computing problems can be simulated by a Turing machine. If an algorithm executed using paper and pencil can solve a computing problem, then a Turing machine can also solve it.
- **Limitation:** Some problems[1] cannot be solved by any Turing machine, rendering them uncomputable. This property allowed Turing to successfully resolve Hilbert's Entscheidungsproblem, demonstrating that there may not exist an algorithm for determining whether a given statement is provable based on axioms and logical rules.

Although the original motivation behind the Turing machine was neither to build real-world computers nor to study computational complexity, it is regarded as the foundation of computer science and the starting point of computational theory. Any computing device must be designed and built to meet at least the requirements of the Turing machine computational model; otherwise, such devices might fail to solve certain computing problems that humans can handle using paper and pencil.

3.2.4 Turing Tape

We break down the Turing machine into three key concepts as preliminaries. The first is the Turing tape. The Turing tape resembles a paper tape and is used in the computational model to store symbols (Figure 3.2).

- Each Turing tape has infinite length and is divided into cells arranged in one row. Each cell is designed to carry only one symbol.
- Each Turing tape also includes a Turing head that can move left (L), move right (R), or remain stationary (S).
- When the head is positioned over a cell, it can read the symbol in that cell or write a new symbol into it. The symbol under the head is referred to as the "current symbol" in this book.

---

[1] No need to expand this area since the problems are very abstracted.

3.2 Computational Models: Background and Preliminaries

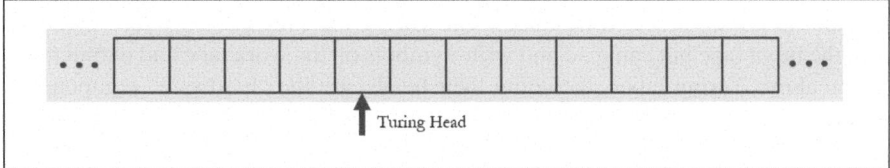

Fig. 3.2 Turing tape composed of cells to carry symbols and a Turing head

A Turing machine has various slightly different definitions, and one of them concerns the symbols. Although a Turing machine can write any symbol on the Turing tape, a definition with four basic symbols suffices for practical use:

- The symbol "$\triangleright$" represents "start".
- The symbol "$\square$" represents "blank" or empty.
- The bits 0 and 1 represent data.

Another variation in the definition concerns the number of Turing tapes. A Turing machine may have multiple Turing tapes, each serving a distinct function or purpose. For illustration, we focus on a three-tape Turing machine, which consists of the following tapes:

- **Input Tape:** The input, such as the problem instance, is written on this tape and read by the Turing machine.
- **Work Tape:** All intermediate data generated during computation (not the final output) is written on this tape.
- **Output Tape:** The output, such as the solution to the input instance, is written on this tape. If the Turing machine is to solve a decision problem, only one bit (1 or 0) will be written on this tape.

The comparison of these tapes is given in Table 3.1.

Table 3.1 Differences of Turing tapes. The input tape indicates that the first cell contains the "start" symbol, followed by an arbitrary sequence of cells containing 0 or 1. The other cells are blank.

	Input Tape	Work Tape	Output Tape
Initialization	$\triangleright \{0,1\}^* \square^*$	$\triangleright \square^*$	$\triangleright \square^*$
Action	Read only	Read and Write	Read and Write

The Turing machine, using symbols and Turing tapes, works together as follows: During initialization before the machine starts, all Turing heads are positioned at the start symbol. The other cells on the work tape and the output tape are initialized with blank symbols, while the input tape contains a bit string $\{0,1\}^*$ representing the input (e.g., the problem instance). The Turing machine can only read symbols from the input tape but can read and write symbols on the work tape and output tape.

The above Turing tapes, including their heads, are the "hardware" components of Turing machines. Next, we describe the "software" components (i.e., algorithms) include instructions and Turing states, which specify how to run a Turing machine.

3.2.5 Instruction and Turing State

A Turing instruction tells a Turing machine what to do after reading Turing tapes each time. It is depicted as follows.

Step 1	Read Tapes	$\rightarrow$	Instruction
Step 2	Read Tapes	$\rightarrow$	Instruction
$\vdots$		$\vdots$	
Step N	Read Tapes	$\rightarrow$	Instruction

The instruction consists of two parts:

- **Writing:** Specifies what to write on the Turing tapes (work tape and output tape only). The symbols that can be written on tapes are $\{0, 1, \Box\}$.
- **Moving:** Describes how to move the Turing heads (input tape, work tape, and output tape). Each Turing head can move at most one cell in each step.

Each reading case has exactly one writing-moving instruction that specifies what to write on the Turing tapes and how to move the Turing heads. We remark that designing a specific Turing machine to solve a computing problem is essentially designing instructions, collectively known as an algorithm.

Nevertheless, a basic instruction is insufficient for a comprehensive definition of Turing machines. Given the presence of four symbols across all three Turing tapes, the current symbols (where heads are located) result in a maximum of $4^3 = 64$ distinct reading cases. At most, there are 64 related instructions. To address this constraint, the concept of a Turing state was introduced. In essence, each state is written on a paper sheet with a 64×3 table (64 rows and 3 columns, See Figure 3.3). Each row in this table corresponds to an index, a reading case, and a unique instruction. There are at most 64 cases, but the actual number may be fewer.

A Turing machine employs multiple states (multiple paper sheets) to increase its computational power. After incorporating the state concept, in addition to writing and moving, the instructions also specify:

- **Changing:** Which state should be called in the next step (state 1, state 2, $\cdots$).

With the help of multiple states, the same reading case from the reading tapes can have different writing-moving instructions.

3.2 Computational Models: Background and Preliminaries

This paper sheet is for state: XXX

Index	Read Case	Instruction
1	If the reading case is _____ ,	do the instruction as _____
2	If the reading case is _____ ,	do the instruction as _____
3	If the reading case is _____ ,	do the instruction as _____
4	If the reading case is _____ ,	do the instruction as _____
5	If the reading case is _____ ,	do the instruction as _____
6	If the reading case is _____ ,	do the instruction as _____
7	If the reading case is _____ ,	do the instruction as _____
8	If the reading case is _____ ,	do the instruction as _____
9	If the reading case is _____ ,	do the instruction as _____
10	If the reading case is _____ ,	do the instruction as _____
11	If the reading case is _____ ,	do the instruction as _____
12	If the reading case is _____ ,	do the instruction as _____
⋮	⋮	⋮
58	If the reading case is _____ ,	do the instruction as _____
59	If the reading case is _____ ,	do the instruction as _____
60	If the reading case is _____ ,	do the instruction as _____
61	If the reading case is _____ ,	do the instruction as _____
62	If the reading case is _____ ,	do the instruction as _____
63	If the reading case is _____ ,	do the instruction as _____
64	If the reading case is _____ ,	do the instruction as _____

Fig. 3.3 A straightforward example of Turing state

In summary, Turing states play a crucial role in guiding the actions of a Turing machine. With multiple states incorporated, Turing machines become more adept at processing and manipulating information. Moving forward, we will formalize these instructions and states using a mathematical function called the transition function.

3.2.6 Transition Function

A transition function serves to represent the instruction:

$$Current\ State \times Reading\ Case \rightarrow Writing \times Moving \times Changing$$

through a mathematical function. The key parameters are defined as:

- Q: The set of states.
- Σ_{read}: The set of all possible symbols (reading cases) in three tapes $(\sigma_i, \sigma_w, \sigma_o)$.

$$\Sigma_{read} = \{(\sigma_i, \sigma_w, \sigma_o) : \sigma_i, \sigma_w, \sigma_o \in \{\triangleright, \square, 0, 1\}\}$$

- Σ_{write}: The set of all possible symbol pairs to be written on the work tape and the output tape.

$$\Sigma_{write} = \{(W, O) : W, O \in \{\square, 0, 1\}\}$$

- $\{L, S, R\}^3$: The movement of three tape heads, where L represents "move left", S represents "stop without moving", and R represents "move right".

Now, the general description of a transition function δ is described as follows:

$$\delta : Q \times \Sigma_{read} \to \Sigma_{write} \times \{L, S, R\}^3 \times Q,$$

where the input is the current state and current symbols (reading case), and the output denotes one of the instructions.

It is essential to note that we do not require a mathematical formula to express this function, but rather a set of tables (or paper sheets) that list all pairs of inputs and outputs. Furthermore, this transition function serves as the only fundamental operation in Turing machines, representing a mapping computation: it determines the output for a given input based on these tables. We also emphasize that this transition function is not the only function defined in all known Turing machines.

3.3 Computational Models: Turing Machines

Based on the previously introduced notations, syntax, and terms, we are now ready to define Turing machines and their variants in this section.

3.3.1 Turing Machines

Definition 3.3.1 (Turing Machines). *A Turing machine is a computing machine that consists of Turing tapes and a set of transition functions.*

The above definition is an intensional one based on computing machines. To aid in understanding the two complex components of Turing machines, we have structured their notations and terms introduced in the previous section as follows.

3.3 Computational Models: Turing Machines

Overview

$$\text{Turing Tapes} = \begin{cases} \text{Tape} \begin{cases} \text{Cells: Carrying Symbols} \\ \text{Symbols: Start } (\triangleright), \text{Blank } (\square), \text{Data } (0, 1) \end{cases} \\ \text{Head} \begin{cases} \text{Move Left, Move Right, Stop} \\ \text{Read, Write} \end{cases} \end{cases}$$

$$\text{Transition Functions} = \begin{cases} \text{Input} \begin{cases} \text{Current State} \\ \text{Current Reading Case } \Sigma_{read} \end{cases} \\ \text{Output} \begin{cases} \text{Written Symbols on Two Tapes } \Sigma_{write} \\ \text{Movement of Three Turing Heads} \\ \text{New State} \end{cases} \end{cases}$$

! Attention

When studying Turing machines, it is important to focus on understanding their fundamental operations rather than trying to design a Turing machine to solve a specific computing problem.

3.3.2 Deterministic Turing Machines

Definition 3.3.2 (Deterministic Turing Machines). *A 3-tape deterministic Turing machine is a* (Q, Σ, δ)-*Turing machine where*

- *It has input tape, work tape, and output tape.*
- *Q is a finite set of states including a start state q_{start} and a halt state q_{halt}.*
- *Σ is a set of symbols $\{\triangleright, 0, 1, \square\}$ on tapes.*
- *$\delta : Q \times \Sigma_{read} \to \Sigma_{write} \times \{L, S, R\}^3 \times Q$ is a transition function.*

The machine begins with the start state q_{start} (in the first step) and stops when the state is q_{halt} (in the last step). Note that this might be just a partial function where both the domain and the codomain are strict subset of $Q \times \Sigma_{read}$ and $\Sigma_{write} \times \{L, S, R\}^3 \times Q$.

We say that a deterministic Turing machine can solve a computing problem if it halts in a finite number of steps and outputs a problem solution for every input problem instance. If a deterministic Turing machine cannot solve a problem, it means that the machine either does not halt or halts but leaves nothing on the output tape (i.e., no output). Note that "output" is an action that occurs after "halt".

3.3.3 Probabilistic Turing Machines

Definition 3.3.3 (Probabilistic Turing Machines). *A 3-tape probabilistic Turing machine is a $(Q, \Sigma, \delta_0, \delta_1)$-Turing machine where*

- *It has input tape, work tape, and output tape.*
- *Q is a finite set of states including a start state q_{start} and a halt state q_{halt}.*
- *Σ is a set of symbols $\{\triangleright, 0, 1, \square\}$ on tapes.*
- *$\delta_0, \delta_1 : Q \times \Sigma_{read} \to \Sigma_{write} \times \{L, S, R\}^3 \times Q$ are two transition functions.*

If both transition functions have defined transitions for the same input, the machine will follow one of the two transitions by making a random choice, with each being selected with probability $\frac{1}{2}$.

Intuitively, each state will have two paper sheets, with one paper sheet containing the "0" symbol representing δ_0, and the other containing the "1" symbol representing δ_1. The random choice decides which paper sheet will be chosen to follow the instruction.

Suppose the machine halts after N steps. A probabilistic Turing machine will return a single computation result, which depends on the sequence of choices (namely, either δ_0 or δ_1 in each step).

The definition of probabilistic Turing machines requires them to be able to make random choices. A variant definition can be made by adding a fourth Turing tape that carries random bits, allowing the Turing machine to read a random bit from this tape to determine whether to follow the transition function δ_0 or δ_1. Each random bit in each cell is read only once, and the Turing head should move right to read the next bit for subsequent use.

3.3.4 Non-Deterministic Turing Machines

Definition 3.3.4 (Non-Deterministic Turing Machines). *A 3-tape non-deterministic Turing machine is a $(Q, \Sigma, \delta_0, \delta_1)$-Turing machine where*

- *It has input tape, work tape, and output tape.*
- *Q is a finite set of states including a start state q_{start} and a halt state q_{halt}.*
- *Σ is a set of symbols $\{\triangleright, 0, 1, \square\}$ on tapes.*
- *$\delta_0, \delta_1 : Q \times \Sigma_{read} \to \Sigma_{write} \times \{L, S, R\}^3 \times Q$ are two transition functions.*

If both transition functions have defined transitions for the same input, the machine will follow both transitions simultaneously.

We say that a non-deterministic Turing machine can solve a computing problem if there exists a sequence of choices that allows the machine to halt in a finite number of steps and output a problem solution for every input problem instance. We do not

3.3 Computational Models: Turing Machines

care which specific sequence returns a problem solution, as long as such a sequence exists within this type of machine.

One intuitive way to understand this concept is through cloning theory and the theory of parallel universes. When both transition functions have defined transitions for the same input, we imagine that the Turing machine is cloned into twice as sub-machines, with each sub-machine following one of the transition functions. In the first step, there is a single machine. The number of machines doubles to two in the second step, four in the third step, and 2^k sub-machines in the k-th step. Each sub-machine produces an output, and the correct problem solution is intelligently selected from one of these outputs by the non-deterministic Turing machine.

It seems that this kind of non-deterministic Turing machine (NDTM) cannot exist in our universe. Even if a computing machine were as small as an atom, the entire Earth could only accommodate approximately 2^{172} such machines. However, an NDTM must support an arbitrary number of cloning instances.

3.3.5 Quantum Turing Machines

The notions of quantum computing and quantum computers began in the early 1980s. A quantum Turing machine is a computational model proposed to represent quantum computing.

A quantum Turing machine is also defined with Turing tapes and a set of transition functions, but its transition functions are more advanced, capturing the features of quantum computing. We do not intend to introduce the quantum Turing machine in detail, as its definition is significantly more complex and requires extensive mathematical preliminaries. Instead, we highlight that a quantum Turing machine is analogous to a probabilistic Turing machine in that it may return incorrect outputs. However, a quantum Turing machine offers greater computational power than a probabilistic Turing machine.

3.3.6 Comparisons of Different Turing Machines

So far, we have introduced deterministic Turing machines (DTM), probabilistic Turing machines (PTM), non-deterministic Turing machines (NDTM), and quantum Turing machines (QTM). These are not the only variant definitions, but they are the most important ones with clear distinctions. We present two types of comparisons in Table 3.2.

The first comparison concerns the computational power of each type of Turing machine. Let DTM represent the Turing machine with standard computational power. The comparison of computational power is as follows.

- PTM is stronger compared to DTM. We can use probabilistic algorithms (within PTM) and deterministic algorithms (within DTM) to illustrate the difference.

Table 3.2 Comparison of variant Turing machines

	DTM	PTM	QTM	NDTM
Computational Power	Standard	Advanced	Optimized	Maximum
Realizable	Yes	Yes	Maybe	Maybe Not

In the literature, researchers have discovered that some problems can be solved efficiently using probabilistic algorithms. One of the most interesting examples is the decision problem known as the primality test problem. Given an integer x, the problem asks whether x is prime. It has been found that a well-designed probabilistic algorithm is more efficient than any known deterministic algorithm for this problem.

- QTM is stronger than PTM. In 1994, Peter Shor discovered a novel algorithm within QTM that can efficiently solve the factorization problem. However, all known algorithms within PTM fail to solve this problem efficiently.
- NDTM is the strongest among all four Turing machines. Many computing problems can be efficiently solved by NDTM, but it remains unknown whether they can be efficiently solved using QTM. One example is the Hamiltonian Cycle problem, which asks whether a cycle exists that visits each vertex exactly once and returns to the starting vertex. This can be visualized as finding a path that traverses every point in a graph exactly once without lifting the pen and returns to the starting point.

We note that these assessments of computational power are based on human knowledge rather than the inherent computational power of each Turing machine.

The second comparison concerns the realization of each type of Turing machine. DTM and PTM can be implemented in the physical world by humans. Our current digital computers are computing devices that can capture these two types of Turing machines. The computing devices that can capture QTM are called quantum computers, but it remains unknown whether humans can eventually build a general-purpose computing device that fully meets the definition of QTM. As for NDTM, it is physically infeasible (or unknown) whether humans can construct computing devices that capture NDTM.

3.4 The Church–Turing Thesis: Equivalent Capabilities

In the course of human scientific advancement, certain mathematical problems, known as computing problems, remain unsolved. These unsolved problems are categorized as open problems. As research progresses, new open problems may emerge, and some of them may eventually be solved by humanity before human extinction. Let $S_\mathbb{H}$ be the set containing all computing problems that humans can solve. It seems impossible to determine the size of this set.

After general-purpose computing devices were invented to replace humans in solving computing problems, a fundamental question arises: how powerful are these computing devices? Using Turing machines as an example, the key question is:

> **? Question**
>
> *Can Turing machines solve all computing problems in the set $S_\mathbb{H}$?*

The Church-Turing thesis is a fundamental concept in computer science and mathematics, proposing the equivalence of different models of computation. Formulated independently by Alonzo Church and Alan Turing in the 1930s, the thesis states:

> **Church-Turing Thesis**
>
> *Turing machines can solve all computing problems in the set $S_\mathbb{H}$.*

This thesis essentially asserts that any computation feasibly executable by humans using pencil and paper can be replicated by a Turing machine, given sufficient time and resources.

The advantage of using Turing machines to replace humans is that Turing machines, with their formal definitions, have a much clearer boundary of computing ability than humans. The Church-Turing thesis allows us to focus on whether a computing problem can be solved by a Turing machine. This is particularly crucial in cryptography. Without this thesis, we might encounter a situation where:

- An adversary can break a cryptographic scheme using pencil and paper, while
- This scheme cannot be broken by all special-purpose computing machines.

In other words, the Church-Turing thesis can be regarded as the first step in scientific research for formally determining whether a computing problem (including breaking a cryptographic scheme) is solvable. The answer to this question reflects the reality of our physical world.

3.5 How to Classify Computing Problems, Revisited

Let $S_\mathbb{P}$ be the set of all computing problems represented using sets:

$$S_\mathbb{P} = \{S_{P_1}, S_{P_2}, S_{P_3}, \cdots\},$$

where S_{P_i} is the set representation for the computing problem P_i. Initially, we can classify the set of computing problems $S_\mathbb{P}$ into subsets with similar structures of problem solutions, including decision problems and search problems.

Overview

$$S_\mathbb{P} = \begin{cases} \text{Decision Problems} \begin{cases} \text{Solvable Decision Problems} \\ \text{Unsolvable Decision Problems} \end{cases} \\ \text{Search Problems} \begin{cases} \text{Solvable Search Problems} \\ \text{Unsolvable Search Problems} \end{cases} \\ \ldots \end{cases}$$

Let $S_\mathbb{P}^D$ and $S_\mathbb{P}^S$ be the subsets of $S_\mathbb{P}$ containing all decision problems and search problems, respectively. We can further divide them into subsets based on whether a problem can be solved or not by a specific-purpose computing machine. Here, "solvable" or "unsolvable" is determined based on whether a problem can be solved but a formal definition is still missing.

In this chapter, we have introduced characteristics that determine the definition of solvable problems:

- The solution relates to a specific problem instance or to any problem instance.
- The solution depends on whether it is computed by a given specific-purpose computing machine or by selecting a machine from a set of computing machines.
- The solution depends on the definition of the set of computing machines.

These characteristics determine the size of $S_\mathbb{P}^D$ and $S_\mathbb{P}^S$. So far, this is what we can divide computing problems into subsets with the concepts of computing machines.

Given a set of computing machines $S_\mathcal{C}$ under computational model $\mathcal{C}$, a computing problem P is called solvable if there exists a specific-purpose computing machine $\mathcal{M} \in S_\mathcal{C}$ that can find a problem solution to any problem instance in P. Let $S_\mathbb{P}$ be the set of all computing problems and $S_\mathbb{P}^\mathcal{C} \subseteq S_\mathbb{P}$ be the subset of solvable computing problems under $\mathcal{C}$. The consequential question asks whether different computational models $\mathcal{C}$ will determine the size of $S_\mathbb{P}^\mathcal{C}$.

This chapter introduced four types of Turing machines: DTM, PTM, QTM, and NDTM. All specific-purpose Turing machines of the same type can be treated as a set of computing machines, namely $\mathcal{C}_{DTM}, \mathcal{C}_{PTM}, \mathcal{C}_{QTM}, \mathcal{C}_{NDTM}$. Then, we have four subsets of solvable problems:

$$S_\mathbb{P}^{\mathcal{C}_{DTM}}, \ S_\mathbb{P}^{\mathcal{C}_{PTM}}, \ S_\mathbb{P}^{\mathcal{C}_{QTM}}, \ S_\mathbb{P}^{\mathcal{C}_{NDTM}}.$$

Intuitively, these four subsets should be different, but they are actually equivalent. That is, a deterministic Turing machine can solve any computing problem that a non-deterministic Turing machine can. The reason is that these machines can perform computations without restrictions on time (operation steps) and space (Turing tapes). Given any non-deterministic Turing machine, there exists a deterministic Turing machine that can simulate it and return the same computational result. We are not going to expand on the reasons since it is beyond the scope of this book, which is intended to help beginners understand cryptographic definitions.

The current classifications of solvable computing problems based on Turing machines are independent of different variants of Turing machines. This result arises from the limitations of the definition of solvability, which does not take into account resource costs, such as the number of transitions executed and the number of cells used.

3.6 Review Questions

? Question 5

Compare the difference of computing machines: ASIC and CPU.

? Question 6

Is proposing an algorithm to solve a computing problem generally easier than implementing a specific-purpose computing machine to solve the same problem? Justify your answer with examples.

? Question 7

Let P be a computing problem where any bit string is an instance. Let $\mathcal{A}$ be a probabilistic algorithm designed to solve problem P. It is known that for any n-bit input instance x, if the first k most significant bits of x are zero, then $\mathcal{A}$ can find a solution to x with probability $\frac{1}{2^{n-k}}$ on average. What is the average probability of $\mathcal{A}$ finding solutions to 10-bit instances?

? Question 8

Let $S_\mathcal{C}$ be a set of computing machines under a computational model $\mathcal{C}$. What are shared characteristics of elements inside this set?

? Question 9

Let $S_\mathcal{C}$ be a set of computing machines under a computational model $\mathcal{C}$. Let x be a problem instance of a computing problem P. Justify the reason why it is hard to know whether y satisfying $R(x, y) = 1$ can be found with a computing machine from the set $S_\mathcal{C}$.

? Question 10

Let $S_\mathcal{C}$ be a set of computing machines under a computational model $\mathcal{C}$. Let S be a set of computing problems. How to break down the set S into subsets with the help of $S_\mathcal{C}$?

? Question 11

Let P be a computing problem. If P can be solved by a non-deterministic Turing machine, it can also be solved by a deterministic Turing machine. Is this true?

? Question 12

Let $\mathcal{M}_1$ and $\mathcal{M}_2$ be two deterministic Turing machines. Although they appear similar in their definitions, they perform different tasks. Specifically, $\mathcal{M}_1$ checks if the first bit of the input is 1, while $\mathcal{M}_2$ checks if the second bit of the input is 1. Can you construct these two machines using the definitions of deterministic Turing machines?

? Question 13

Alice said "Alan Turing invented Turing machines aiming to build computers and study computational complexity". Correct Alice's statement if it is wrong.

Chapter 4
Computational Complexity

Abstract Let S be the set of computing problems that can be solved by a Turing machine. This chapter introduces how to further classify this set using complexity as a new characteristic based on computational resources. Complexity can be defined in many ways. As a consequence, a significant number of subsets of solvable computing problems can be derived from the set S.

4.1 Roadmap: We Are Here

We believe it is beneficial to provide a roadmap (Figure 4.1) outlining all the knowledge covered in this book, particularly in the previous two chapters and this one. This roadmap will help beginners stay oriented despite the significant number of notations, syntax, and terms introduced and yet to be introduced in this chapter.

In Chapter 2, we introduced what a computing problem is. Each computing problem P can be abstracted using a relation function R and interpreted as a set of instance-solution pairs (x, y) satisfying $R(x, y) = 1$.

In Chapter 3, we introduced computing machines and their abstraction called computational models. Computing machines can be classified into specific-purpose computing machines and general-purpose computing machines, where the former is also known as algorithms that run on the latter. We run algorithms on a (general-purpose) computing machine to solve computing problems. An algorithm should return an output, which we expect to be the solution to the given problem instance. On the other hand, computational models were proposed to define the limits of theoretical computation. Turing machines are the most well-known computational models, and the Church-Turing thesis states that they can solve all computing problems that humans can solve with pencil and paper.

Now, we are gradually introducing the computational complexity of an algorithm or a Turing machine in solving a computing problem. The following knowledge in this chapter consists of three parts:

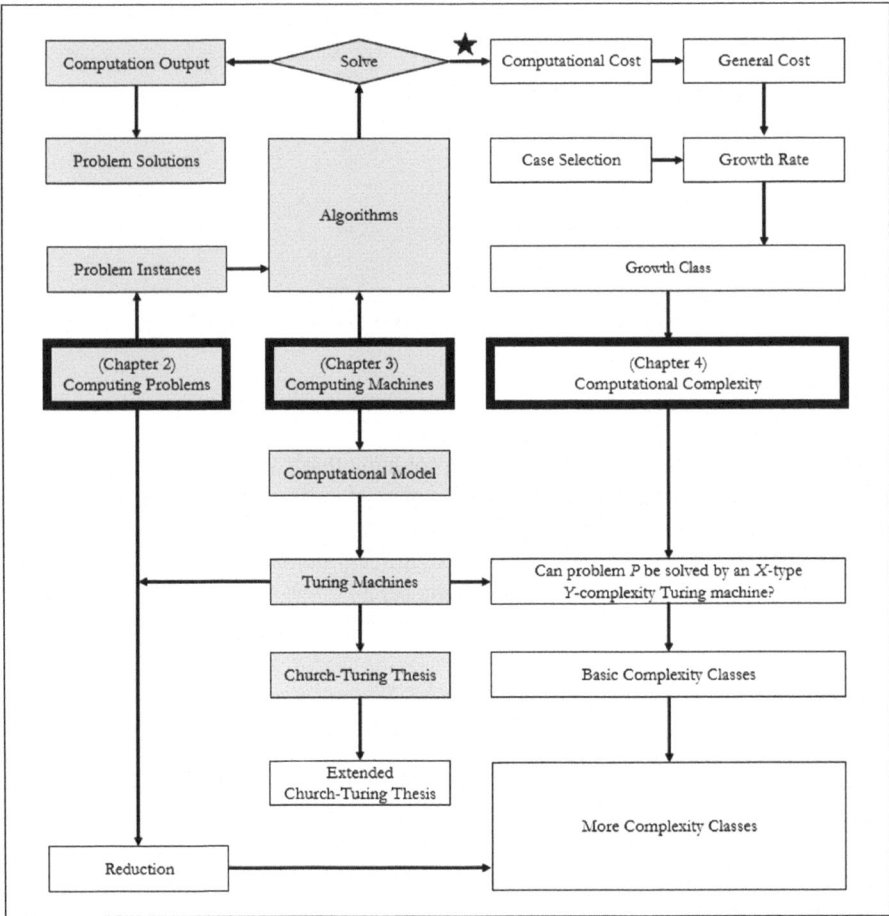

Fig. 4.1 We are here ★. All white fields will be introduced in this chapter.

- The first part introduces notations, syntax, and terms related to complexity. The key terms include computational cost, general cost, case selection, growth rate, and growth class.
- The second part introduces new Turing machines after adding complexity to definitions, referred to as X-type Y-complexity Turing machines. Here, X-type refers to deterministic, probabilistic, or non-deterministic. Y-complexity will be the newly defined term.
- The third part introduces many sets of solvable computing problems under different definitions, commonly referred to as complexity classes. The primary difference is determined by Turing machines with different X and Y.

4.2 Solving Problems: From Cost to Complexity

4.2.1 Computational Cost

Computational cost quantifies the amount of resources required by an algorithm in solving a computing problem. The main resources we are concerned with are time and/or space, explained as follows:

- **Time.** How long does it take to produce an output? In practice, when running the algorithm on a physical computing machine, the time cost refers to seconds, minutes, months, or years that we must wait until we see an output. In theory, the time cost is determined by operations inside the algorithm. For example, it takes 95 modular additions and 27 modular multiplications.
- **Space.** How much intermediate storage does the algorithm require? In practice, when running the algorithm on a physical computing machine, the space cost refers to the required random-access memory (RAM). In theory, the space cost is determined by the number of variables defined within the algorithm.

Computational cost reflects the efficiency of an algorithm when solving a computing problem on a machine. When comparing the efficiency of two algorithms, we can use time or space cost, either in theory or in practice, as long as the comparison is fair enough.

Given an algorithm that can solve a computing problem P, namely finding a problem solution to any input problem instance, we stress that the computational cost may vary depending on the input instance. In particular, the instance length and the instance case significantly affect the computational cost.

- **Instance length:** It refers to the bit length of instance x to be solved. It has been shown that the cost of finding solutions for problem instances may increase as the instance length grows. Taking the simple example of counting 1-bits in a given bit string, it is obvious that the number of counting operations is linear in the bit length of the given instance. We also note that some special problems have constant computational cost. For example, the problem of deciding whether the input integer is even or odd. This can be done by checking the least significant bit of the input string.
- **Instance case:** It refers to determining which instance to solve among all problem instances of the same length. It has been shown that finding solutions to different instances could require different amounts of computation even if instances have the same length. A simple example is the exhaustive search algorithm to solve the discrete log problem defined over a group $(\mathbb{G}, g, p)$, where all instances have the same length. Consider the search algorithm that guesses a solution to the instance $x = (g, g^a)$ by sequentially guessing from 1 to p. It is easy to see that finding a solution to the instance $x = (g, g^{1205})$ requires $1,205$ operations fewer than finding a solution to the instance $x = (g, g^{9527})$, which requires $9,527$ operations.

In computational models like Turing machines, the resource costs are slightly different yet conceptually similar. These costs include the number of computational steps (time complexity) and the number of cells used in the work tape (space complexity). Before introducing new computational models, we will use an algorithm (which is more beginner-friendly) instead of a Turing machine when introducing related terms.

4.2.2 Concrete Cost and General Cost

Let $\mathcal{A}$ be an algorithm that can solve the computing problem P, and let x be a specific instance of P. We consider the following two questions related to computational cost (either time or space):

> **? Questions**
>
> 1. What is the computational cost of <u>finding a solution to x</u> by algorithm $\mathcal{A}$?
> 2. What is the computational cost of <u>solving problem P</u> by algorithm $\mathcal{A}$?

The first question is about the concrete cost, denoted by $C(x)$, which represents the computational cost of finding a problem solution for a specific problem instance using the algorithm $\mathcal{A}$. The answer to this question is a fixed number of operations such as 2^{10}, 2^{20}, or one million operations, depending on the algorithm and the instance. Answering the first question is straightforward.

The second question refers to general cost, denoted by $C_\mathcal{A}(P)$, which represents the computational cost without specifying instances. The answer to this question is not obvious because the computational cost varies and depends on both instance length and instance case. Let $x_{i,j}$ denote the j-th instance of i-bit length, ordered according to a certain sorting rule. Theoretically, the computational cost of $C_\mathcal{A}(P)$ can be expressed as follows.

$$C_\mathcal{A}(P) = \begin{pmatrix} C(x_{1,1}), C(x_{1,2^1}) \\ C(x_{2,1}), C(x_{2,2}), C(x_{2,3}), C(x_{2,2^2}) \\ C(x_{3,1}), C(x_{3,2}), C(x_{3,3}), C(x_{3,4}), \cdots\cdots, C(x_{3,2^3}) \\ \vdots \end{pmatrix},$$

where the i-th row in the matrix $C_\mathcal{A}(P)$ contains the computational cost of all i-bit instances, and there are at most 2^i instances in this row.

The general cost presented in $C_\mathcal{A}(P)$ is not straightforward due to two reasons.
- Firstly, it is not easy to identify a clear pattern in the concrete costs because each cost may vary depending on instance length and instance case.

4.2 Solving Problems: From Cost to Complexity

- Secondly, this general cost necessarily includes an infinite number of concrete costs. It is impossible to list all of them and therefore we cannot see the omitted concrete costs in the presentation.

Therefore, answering the second question is neither easy nor straightforward. A clever approach is needed to simplify $C_\mathcal{A}(P)$ before conveying how heavy or light the general cost is.

4.2.3 Case Selection and Growth Rate

As seen in the definition of $C_\mathcal{A}(P)$, the computational cost for instances of the same length cannot be uniquely determined by a single value because it also depends on instance cases.

The first step in simplifying $C_\mathcal{A}(P)$ is choosing a representative case to approximate the computational cost for instances of the same length. We consider the computational costs

$$C(x_{n,1}), C(x_{n,2}), C(x_{n,3}), \cdots, C(x_{n,2^n})$$

for all n-bit instances when finding their solutions. Let C_n be a single representative value for $(C(x_{n,1}), C(x_{n,2}), \cdots, C(x_{n,2^n}))$, which consists of 2^n values. There are three common approaches used in the literature to calculate and represent C_n, namely the Best Case, the Worst Case, and the Average Case.

- **Best Case:** We consider the instance case with the minimal cost and define

$$C_n = \min\{C(x_{n,1}), C(x_{n,2}), C(x_{n,3}), \cdots, C(x_{n,2^n})\}.$$

- **Worst Case:** We consider the instance case with the maximum cost and define

$$C_n = \max\{C(x_{n,1}), C(x_{n,2}), C(x_{n,3}), \cdots, C(x_{n,2^n})\}.$$

- **Average Case:** We consider all instance cases and calculate the average by

$$C_n = \frac{C(x_{n,1}) + C(x_{n,2}) + C(x_{n,3}) + \cdots + C(x_{n,2^n})}{2^n}.$$

Any of the above approaches can be chosen to represent the computational cost C_n as long as the choice of case representation is sound and convincing. It is important to note that the representation of the computational cost C_n differs significantly between complexity theory and cryptography. Moreover, these are not the only approaches for representing the computational cost C_n for n-bit instances.

With the above simplified measurement, the computational cost of solving the computing problem P using the algorithm $\mathcal{A}$ is denoted by

$$C_\mathcal{A}^{case}(P) = (C_1, C_2, C_3, C_4, C_5, C_6, \cdots).$$

The general cost using a one-dimensional array is much simpler than that using the original two-dimensional matrix. However, since this array has an infinite length, it is still difficult to evaluate the computational cost of using $\mathcal{A}$ to solve the problem unless most C_i values are known. Obviously, such an array cannot be used to represent the computational cost of solving a computing problem.

The second step in simplifying $C_\mathcal{A}(P)$ is defining a function formula $f(n)$ to represent $C_\mathcal{A}^{case}(P)$. We refer to this function as the growth rate in this book, which describes how fast C_n grows as the index n (or instance length) grows. The growth rate helps us understand the difficulty of solving the computing problem, as it allows us to compute the computational cost $C_i = f(i)$ for any instance length i directly from this formula.

With the use of growth rate, we can state as follows to answer the question related to the general cost:

Statement

The algorithm $\mathcal{A}$ can solve the computing problem P with growth grate $f(n)$.

This statement clearly describes the relation between the computational cost and the instance length n. Given any instance length i, we can immediately determine the corresponding computational cost by computing $f(i)$. Compared to the cost represented in $C_\mathcal{A}^{case}(P) = (C_1, C_2, C_3, C_4, C_5, C_6, \cdots)$, expressing the growth rate as a function is more succinct and clear, while still providing sufficient information to describe the computational cost of solving a computing problem.

In the above statement, we do not know how $f(n)$, the resource cost for n-bit instances, is measured. It can be the best case, the worst case, or the average case. Nor do we know what resource is being measured. It can refer to time, space, or other resources. What we want to emphasize here is that if $f(n)$ refers to time cost only, the space cost of algorithm $\mathcal{A}$ might be extremely large. Similarly, if $f(n)$ represents space cost only, the time cost of algorithm $\mathcal{A}$ might be extremely large.

4.2.4 Growth Class

The growth rate, denoted by $f(n)$, is used to represent the computational cost of solving the computing problem P. Suppose we can compute this function $f(n)$. This leads to the following question:

4.2 Solving Problems: From Cost to Complexity

> **? Question**
>
> *Is the growth rate $f(n)$ fast or slow among all algorithms that can solve P?*

The above question is interesting because we are interested in knowing whether the algorithm $\mathcal{A}$ is an efficient algorithm or not when compared to other potential algorithms that can solve the computing problem P. Unfortunately, it is very challenging to answer this question because the number of growth rates is infinite (we have an infinite number of function formulas) and there is no clear rule to quantify what is fast or slow.

To provide a straightforward answer to the above question, we introduce the concept of a growth class, which we refer to in this book as a set of growth rates that share common characteristics based on well-defined rules. That is, all growth rates, which are infinite in number, have been classified into a few sets, each of which is called a growth class. Consider the case where all growth rates are classified into the following six growth classes:

$$\{GC_1, GC_2, GC_3, GC_4, GC_5, GC_6\},$$

where growth rates in GC_6 grow the fastest among them. Growth rates from two different growth classes will be considered as having "significantly different costs" under the well-defined rules.

By replacing growth rate with growth class, we can change the statement with growth rate to statement with growth class as follows.

> **Statement**
>
> The algorithm $\mathcal{A}$ can solve the computing problem P with growth class GC_i.

Although this statement lacks precision, it provides two advantages.

- Firstly, the statement is compact without providing the growth rate $f(n)$, which might be very complicated to be calculated (or impossible to be calculated).
- Secondly, we can roughly evaluate how good algorithm $\mathcal{A}$ is from the description without looking into the growth rate $f(n)$. This is because there are only six growth classes compared to an infinite number of growth rates.

In the above introduction, we did not specify the rules for defining growth classes, since there exist multiple ways to define them. In the following subsections, we introduce three types of growth classes.

4.2.5 Growth Classes: Big O

Let $f(n), g(n) > 0$ be two functions in integer n (≥ 1) satisfying

$$f(n) = O(g(n)).$$

The big O notation means that there exist $n_0 > 0, c > 0$ such that for every $n > n_0$,

$$f(n) \leq c \cdot g(n).$$

That is, the growth rate $f(n)$ is not faster than the growth rate $c \cdot g(n)$ when $n > n_0$.

A Variant Definition. The definition of the big O notation can even omit the integer n_0. This is because we can choose another c' to replace c such that $f(n) \leq c' \cdot g(n)$ holds for all $n \geq 1$. The approach is briefly explained as follows.

Let f_{max}, g_{min} be two values satisfying

$$0 < f(n) \leq f_{max} \text{ for all } n \in [1, n_0]$$
$$0 < g_{min} \leq g(n) \text{ for all } n \in [1, n_0].$$

We can set c' as

$$c' = c + \frac{f_{max}}{g_{min}}.$$

It is not hard to verify that

$$\frac{f(n)}{f_{max}} \leq 1 \leq \frac{g(n)}{g_{min}} \text{ for all } n \in [1, n_0].$$

Then, we have

$$f(n) \leq \frac{f_{max}}{g_{min}} \cdot g(n) \leq c \cdot g(n) + \frac{f_{max}}{g_{min}} \cdot g(n) = c' \cdot g(n) \text{ for all } n \in [1, n_0].$$
$$f(n) \leq c \cdot g(n) \leq c \cdot g(n) + \frac{f_{max}}{g_{min}} \cdot g(n) = c' \cdot g(n) \text{ for all } n \geq n_0.$$

Therefore, we have

$$f(n) \leq c' \cdot g(n) \text{ for all } n \geq 1.$$

In this book, the standard definition and this variant definition for the big O notation will be both used without emphasizing the equivalence again.

The Big O Growth Classes. We can define the following six growth classes with the big O notation:

$$O(1), \quad O(\log n), \quad O(n), \quad O(n^k), \quad O(2^{n^\epsilon}), \quad O(2^n).$$

The definition of each growth class is described as follows.

- We write $f(n) = O(1)$ if there exists $c > 0$ such that for every $n \geq 1$,

4.2 Solving Problems: From Cost to Complexity

$$f(n) \leq c.$$

- We write $f(n) = O(\log n)$ if there exists $c > 0$ such that for every $n \geq 1$,

$$f(n) \leq c \cdot \log n.$$

- We write $f(n) = O(n)$ if there exists $c > 0$ such that for every $n \geq 1$,

$$f(n) \leq c \cdot n.$$

- We write $f(n) = O(n^k)$ if there exist $c > 0$ and $k > 1$ such that for every $n \geq 1$,

$$f(n) \leq c \cdot n^k.$$

- We write $f(n) = O(2^{n^\epsilon})$ if there exist $c > 0$ and $0 < \epsilon < 1$ such that for every $n \geq 1$,

$$f(n) \leq 2^{c \cdot n^\epsilon}.$$

- We write $f(n) = O(2^n)$ if there exists $c > 0$ such that for every $n \geq 1$,

$$f(n) \leq 2^{c \cdot n}.$$

We use $2^{c \cdot n}$ instead of $c \cdot 2^n$ as the former is easier to include the growth rate 3^n.

In this book, the above six growth classes are named as follows.

Growth Classes	Names
$O(1)$	Upper Bound Constant Growth Class
$O(\log n)$	Upper Bound Logarithmic Growth Class
$O(n)$	Upper Bound Linear Growth Class
$O(n^k)$	Upper Bound Polynomial Growth Class
$O(2^{n^\epsilon})$	Upper Bound Sub-exponential Growth Class
$O(2^n)$	Upper Bound Exponential Growth Class

The relations of the above six growth classes satisfy

$$O(1) \subseteq O(\log n) \subseteq O(n) \subseteq O(n^k) \subseteq O(2^{n^\epsilon}) \subseteq O(2^n).$$

That is, if $f(n) = 9n + 5$, we can write

$$f(n) = O(n), \text{ or, } f(n) = O(n^k), \text{ or, } f(n) = O(2^{n^\epsilon}), \text{ or, } f(n) = O(2^n).$$

We remark that more growth classes can be defined with the big O notation besides the above six classes. However, these six classes have included the most important ones for computational complexity and cryptography.

4.2.6 Growth Classes: Big Ω

Let $f(n), g(n) > 0$ be two functions in integer $n\ (\geq 1)$ satisfying

$$f(n) = \Omega(g(n)).$$

The big Ω notation means that there exist $n_0 > 0, c > 0$ such that for every $n > n_0$,

$$c \cdot g(n) \leq f(n).$$

The growth rate $f(n)$ is not slower than the growth rate $c \cdot g(n)$. Similarly, the definition of the big Ω notation can also omit the integer n_0 with the same reason as for the big O notation.

The Big Ω Growth Classes. We can define the following six growth classes with the big Ω notation:

$$\Omega(1),\ \Omega(\log n),\ \Omega(n),\ \Omega(n^k),\ \Omega(2^{n^\epsilon}),\ \Omega(2^n).$$

The definition of each growth class is described as follows.

- We write $f(n) = \Omega(1)$ if there exists $c > 0$ such that for every $n \geq 1$,

$$c \leq f(n).$$

- We write $f(n) = \Omega(\log n)$ if there exists $c > 0$ such that for every $n \geq 1$,

$$c \cdot \log n \leq f(n).$$

- We write $f(n) = \Omega(n)$ if there exists $c > 0$ such that for every $n \geq 1$,

$$c \cdot n \leq f(n).$$

- We write $f(n) = \Omega(n^k)$ if there exist $c > 0$ and $k > 1$ such that for every $n \geq 1$,

$$c \cdot n^k \leq f(n).$$

- We write $f(n) = \Omega(2^{n^\epsilon})$ if there exist $c > 0$ and $0 < \epsilon < 1$ such that for every $n \geq 1$,

$$2^{c \cdot n^\epsilon} \leq f(n).$$

- We write $f(n) = \Omega(2^n)$ if there exists $c > 0$ such that for every $n \geq 1$,

$$2^{c \cdot n} \leq f(n).$$

In this book, the above six growth classes are named as follows.

4.2 Solving Problems: From Cost to Complexity

Growth Classes	Names
$\Omega(1)$	Lower Bound Constant Growth Class
$\Omega(\log n)$	Lower Bound Logarithmic Growth Class
$\Omega(n)$	Lower Bound Linear Growth Class
$\Omega(n^k)$	Lower Bound Polynomial Growth Class
$\Omega(2^{n^c})$	Lower Bound Sub-exponential Growth Class
$\Omega(2^n)$	Lower Bound Exponential Growth Class

The relations of the above six growth classes satisfy

$$\Omega(1) \supseteq \Omega(\log n) \supseteq \Omega(n) \supseteq \Omega(n^k) \supseteq \Omega(2^{n^c}) \supseteq \Omega(2^n).$$

That is, if $f(n) = 2n^3 + 7$, we can write

$$f(n) = \Omega(1), \text{ or } f(n) = \Omega(\log n), \text{ or, } f(n) = \Omega(n), \text{ or, } f(n) = \Omega(n^k).$$

4.2.7 Growth Classes: Big Θ

Let $f(n), g(n) > 0$ be two functions in integer n (≥ 1) satisfying

$$f(n) = \Theta(g(n)).$$

The big Θ notation means that there exist $n_0 > 0, c_1, c_2 > 0$ such that for every $n > n_0$,

$$c_1 \cdot g(n) \leq f(n) \leq c_2 \cdot g(n).$$

It means that the growth rate $f(n)$ grows as fast as the growth rate $g(n)$. Similarly, the definition of the big Θ notation can also omit the integer n_0 with the same reason as for the big O notation.

The Big Θ Growth Classes. We can define the following six growth classes with the big Θ notation:

$$\Theta(1), \Theta(\log n), \ \Theta(n), \ \Theta(n^k), \ \Theta(2^{n^c}), \ \Theta(2^n).$$

The definition of each growth class is described as follows.

- We write $f(n) = \Theta(1)$ if there exist $c_1, c_2 > 0$ such that for every $n \geq 1$,

$$c_1 \leq f(n) \leq c_2.$$

- We write $f(n) = \Theta(\log n)$ if there exist $c_1, c_2 > 0$ such that for every $n \geq 1$,

$$c_1 \cdot \log n \leq f(n) \leq c_2 \cdot \log n.$$

- We write $f(n) = \Theta(n)$ if there exist $c_1, c_2 > 0$ such that for every $n \geq 1$,

$$c_1 \cdot n \leq f(n) \leq c_2 \cdot n.$$

- We write $f(n) = \Theta(n^k)$ if there exist $c_1, c_2 > 0$ and $k > 1$ such that for every $n \geq 1$,
$$c_1 \cdot n^k \leq f(n) \leq c_2 \cdot n^k.$$

- We write $f(n) = \Theta(2^{n^\epsilon})$ if there exist $c_1, c_2 > 0$ and $0 < \epsilon < 1$ such that for every $n \geq 1$,
$$2^{c_1 \cdot n^\epsilon} \leq f(n) \leq 2^{c_2 \cdot n^\epsilon}.$$

- We write $f(n) = \Theta(2^n)$ if there exist $c_1, c_2 > 0$ such that for every $n \geq 1$,
$$2^{c_1 \cdot n} \leq f(n) \leq 2^{c_2 \cdot n}.$$

In this book, we call the above six growth classes with names given as follows.

Growth Classes	Names
$\Theta(1)$	Tight Bound Constant Growth Class
$\Theta(\log n)$	Tight Bound Logarithmic Growth Class
$\Theta(n)$	Tight Bound Linear Growth Class
$\Theta(n^k)$	Tight Bound Polynomial Growth Class
$\Theta(2^{n^\epsilon})$	Tight Bound Sub-exponential Growth Class
$\Theta(2^n)$	Tight Bound Exponential Growth Class

There is no overlap in any two tight bound growth classes above. That is, if $f(n) = 2n^3 + 7$, we can only write $f(n) = \Theta(n^k)$. In other words, each growth rate will fall into one growth class only. This is different from the growth classes defined with the big O notation and the big Ω notation.

We have completed the introduction to three growth classes using O, Ω, and Θ. In short, if two growth rates $f_1(n), f_2(n)$ are both equal to $O(n^k)$, meaning they share the same characteristic, then they belong to the same growth class. It is worth noting that there are other growth classes, such as the small o notation, which represents a strictly upper bound on the growth rate of a function. We omit the discussion of these additional growth classes since they are not commonly applied in cryptographic contexts.

4.2.8 Growth Class: Polynomial Time $O(n^k)$

Among all proposed growth classes in the literature, the most important class is:

$$O(n^k),$$

where k is a positive constant integer. This class is also known as polynomial time or polynomial size in n, and n represents instance length in computational cost. That is, we can further simplify all growth rates into two classes:

- **Polynomial-Time Class**: Any growth rate expressed as $f(n) = O(n^k)$.
- **Non-Polynomial-Time Class**: All growth rates that cannot be expressed as the formula $f(n) = O(n^k)$ for any constant integer k.

It is believed by the complexity and cryptology community that these two growth classes are the best for distinguishing between efficient and inefficient algorithms if only two classes are allowed to be used. We emphasize that the non-polynomial-time class is not equivalent to $2^{\Omega(n^\epsilon)}$, but it is a superset of it. The non-polynomial-time class cannot be defined using O, Ω, or Θ. However, this is not important for learning cryptographic definitions.

From now on, these growth classes will be referred to as computational complexity in solving computing problems. In general, computational complexity refers to the amount of resources required to run an algorithm or a Turing machine for solve computing problems. It consists of time complexity and space complexity. It focuses more on how fast resource consumption grows as the instance length increases, rather than the exact resource usage for specific instances.

4.3 Computational Models: Adding Complexity

In this section, we discuss how polynomial-time complexity is incorporated into various types of Turing machines. Here, time complexity refers to the number of computational steps (transitions) required by Turing machines.

4.3.1 Polynomial-Time Turing Machines

Previously, we introduced deterministic Turing machines (DTM), probabilistic Turing machines (PTM), and non-deterministic Turing machines (NDTM). We now incorporate "polynomial time" into these computational models. More precisely, this characteristic restricts Turing machines to halt after a polynomial number of computational steps, which depend on the input instance length. The definitions of the three new Turing machines are as follows:

> **Definition 4.3.1** (Deterministic Polynomial-Time Turing Machines). *A Turing machine is a deterministic polynomial-time Turing machine if it satisfies the following conditions:*
>
> - *It is a deterministic Turing machine.*
> - *For any input instance of length n, the machine halts in a number of steps that is polynomial in n.*

Definition 4.3.2 (Probabilistic Polynomial-Time Turing Machines). *A Turing machine is a probabilistic polynomial-time Turing machine if it satisfies the following conditions:*

- *It is a probabilistic Turing machine.*
- *For any input instance of length n, the machine halts in a number of steps that is polynomial in n.*

Definition 4.3.3 (Non-Deterministic Polynomial-Time Turing Machines). *A Turing machine is a non-deterministic polynomial-time Turing machine if it satisfies the following conditions:*

- *It is a non-deterministic Turing machine.*
- *For any input instance of length n, the machine halts in a number of steps that is polynomial in n.*

The above three Turing machines will be used to classify solvable computing problems into efficiently solvable and inefficiently solvable categories. Specifically, computing problems that cannot be solved by polynomial-time Turing machines will be considered "inefficiently solvable". In the context of solving a computing problem, it is important to note that a polynomial-time Turing machine should halt within a polynomial number of steps and produce a solution for every input instance.

4.3.2 Polynomial-Size Circuit Family

There is a long story before we introduce the term in the title of this subsection, but we have to provide sufficient background. We start with deterministic polynomial-time Turing machines and then gradually move to this term.

A deterministic polynomial-time Turing machine designed to solve a computing problem is a machine that can compute a solution for every input instance within a polynomial number of steps, regardless of the instance length. In the literature, researchers have found that there are some computing problems exhibiting the following features:

- These problems cannot be solved by any deterministic polynomial-time Turing machine (DPTTM).
- These problems are solvable by a DPTTM with adaptive strings. The adaptive strings, denoted by $\{\alpha_n\}_{n\in\mathbb{N}}$, are of polynomial size, meaning that the bit length of α_n is polynomial in n. In particular, α_n will be used as additional input (advice) to the Turing machine for computing solutions to every problem instance of length n. Let x be an instance of length n. We can interpret this as the input tape in this type of Turing machine containing $x|\alpha_n$ instead of just x.

4.3 Computational Models: Adding Complexity

Suppose we intend to propose a DPTTM with polynomial-size adaptive strings to solve the computing problem P. The string is considered adaptive because we can select any string α_n we wish for n-bit instances related to P, ensuring that the length of α_n remains polynomial in n. The source of α_n is not considered in this computational model. We assume there is a God. When we are asked to design a DPTTM with polynomial-size adaptive strings to solve a computing problem, we can ask God to place any string of our wish into α_n for us.

We remark that it is trivial to define such a computational model if the length of α_n is not bounded. The number of instances of length n is at most 2^n. If the length of α_n is not bounded, we can let α_n store solutions to all instances whose number is exponential in n. With this adaptive string α_n, it is easy to design a Turing machine to compute a problem solution to any n-bit instance by retrieving it from α_n. Therefore, to study the novelty of this computational model, we must restrict α_n to polynomial length.

Example. We refer to an example from [26] (page 41) to show that adaptive strings can be highly powerful and useful for DPTTMs in solving computing problems. Let $f : \mathbb{N} \to \{0,1\}$ be a Boolean function that is uncomputable by any DPTTM. Let $f' : \{0,1\}^* \to \{0,1\}$ be another Boolean function defined as

$$f'(x) = f(|x|).$$

We have that $f'(x)$ is also uncomputable by any DPTTM. However, by setting $\alpha_n = f(n)$ (God will provide it to us), we can easily propose a DPTTM with polynomial-size adaptive strings to solve the problem f' by simply returning the advice α_n as the problem solution to any problem instance x satisfying $|x| = n$. This is because we have

$$f'(x) = f(|x|) = f(n) = \alpha_n.$$

This adaptive string α_n contains only one bit for every $n \in \mathbb{N}$ and satisfies the polynomial size requirement. Therefore, we obtain a computing problem that is uncomputable by a DPTTM but computable by a DPTTM with polynomial-size adaptive strings.

The DPTTM with polynomial-size adaptive strings is an unrealistic computational model. This is because even the strings $\{\alpha_n\}_{n \in \mathbb{N}}$ are indeed useful, we might not be able to find God to obtain these strings.

In computational complexity, defining computational models with polynomial-size adaptive strings is known as non-uniform computation. A uniform computation is a method of solving problems that remains the same regardless of input length, such as the deterministic polynomial-time Turing machine. A non-uniform computation is the manner of solving problems with respect to input length, such as the deterministic polynomial-time Turing machine with polynomial-size adaptive strings. That is, the approaches of computing problem solutions to instances of different length are not identical in non-uniform computations.

Another approach of defining a non-uniform computation is through the concept of circuits. A circuit is a non-uniform computational model where

- The fundamental computational unit is a logic gate, such as AND gate, OR gate, and NOT gate, where the input space is $\{0,1\} \times \{0,1\}$ and the output space is $\{0,1\}$, while a NOT gate has a single-bit input.
- Computation proceeds by connecting all gates into a directed acyclic graph using wires, as shown in the following figure, where the input consists of a three-bit string $x_1 x_2 x_3$ and produces a two-bit output string $y_1 y_2$.

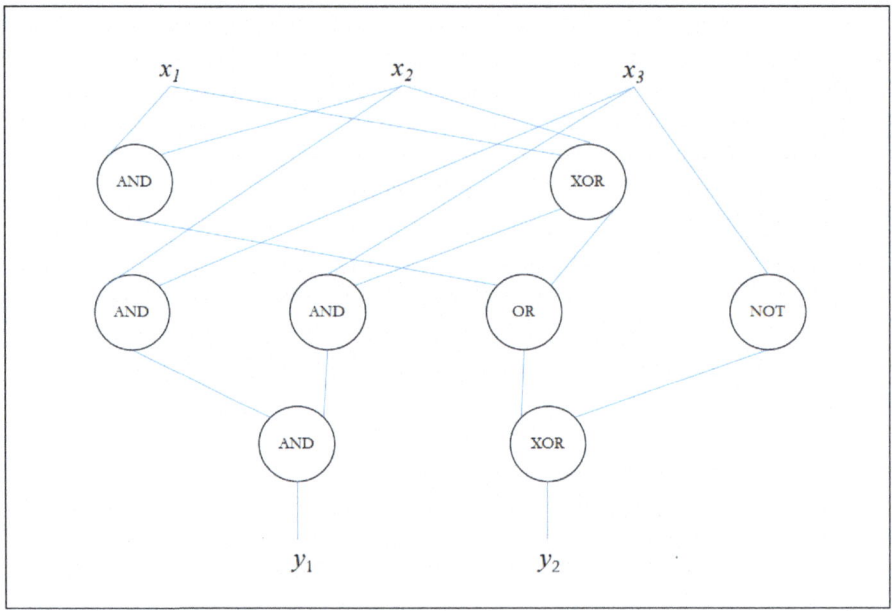

A circuit can be regarded as a model analogous to a Turing machine for solving computing problems. The key difference is that a circuit is designed for a fixed input length, whereas a Turing machine can process inputs of varying lengths. In the context of complexity, the computational complexity of Turing machines is measured by the number of computational steps, whereas circuit complexity can be measured by the total number of gates (circuit size) or the depth of the circuit. A circuit whose circuit size is polynomial in n for n-bit inputs is equivalent to a deterministic polynomial-time Turing machine for finding solutions to n-bit instances.

Let $\mathcal{C}_n$ denote a circuit proposed to find solutions to n-bit instances for computing problem P. We have

Statement

A deterministic polynomial-time Turing machine with polynomial-size adaptive strings is equivalent to $\{\mathcal{C}_n\}_{n \in \mathbb{N}}$, which denotes a circuit family, and the circuit size in $\mathcal{C}_n$ is polynomial in n.

In summary, a polynomial-size circuit family is equivalent to a deterministic polynomial-time Turing machine with polynomial-size adaptive strings, which is also known as a non-uniform deterministic polynomial-time Turing machine. This is a computational model that is stronger than the deterministic polynomial-time Turing machine. This computational model and its variants are frequently adopted in security definitions for cryptographic protocols (such as MPC), which is why we introduce it here.

4.4 Complexity Class (1): Classifying Computing Problems

The term complexity class is mainly related to the following question:

> **? Question**
>
> *What kinds of Z-type computing problems can be solved by X-type Y-complexity Turing machines?*

- "X" in the X-type refers to the type of computational models such as deterministic, probabilistic, non-deterministic, and quantum.
- "Y" in the Y-complexity refers to the rule of defining computational complexity (growth class) with polynomial time being the primary rule. However, the measurement of time cost is missing here, which could be based on the worst case, the best case, the average case, or other measurements.
- "Z" in the Z-type refers to the type of computing problems, including decision problems and search problems.

Given (X, Y, Z), those computing problems solvable by the same type of computational models will be collected as a set and this set is called complexity class. Therefore, a complexity class is a set of solvable computing problems with well-defined common characteristics.

We are now ready to introduce some complexity classes. Notice that the complexity classes in this book are mainly given for decision problems only. As we introduced previously, a decision problem P is equivalent to a membership problem asking whether $x \in L$ for a formal language L associated with P. All complexity classes consisting of decision problems are defined in terms of formal languages and membership problems.

4.4.1 $\mathcal{P}$ and $\mathcal{NP}$

This subsection introduces the most famous complexity classes $\mathcal{P}$ and $\mathcal{NP}$.

Definition 4.4.1 (Complexity Class $\mathcal{P}$). *A language L is in $\mathcal{P}$ (deterministic Polynomial-time) if for every integer n, every n-bit string x, there exists a deterministic Turing machine, denoted by DTM, such that*

- *$DTM(x) = 1$ if and only if $x \in L$.*
- *DTM halts in polynomial steps in n.*

Definition 4.4.2 (Complexity Class $\mathcal{NP}$). *A language L is in $\mathcal{NP}$ (Non-deterministic Polynomial-time) if for every integer n, every n-bit string x, there exists a non-deterministic Turing machine, denoted by NDTM, such that*

- *$NDTM(x) = 1$ if and only if $x \in L$.*
- *NDTM halts in polynomial steps in n.*

In these two definitions, the Turing machines can find solutions to every instance meeting complexity requirements. The definition therefore is given based on the worst case. The if-and-only-if condition indicates that the success probability is 1 without any error in computations by Turing machines.

We revisit the definition of $\mathcal{NP}$. The definition of $\mathcal{NP}$ is exactly the same as the definition of $\mathcal{P}$ except that a deterministic Turing machine is replaced with a non-deterministic Turing machine. One might find this definition unintuitive and impractical, since a non-deterministic polynomial-time Turing machine is not a physically realizable model. This definition is indeed confusing. A variant definition of $\mathcal{NP}$ is introduced below, providing an alternative perspective that helps beginners grasp the significance of this complexity class.

Suppose that the language L is in $\mathcal{NP}$. Then for any bit string x we have:

- If $x \in L$, there exists a sequence of choices (of transition functions), denoted by y, such that a deterministic Turing machine following this sequence of choices will halt and output 1.
- If $x \notin L$, any deterministic Turing machine following any sequence of transitions either does not halt or halts with output 0. That is, the machine must either fail to halt or halt with output 0 only.

There might be no deterministic polynomial-time Turing machine that can compute the sequence y for a given $x \in L$. However, it is straightforward for a deterministic polynomial-time Turing machine to verify $x \in L$ with a given y by simply following the sequence y in computation.

Based on the above observations, we can redefine $\mathcal{NP}$ as follows.

Definition 4.4.3 (Variant Definition of Complexity Class $\mathcal{NP}$). *A language L is in $\mathcal{NP}$ if for every integer n, every n-bit string x, there exists a deterministic Turing machine, denoted by DTM, such that*

4.4 Complexity Class (1): Classifying Computing Problems

- *There exists a bit string y satisfying $DTM(x, y) = 1$ if and only if $x \in L$, where the string length $|y|$ is polynomial in n.*
- *DTM halts in polynomial steps in n.*

Using the above variant $\mathcal{NP}$ definition, we can define a specific type of search problem based on a given language $L \in \mathcal{NP}$. In particular, we have:

- Any string $x \in L$ is a problem instance of this search problem.
- Any string y satisfying $\text{DTM}(x, y) = 1$ is a problem solution to the instance x.

For any language $L \in \mathcal{NP}$ and any problem instance $x \in L$, an NDTM can compute a problem solution in polynomial steps while a DTM can only verify a problem solution in polynomial steps. Suppose we use exhaustive search method to find a problem solution to a given $x \in L$. Roughly speaking, no deterministic Turing machine can complete the search, halt in polynomial steps, and output a problem solution to instance x, while a non-deterministic Turing machine can do this. Therefore, if $\mathcal{P} = \mathcal{NP}$, it means that computing a problem solution y for a given instance x is as easy (within polynomial time) as verifying a problem solution for given (x, y). If L is the language consisting of all true mathematical theorems that have proofs, the result $\mathcal{P} = \mathcal{NP}$ means that finding a proof to a new and true mathematical theorem is as easy as verifying a given proof. Intuitively, if one believes finding a proof for a mathematical theorem is definitely harder than verifying a proof, one should then conclude that $\mathcal{P} \neq \mathcal{NP}$.

4.4.2 $\mathcal{BPP}$, $\mathcal{BQP}$, and $\mathcal{P}_{/poly}$

This subsection introduces another three complexity classes defined using other Turing machines.

Definition 4.4.4 (Complexity Class $\mathcal{BPP}$). *A language L is in $\mathcal{BPP}$ (Bounded-error Probabilistic Polynomial-time) if for every integer n, every n-bit string x, there exists a probabilistic Turing machine, denoted by PTM, such that*

- $\Pr[PTM(x) = 1] \geq \frac{2}{3}$ *if $x \in L$.*
- $\Pr[PTM(x) = 0] \geq \frac{2}{3}$ *if $x \notin L$.*
- *PTM halts in polynomial steps in n.*

The error is bounded by less than $1/3$. However, the success probability $2/3$ mentioned above can be replaced by any probability c, as long as $c > 1/2$ and c is independent of n. This is because we can run the PTM polynomially many times and take the majority vote of all outputs as the final result. Furthermore, running PTM multiple times will still halt in polynomial steps.

Definition 4.4.5 (Complexity Class $\mathcal{BQP}$). *A language L is in $\mathcal{BQP}$ (Bounded-error Quantum Polynomial-time) if for every integer n, every n-bit string x, there exists a quantum Turing machine, denoted by QTM, such that*

- $\Pr[QTM(x) = 1] \geq \frac{2}{3}$ *if* $x \in L$.
- $\Pr[QTM(x) = 0] \geq \frac{2}{3}$ *if* $x \notin L$.
- *QTM halts in polynomial steps in n.*

Similar to the $\mathcal{BPP}$ complexity class, the probability $2/3$ can be replaced with any probability that is fixed and larger than $1/2$.

Definition 4.4.6 (Complexity Class $\mathcal{P}_{/poly}$). *A language L is in $\mathcal{P}_{/poly}$ if for every integer n, every n-bit string x, there exists a deterministic Turing machine with polynomial-size adaptive strings $\{\alpha_n\}_{n \in \mathbb{N}}$, denoted by DTM_a, such that*

- $DTM_a(x, \alpha_{|x|}) = 1$ *if and only if* $x \in L$.
- DTM_a *halts in polynomial steps in n.*

Here, $\{\alpha_n\}_{n \in \mathbb{N}}$ is a sequence of advice strings and $|\alpha_n|$ is polynomial in n.

Research in complexity theory has successfully shown the following relations among the complexity classes ($\mathcal{P}$, $\mathcal{BPP}$, $\mathcal{P}_{/poly}$, $\mathcal{BQP}$) in the literature:

$$\mathcal{P} \subseteq \mathcal{BPP} \subseteq \mathcal{BQP}$$

$$\mathcal{P} \subseteq \mathcal{BPP} \subset \mathcal{P}_{/poly}$$

The relation between $\mathcal{BQP}$ and $\mathcal{P}_{/poly}$ is still unknown. We use two general complexity classes A and B in the following discussions to help beginners understand the relation using the symbols "$\subseteq$" and "$\subset$" we mentioned.

- $A \subseteq B$ means that (1) any problem in class A is proved to be also in class B, and (2) there is at least one language L in complexity class B, but it is currently unknown whether $L \in A$ or $L \notin A$.
- $A \subset B$ means that (1) any problem in class A is proved to be also in class B, and (2) there is at least one language L in complexity class B but not in A.

The result $\mathcal{P} \subseteq \mathcal{BPP} \subset \mathcal{P}_{/poly}$ shows different computational powers of variants of polynomial-time Turing machines. Deterministic polynomial-time Turing machines with polynomial-size adaptive strings are more powerful than the other two computational models for defining $\mathcal{P}$ and $\mathcal{BPP}$ because the former can solve more decision problems within polynomial steps.

4.5 Complexity Class (2): Adding Reduction

In the context of solving computing problems, "solvable/unsolvable" and "complexity" are two characteristics adopted in classifying computing problems. This section introduces another characteristic called "reduction" to refine classification.

4.5.1 Reduction in Complexity Theory

Given a new computing problem P_{new}, we are asked to investigate whether this problem can be solved by a deterministic polynomial-time Turing machine. Assume that we suspect the answer is negative, but we are not able to analyze its lower bound time complexity to prove it. What alternative approach can we take? The concept of *reduction* is one of the most widely used methods to address this issue.

Reduction is used to connect the computational complexity of solving two different computing problems. In particular, reduction is used to prove a lower bound on the computational complexity of a problem, primarily in terms of time complexity. More precisely, let P_{old} be an old (existing) problem and P_{new} be a new problem. The purpose of a reduction is to obtain the following statement:

Statement

The old problem P_{old} is (polynomial-time) reducible to the new problem P_{new}.

This statement means that if the new problem P_{new} is solvable (by a polynomial-time Turing machine), then the old problem P_{old} must also be solvable. Roughly speaking, solving the new problem is not easier than solving the old problem. If the time complexity of solving problem P_{old} is not polynomial, it follows that the new problem P_{new} cannot be solved in polynomial time either. The above introduction to reduction is not very clear for beginners because the meaning of "reducible" is not clear so far. The details will be discussed in detail later in this chapter. The purpose of this introduction is to clarify the relationship between two problems in the context of reduction.

Reduction serves as an alternative method for proving that a computing problem cannot be solved in polynomial time by a Turing machine. This method plays a crucial role in computational complexity, particularly in cases where analyzing lower bounds on the computational complexity of certain problems within a computational model is challenging.

We now clarify the meaning of reduction. In short, the term "reducible" refers to the fact that a problem instance x_{old} of P_{old} can be used to generate a corresponding problem instance x_{new} of P_{new}, such that the problem solution y_{new} of

x_{new} can be transformed back into the solution y_{old} of x_{old}. The above statement may seem confusing because without further explaining the meaning of reduction, it is unclear which problem is harder, especially when we replace P_{old}, P_{new} with P_A, P_B, respectively.

If the studied problem is P_{new}, people might prefer a description where the problem P_{new} appears as the subject of the sentence. This practice is frequently used in cryptography. An alternative way to present reduction is given below.

Statement

Solving the new problem P_{new} can be reduced to solving the old problem P_{old}.

We prefer to use this "solving" statement with P_{new} in the subject in the following introduction especially for cryptography. The purpose is to maintain consistency with a related concept known as security reduction in cryptography.

We note that "reducible" and "reduced" appear to be used with some inconsistency in many research papers. That is, when authors said "P_A is reducible to P_B" in their papers, they might actually mean "solving P_A can be reduced to solving P_B". Both usages are correct because the meanings of "reducible" and "reduced" are interpreted inconsistently by different authors. We believe this inconsistency will likely be resolved in two hundred years, but not anytime soon. Beginners must be mindful of this distinction and interpret its meaning based on context.

4.5.2 $y \leftarrow \mathcal{A}^{\mathcal{B}}(x)$

Although it may seem unconventional, we first need to explain the syntax of this subsection's title using algorithms. Then, we abstract the concept of algorithms into computing machines.

In Section 3.1.4, we introduced the meaning of $y \leftarrow \mathcal{A}(x)$. On input x to the algorithm $\mathcal{A}$, this algorithm returns an output denoted by y. In the new syntax appearing in the title of this subsection, $\mathcal{B}$ denotes another algorithm. The meaning of the syntax $y \leftarrow \mathcal{A}^{\mathcal{B}}(x)$ can be explained as follows:

- On input x to the algorithm $\mathcal{A}$, it will return an output denoted by y.
- Before returning the output y, the algorithm $\mathcal{A}$ can make any input to the algorithm $\mathcal{B}$ and use its output to compute y.

We introduce this syntax because it is the core definition that will be used in reduction. This syntax can be extended to accommodate additional requirements or restrictions. For example,
$$y \leftarrow \mathcal{A}^{\mathcal{B}(z,\cdot)}(x).$$

4.5 Complexity Class (2): Adding Reduction

In this syntax, the input to the algorithm $\mathcal{B}$ should be a pair consisting of z and another arbitrary value denoted by "·". It means that if the algorithm $\mathcal{A}$ would like to make any input denoted by w to $\mathcal{B}$, this algorithm will run with (z, w) as the input[1]. In this process, the algorithm $\mathcal{A}$ is not required to know z.

In the context of computational models, the syntax $y \leftarrow \mathcal{A}^{\mathcal{B}}(x)$ has more meanings and restrictions.

- $\mathcal{B}$ is treated as an oracle machine. This oracle is a black box that will return $\mathcal{B}(x')$ for any input x'. The meaning of black box is that any intermediate computational results inside this oracle cannot be seen or captured by other machines such as the computing machine $\mathcal{A}$.

- The notation $\mathcal{A}^{\mathcal{B}}$ denotes a computing machine $\mathcal{A}$ with oracle access to $\mathcal{B}$. The input to the oracle $\mathcal{B}$ is referred to as queries. The computing machine $\mathcal{A}$ can make as many queries to the oracle $\mathcal{B}$ as possible within limited time.

This syntax, namely $y \leftarrow \mathcal{A}^{\mathcal{B}}(x)$, will also be adopted in the security definition of cryptography. In particular, the terms "oracle" and "query" will be adopted in security definitions. Now, we are ready to introduce several reductions in the next two subsections. It is important to note that there exist many types of reductions, each with distinct definitional details.

4.5.3 Cook Reduction

The first reduction we introduce here is called Cook reduction that was originally given by the researcher Stephen Cook.

> **Definition 4.5.1** (Cook Reduction). *A problem P_A is Cook-reducible to a problem P_B if for every computing machine $\mathcal{B}$ that can solve problem P_B, there exists a polynomial-time computing machine $\mathcal{A}^{\mathcal{B}}$ which returns a problem solution to any instance of P_A.*

In the Cook reduction, the machine $\mathcal{A}$ can make a polynomial number of queries to the oracle $\mathcal{B}$ as long as the machine $\mathcal{A}$ halts in polynomial time. The problems P_A and P_B in a Cook reduction can be decision problems, search problems, or others. The Cook reduction is a deterministic reduction. The proposed machine $\mathcal{A}$ with oracle access to $\mathcal{B}$ must return a correct solution to the problem.

Suppose we need to give a Cook reduction to prove that solving (new) problem P_B is not easier than solving (well studied and old) problem P_A. Our task is to construct a computing machine $\mathcal{A}$ to solve problem P_A. It should work as follows.

- We are first given an oracle $\mathcal{B}$ that can solve problem P_B.
- We are also given a problem instance x_A (variable) of P_A.

---
[1] Other references might present $\mathcal{B}(z, \cdot)$ in a different way as $\mathcal{B}_z(\cdot)$.

- Our aim is to show how to compute the solution y_A to x_A.
- We generate instances of problem P_B based on x_A.
- We query the generated instances of problems P_B to the oracle $\mathcal{B}$.
- Compute a problem solution y_A with responses from the oracle $\mathcal{B}$.

The Cook reduction is also known as Turing reduction in the literature. This reduction is considered as a general notion of reduction. The Cook reduction is much more similar to security reduction in cryptography than the other two reductions with further restrictions introduced in the next subsection.

4.5.4 Karp Reduction and Levin Reduction

The Karp reduction was originally proposed by the researcher Richard Karp, and the Levin reduction was independently introduced by Leonid Levin. They can be seen as two special cases of Cook reduction, with additional restrictions on the oracle and the reduction process. One key difference is that the Karp reduction focuses on reductions between decision problems, while the Levin reduction applies to search problems.

Definition 4.5.2 (Karp Reduction). *A decision problem P_A is Karp-reducible to a decision problem P_B if there exists a polynomial-time machine $\mathcal{A}$ such that*

- *The machine returns $\mathcal{A}(x)$ for any string x.*
- *$\mathcal{A}(x_A) \in L_B$ if and only if $x_A \in L_A$.*

Here, L_A, L_B are languages defined over the decision problems P_A, P_B.

The polynomial-time machine $\mathcal{A}$ is mainly defined for transforming an instance x_A of problem P_A to an instance of problem P_B. In the Karp reduction, there is no oracle in its definition, but we still need such an oracle that given input $\mathcal{A}(x_A)$ it returns either 1 or 0. Furthermore, this reduction completes immediately after a single query to the oracle because $\mathcal{A}(x_A)$ and x_A in a Karp reduction must either both be true instances or both false instances. We note that a Cook reduction allows multiple queries to the oracle and may require additional computations on responses from oracle to obtain problem solution.

The Karp reduction is also known as many-to-one reduction in the literature because every instance in L_A can be mapped to an instance in L_B, and it allows different instances in L_A to be mapped to the same instance in L_B.

Definition 4.5.3 (Levin Reduction). *A search problem P_A is Levin-reducible to a search problem P_B if there exist two polynomial-time machines $\mathcal{A}_I, \mathcal{A}_S$ such that*

- $x_B = \mathcal{A}_I(x_A) \in P_B$ *if and only if* $x_A \in P_A$.
- $y_A = \mathcal{A}_S(x_A, y_B)$ *is a problem solution to* x_A *if* y_B *is a problem solution to* x_B.

The polynomial-time machine $\mathcal{A}_I$ is defined for transforming an instance x_A of problem P_A to an instance of problem P_B. On the other hand, the polynomial-time machine $\mathcal{A}_S$ is defined for transforming a solution y_B of problem P_B back to a solution of problem P_A. In the Levin reduction, only one query is allowed. The response (namely y_B) from the oracle does not need to be solution to instance x_A. Upon receiving y_B from the oracle, the machine $\mathcal{A}_S$ can compute y_A for instance x_A using y_B.

4.5.5 $\mathcal{NP}$-Complete, $\mathcal{NP}$-Intermediate, and $\mathcal{NP}$-Hard

Building on complexity classes $\mathcal{P}$ and $\mathcal{NP}$, we introduce three complexity classes associated with reduction.

Definition 4.5.4 (Complexity Class $\mathcal{NP}$-Complete). *A language L is in the complexity class $\mathcal{NP}$-Complete if*

- *The language L is in the complexity class $\mathcal{NP}$.*
- *Any language in $\mathcal{NP}$ is Karp-reducible to the language L.*

Informally speaking, the class $\mathcal{NP}$-Complete consists of the hardest problems in $\mathcal{NP}$ because solving any problem L in the class $\mathcal{NP}$-Complete can be reduced to solving all problems in $\mathcal{NP}$. We remark that this complexity class is defined strictly under the Karp reduction.

Many problems, such as the Subset Sum problem, have been classified as in the class $\mathcal{NP}$-Complete. Solving any of these problems by a deterministic polynomial-time Turing machine would imply that $\mathcal{P} = \mathcal{NP}$. If one believes $\mathcal{P} \neq \mathcal{NP}$, they should not attempt to find a deterministic polynomial-time Turing machine to solve problems in the $\mathcal{NP}$-Complete.

Definition 4.5.5 (Complexity Class $\mathcal{NP}$-Intermediate). *A language L is in the complexity class $\mathcal{NP}$-Intermediate if*

- *The language L is in the complexity class $\mathcal{NP}$.*
- *The language L is neither in $\mathcal{P}$ nor in $\mathcal{NP}$-Complete.*

The complexity class $\mathcal{NP}$-Intermediate is a subset of $\mathcal{NP}$ defined as the set of problems that lie strictly between $\mathcal{P}$ and $\mathcal{NP}$-Complete. Every $\mathcal{NP}$-Complete problem is at least as hard as any $\mathcal{NP}$-Intermediate problem. We remark that if a problem initially believed to be in the $\mathcal{NP}$-Intermediate is later found to be in $\mathcal{P}$, this does not prove $\mathcal{P} = \mathcal{NP}$ but rather that $\mathcal{P}$ contains more problems than previously known. However, if one successfully proves that this problem is not in $\mathcal{P}$, it would immediately imply $\mathcal{P} \neq \mathcal{NP}$.

Definition 4.5.6 (Complexity Class $\mathcal{NP}$-Hard). *A computing problem P is in the complexity class $\mathcal{NP}$-Hard if any language in $\mathcal{NP}$ is Cook-reducible to the computing problem P.*

This complexity class differs significantly from the previously discussed complexity classes. The most significant differences are summarized as follows.

- It is defined using the Cook reduction, in contrast to the Karp reduction used in the definition of $\mathcal{NP}$-Complete problems.
- The definition encompasses both decision problems and search problems. That is, the $\mathcal{NP}$-Hard class also includes search problems.
- The $\mathcal{NP}$-Hard class contains the $\mathcal{NP}$-Complete class. That is, every $\mathcal{NP}$-Hard problem is at least as hard as any $\mathcal{NP}$-Complete problem.
- The $\mathcal{NP}$-Hard class also contains problems outside the $\mathcal{NP}$ class. That is, for certain $\mathcal{NP}$-Hard problems, even given an instance and its solution, we might not be able to verify its correctness in polynomial time. An example of an $\mathcal{NP}$-Hard decision problem is the Traveling Salesman Problem (TSP).

So far, we can rank the hardness of solving problems in four complexity classes as follows:

$$\mathcal{P} \leq \mathcal{NP}\text{-Intermediate} \leq \mathcal{NP}\text{-Complete} \leq \mathcal{NP}\text{-Hard}.$$

This ranking is important because cryptographic schemes must be based on computationally hard problems, and it indicates where such problems can be found. However, this ranking serves only as a reference, since the criteria for defining hard problems in these complexity classes are not directly applicable to cryptography. We will elaborate on this in the next chapter.

4.6 The Extended Church–Turing Thesis: Equivalent Efficiency

In Section 3.4, we previously introduced the Church-Turing thesis. Let $S_\mathbb{H}$ denote the set of all computing problems that humans can solve using pencil and paper. The Church-Turing thesis states that:

Church-Turing Thesis

Turing machines can solve all computing problems in the set $S_\mathbb{H}$.

The Extended Church-Turing (ECT) thesis was proposed in the 1980s as an extension of the Church-Turing thesis. It extends the original thesis by incorporating computational efficiency (complexity). It states that:

> **Extended Church-Turing Thesis**
>
> Every algorithm on any physically realizable devices can be simulated by a Turing machine with polynomial overhead.

That is, if a problem can be solved in polynomial time by an algorithm on any physically realizable device, then a Turing machine can also solve it in polynomial time. This thesis allows us to define efficiently solvable problems using polynomial-time Turing machines while disregarding other computational models for polynomial-time computation.

The Extended Church-Turing thesis was not proposed by Alonzo Church or Alan Turing. Its origins in the literature are not well documented. Furthermore, it remains uncertain whether the ECT thesis is true. The most plausible challenge to the ECT thesis comes from quantum computing. The ECT thesis remains valid unless both of the following conditions are proven:

- We must be able to construct quantum computers capable of handling an arbitrary number of qubits in computation. As of 2022, the most advanced quantum computers can handle only about 400 qubits.
- It must be proven that at least one problem, such as the factorization problem, is solvable in polynomial time by a quantum algorithm but not by a Turing machine. This appears to be at least as difficult as proving $\mathcal{P} \neq \mathcal{NP}$.

We emphasize that both conditions must be proven true to refute the Extended Church-Turing thesis.

Suppose the ECT thesis is true. Since simulating any algorithm in the physical world using a Turing machine incurs only a polynomial overhead, the following statements should hold and be widely accepted.

> **Statement**
>
> Polynomial-Time Turing Machines = Polynomial-Time Algorithms

From now on, beginners should not be confused by statements that use "algorithms" instead of "Turing machines". Although "Turing machines" provide a more formal and precise presentation than "algorithms", they are equivalent under the Extended Church-Turing thesis.

4.7 How to Classify Computing Problems, Summary

In the previous two chapters, we have introduced computing problems, computing machines, and computational models. Based on this knowledge, we can define the set of solvable computing problems as

$$\{P : \text{Any } \_\_\_\_ \text{ problem } P \text{ that can be solved by a Turing machine.}\}$$

Here, "____" represents the characteristics that define the type of computing problem, such as decision and search problems. However, this set cannot be further refined, regardless of the computational model adopted.

By incorporating complexity, the set of solvable computing problems can be further divided into subsets, known as complexity classes, defined as

$$\left\{ P : \begin{array}{l} \text{Any } \_\_\_\_ \text{ problem } P \text{ that can be solved with } \_\_\_\_ \text{ complexity,} \\ \text{considering } \_\_\_\_ \text{ cost and } \_\_\_\_ \text{ case, by a } \_\_\_\_ \text{ Turing machine.} \end{array} \right\}.$$

Here, "____" represents the characteristics used to define the problem type, complexity cost, case, and computational model. Excluding the problem type, the remaining characteristics are explained as follows:

- **Complexity.** The complexity refers to the rules of defining growth classes, including upper bound O, lower bound Ω, tight bound Θ on different growth rate such as n^k and 2^n.
- **Cost.** The cost refers to time cost, space cost, or others for solving problems.
- **Case.** The case refers to the measurement of computational cost under the best case, the worst case, the average case, or others.
- **Computational Model.** Any well-defined computational models, including DTM, PTM, NDTM, QTM, and others that are not introduced in this book.

Another characteristic used to define complexity classes is the concept of reduction. Owing to the diverse characteristics used to define solvable computing problems, more than 500 complexity classes have been identified and cataloged in the Complexity Zoo[2]. The two most well-known complexity classes are $\mathcal{P}$ and $\mathcal{NP}$.

We have completed the classification of solvable computing problems, with no further subdivisions. In the next chapter, we will introduce how these complexity classes are treated in the context of cryptography.

4.8 Review Questions

> **? Question 14**

Alice claims she can use her laptop to run the algorithm $\mathcal{A}$ to solve computing problem P with time cost less than 2.1 seconds. Is Alice's statement correct? Justify your reasons.

---

[2] See https://complexityzoo.net/Complexity_Zoo

? Question 15

Alice and Bob are independently tasked by their supervisor, John, to evaluate the computational cost of solving the computing problem P using a given algorithm $\mathcal{A}$. However, their results differ significantly. Alice concluded that the time complexity is polynomial, whereas Bob determined that it is exponential. Their supervisor found that both results were correct. Justify the reasons.

? Question 16

Let $f_1(n) = O(2^n)$ and $f_2(n) = O(n^2)$ be time complexity of two algorithms $\mathcal{A}_1, \mathcal{A}_2$ proposed for solving the same computing problem P. Then, the second algorithm must be better than the first algorithm. Is this true? Justify your reasons.

? Question 17

Let $f(n)$ be a function within polynomial-time growth rate and $g(n)$ be a function within non-polynomial-time growth rate. Provide examples of $f(n), g(n)$ that demonstrate $f(n)$ is significantly *less* than $g(n)$ when $n = 160$.

? Question 18

Let $f(n)$ be a function within polynomial-time growth rate and $g(n)$ be a function within non-polynomial-time growth rate. Provide examples of $f(n), g(n)$ that demonstrate $f(n)$ is significantly *larger* than $g(n)$ when $n = 160$.

? Question 19

Let $\mathcal{M}$ be a probabilistic polynomial-time Turing machine designed to solve a computing problem P, with a success probability of $\frac{4}{5}$. Is this probability calculated for each individual instance of P, or is it the average success probability over all instances of the same input length?

? Question 20

Can we propose a single circuit to solve a computing problem? Justify your answer. (Note: This question might need external references and reading.)

? Question 21

Let $(\mathbb{G}, g, p)$ be a cyclic group, where $\mathbb{G}$ is the set of group elements, g is a group generator, and p (prime number) is the group order. Let P_1, P_2 be two computing problems defined as follows.

- P_1: On input (g, g^x), compute $x \in \mathbb{Z}_p$.
- P_2: On input $(g, g^x, h, h^{\frac{1}{x}})$ where $h \in \mathbb{G}$ is a random element, compute $x \in \mathbb{Z}_p$.

Prove that solving P_2 can be reduced to solving P_1.

? Question 22

Assuming that $\mathcal{P} \neq \mathcal{NP}$ and the Extended Church-Turing thesis hold, what tasks can hypothetical alien computers, built by alien intelligences, definitely not perform?

? Question 23

Let $S_\mathbb{H}$ be a set of computing problems known by the human. How to break the set $S_\mathbb{H}$ into subsets with problem types, computational models, and time complexity?

? Question 24

Let $S_\mathcal{C}$ be a set of computing machines under a computational model $\mathcal{C}$. Let P be a computing problem. How to break the set $S_\mathcal{C}$ into subsets related to the computing problem P?

Chapter 5
From Computational Complexity to Cryptography: Transition

Abstract This chapter is structured into two sections to facilitate the transition from computational complexity to cryptography. First, we revisit key concepts in computational complexity in order to put forward the most important term "probabilistic polynomial-time algorithms". Next, we explore cryptography, introducing principles that guide the definitions for usability and security. These explanations aim to clarify the concept of probabilistic polynomial-time algorithms and their role in cryptographic definitions.

5.1 Computational Complexity, Revisited

Our review will focus on algorithms, including their characteristics and classifications. We begin by clarifying the concept of algorithms, followed by a discussion of probabilistic algorithms in terms of their notion of solving, cost measurement, and complexity. We then formally define a subset of probabilistic algorithms, known as probabilistic polynomial-time algorithms.

5.1.1 Turing Machines ≈ Algorithms

Overview

Algorithms ⟵ Real-World ⟶ Computing Machines ⟶ Abstracted ⟶ Turing Machines

Computing machines are designed to execute automata-based operations using mechanical or electronic devices to solve computing problems. They can be categorized into general-purpose computing machines and specific-purpose computing machines. Two fundamental concepts associated with computing machines are algorithms and computational models, such as Turing machines.

- **Algorithms:** An algorithm is a well-defined, step-by-step procedure for solving a specific problem or carrying out a computation. Algorithms are implemented and executed on general-purpose computing machines, such as digital computers.
- **Turing Machines:** A Turing machine is a (specific-purpose) theoretical machine consisting of Turing tapes and a set of transition functions. Turing machines have the same computational capabilities as algorithms, enabling them to solve specific problems and perform computations.

While both algorithms and Turing machines aim to solve computing problems, they serve different purposes.

- To solve a computing problem, we typically design an algorithm (that can be executed on a general-purpose computing machine) rather than a Turing machine, even though a Turing machine could, in principle, be designed for the same purpose.
- To determine whether a computing problem is solvable, Turing machines are preferred, as they offer a well-defined theoretical framework. In contrast, algorithms are informal and lack a precise definition of computational capability.

Determining whether a problem is solvable requires computational models rather than physical computing machines. Currently, digital computers are widely used, and quantum computers may emerge in the future. Furthermore, if extraterrestrial life (e.g., aliens) were to visit Earth, they might introduce even more advanced computing machines. All of these computing machines are physical devices, and the algorithms running on them could solve the same computational problem with different time complexities. However, when a well-defined Turing machine is used to solve the same problem, the resulting time complexity remains consistent.

Determining whether a problem is solvable requires computational models rather than algorithms. However, in fields beyond complexity theory, such as cryptography, formal definitions have been relaxed by substituting algorithms for Turing machines. In these contexts, algorithms are often regarded as equivalent to Turing machines. This relaxed approach is justified by the Extended Church-Turing thesis, which asserts the conditional equivalence of algorithms and Turing machines, and has not yet been disproven.

5.1.2 Algorithms and Solve

Generally speaking, when running an algorithm to solve a computing problem, on input an instance, the algorithm will execute, stop, and return an output. The output will be treated as the problem solution to the given input, but the output could

5.1 Computational Complexity, Revisited

be a wrong problem solution (namely, the algorithm fails in finding the problem solution). All algorithms can be classified into two types:

- **Deterministic algorithms:** An algorithm is deterministic if it always produces the same output for a given input across multiple executions.
- **Probabilistic algorithms:** An algorithm is probabilistic if it can produce different outputs for the same input across multiple executions, due to inherent randomness (e.g., random number generation) in its process.

In the classification above, deterministic algorithms correspond to deterministic Turing machines, while probabilistic algorithms correspond to probabilistic Turing machines. Other types of algorithms (Turing machines) are not considered by default, as they are not yet physically realizable.

From now on, we will move all introductions associated with solving problems using probabilistic algorithms, as they are widely adopted in the cryptology community. The detailed reasons will be provided in subsequent sections.

When using probabilistic algorithms to solve computing problems, the success probability can have different definitions as introduced in Section 3.1.6. There are two distinct probability definitions for finding solutions to n-bit instances.

- **At Least 2/3 Probability for Each Instance:** For each input n-bit instance, the output returned by the probabilistic algorithm is a correct solution with probability at least $2/3$, where the probability is calculated based on all tossed random numbers for the input instance.
- **At Least 2/3 Probability on Average:** For a random input n-bit instance, the output returned by the probabilistic algorithm is a correct solution with probability at least $2/3$ on average, where the probability is calculated based on all n-bit instances and tossed random numbers for each instance.

Recall that the complexity class $\mathcal{BPP}$, as introduced in this book, is defined using the first method. In contrast, cryptography especially security definition adopts the second method with some modifications.

5.1.3 Cost Measurement and Complexity

When an algorithm is proposed to solve a computing problem, its computational cost refers to the number of operations that the algorithm needs to take before halting and producing an output. Let $f(n)$ denote the computational cost of solving n-bit instances of the problem. Next, we revisit the methods for measuring the computational cost $f(n)$ and analyzing its complexity.

In previous chapters, we demonstrated that a computing problem may have multiple n-bit instances, and the computational cost can vary depending on the specific instance case. The computational cost is typically measured in at least three ways:

- **Best Case:** The first definition is called best case where $f(n)$ is based on the n-bit instance case that costs the least significant operations.
- **Worst Case:** The second definition is called worst case where $f(n)$ is based on the n-bit instance case that costs the most significant operations.
- **Average Case:** The third definition is called average case where $f(n)$ is based on all n-bit instances and their average cost.

It could be possible that the computational cost is significantly different by the best case, the worst case, and the average case. It is therefore crucial when selecting a approach to measure computational cost. Furthermore, we observe that the measurement is even more complex for probabilistic algorithms as it may also depend on the random numbers used. That is, the computational cost for instance x using random numbers R_1 and R_2 are not the same. As a result, in the worst case, one must consider the n-bit instance and the random number that results in the highest computational cost.

In general, the computational cost $f(n)$ tends to increase as the instance length n grows. Let $f_\mathcal{U}(n)$ and $f_\mathcal{A}(n)$ denote the computational cost of solving n-bit instances of the computing problem P using algorithms $\mathcal{U}$ and $\mathcal{A}$, respectively. Computational complexity theory states that

- **Polynomial-Time:** $f_\mathcal{U}(n)$ is in the polynomial-time class if there exist an integer $k > 0$ and a constant $c > 0$ such that

$$\forall n > 0, f_\mathcal{U}(n) \leq c \cdot n^k.$$

This means that the time cost $f_\mathcal{U}(n)$ can be bounded by a polynomial in n. For example, $f_\mathcal{U}(n) = n^2$ is in this class.

- **Non-Polynomial-Time:** $f_\mathcal{A}(n)$ is in the non-polynomial-time class if[1] there exists an integer $n_0 > 0$ such that

$$\forall k, c > 0, \forall n > n_0, f_\mathcal{A}(n) > c \cdot n^k.$$

This means that the time cost $f_\mathcal{A}(n)$ grows faster than any polynomial in n, and cannot be bounded by any polynomial for sufficiently large n. For example, $f_\mathcal{A}(n) = 2^n$ is in this class.

We analyze these two time complexities because

$$\frac{f_\mathcal{U}(n)}{f_\mathcal{A}(n)} \longrightarrow 0 \text{ (tending to zero)}$$

as n increases. The computational cost $f_\mathcal{A}(n)$ becomes impractically large when compared to $f_\mathcal{U}(n)$ for sufficiently large instances. Consider the example where $f_\mathcal{U}(n) = n^2$ and $f_\mathcal{A}(n) = 2^n$. For $n = 160$, we obtain

---

[1] The condition is informal and not precise. The reason will appear in Section 7.2.3.

5.1 Computational Complexity, Revisited

$$\frac{f_{\mathcal{U}}(160)}{f_{\mathcal{A}}(160)} = \frac{160^2}{2^{160}} \leq \frac{1}{2^{142}}.$$

This probability, 1 in 2^{142}, is so tiny that it is like winning the lottery jackpot several times in a row. For perspective, it is about the same as winning a lottery with 1-in-100-million odds five times consecutively.

5.1.4 Probabilistic Polynomial-Time Algorithms

When a probabilistic algorithm is claimed to solve a computing problem, three concerns arise in complexity theory: (1) The definition of probability for "successfully solving" the problem, (2) The measurement of computational cost, and (3) The complexity of computational cost (namely, time complexity). In particular, the resulting time complexity may be influenced by the cost measurement. Consider the following statement as an example.

Statement

Probabilistic algorithm $\mathcal{U}$ can solve computing problem P in polynomial time.

Without specifying time measurement, it is hard to know how many problem instances the algorithm $\mathcal{U}$ can stop and return a solution within polynomial time. Therefore, when evaluating the effectiveness of a probabilistic algorithm in solving a computing problem, the above statement may become complex, ambiguous, or misleading.

To address this issue, the term "probabilistic polynomial-time algorithms" has been adopted to replace "probabilistic algorithms" in the previous statement.

Definition 5.1.1 (Probabilistic Polynomial-Time Algorithms). *A probabilistic polynomial-time algorithm is a probabilistic algorithm that will stop and return an output within polynomial time relative to the instance length. That is, no matter what the instance case and tossed random number are, the algorithm will stop after polynomial steps in n, where n is the instance length.*

With the help of this term, all probabilistic algorithms can be re-classified into three categories. They are:

- **Probabilistic Polynomial-Time Algorithms.** Given any input instance of length n, these algorithms halt and produce an output within polynomial time in n.
- **Probabilistic Mixed-Time Algorithms.** Given an input instance of length n, a probabilistic algorithm may halt within polynomial time or take non-polynomial

time in n, depending on the instance. That is, the time complexity is polynomial for solving certain instances but non-polynomial for others.

- **Probabilistic Non-Polynomial-Time Algorithms.** Given any input instance of length n, these probabilistic algorithms halt and produce an output in non-polynomial time in n.

The first category will play the most important role or even the exclusive role in cryptographic definitions. We note that the term for the second category is uniquely defined in this book.

In summary, the most important term originating from complexity theory for cryptographic definitions is "probabilistic polynomial-time algorithms". All defined complexity classes are of lesser importance, but the formal definition approaches have been adopted and applied in cryptographic definitions. This is likely because cryptography focuses on whether a particular problem can be solved rather than the size of the set of solvable problems within a complexity class defined by Turing machines.

5.2 Cryptography and Its Algorithms

From now on, we transition into cryptography, first beginning with clarifications of key concepts related to the field and then ending with the use of probabilistic polynomial-time algorithms from computational complexity in cryptography.

5.2.1 Concepts Clarification

Overview

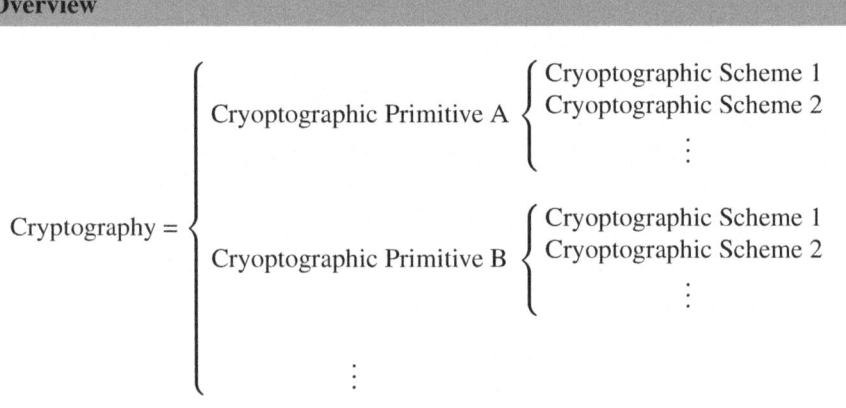

5.2 Cryptography and Its Algorithms

Cryptography is a field that employs mathematics and algorithms to secure information and communications for users against adversaries. The core security protection is via mathematical operations while algorithms conduct these operations automatically inside computing machines. Public-key cryptography, also known as asymmetric cryptography, is a subset of cryptography using pairs of keys, namely public keys and secret keys, for security protection. Each user generates a key pair, denoted by (pk, sk), where pk is the public key shared with others, and sk is the secret key known only to the user who generated it.

Cryptographic primitives are fundamental components in cryptography that offer specific security protections, such as ensuring data integrity or confidentiality. If cryptography is a set, each cryptographic primitive can be seen as an element of the set. Cryptographic primitives are formally described using specific (cryptographic) algorithms in syntax, defining the unique input and output components for each algorithm (without intermediate operations). There is no single primitive that can solve all security concerns. It is important to note that cryptographic primitives cannot be directly used for security protections because they are theoretical constructs or conceptual products only.

Cryptographic schemes (or protocols) are implementations of cryptographic primitives. Here, the implementation is not about coding implementation but pseudocode implementation setting parameters and designing operations for each algorithm within the primitives. Each cryptographic algorithm in schemes or protocols provides a step-by-step procedure for generating outputs based on given inputs using some building blocks. A cryptographic primitive can have various proposed schemes, each with its own advantages and disadvantages. All cryptographic schemes (or protocols) proposed for the same cryptographic primitive should have the same number of algorithms, with each algorithm having the same set of inputs and outputs. However, the same algorithm for the same primitive in different schemes may have different step-by-step procedures.

To develop a new cryptographic primitive and its construction (implementation), the first step is to formally define its syntax, ensuring a common understanding of notations, terms, and processes. Afterwards, researchers and developers can focus on implementing (how to process inputs into output) cryptographic schemes based on this syntax. Since this book focuses on cryptographic definitions, when we mention a cryptographic algorithm, we are mostly referring to an algorithm as defined in the syntax.

Summary

$$\text{Cryptographic Algorithms} = \begin{cases} \text{Syntax only in cryptographic primitives} \\ \text{Having step-by-step procedures in constructions} \end{cases}$$

5.2.2 Cryptography Principle: Use and Abuse

In any proposed cryptographic scheme for a cryptographic primitive, there are two key stakeholders with conflicting interest: users and adversaries.

- **Users:** They seek protections for confidentiality and/or integrity using the given cryptographic scheme. These individuals employ cryptographic algorithms from the given cryptographic scheme to secure various aspects, such as data security, identity security, or computing security. All cryptographic algorithms inside this scheme must be user-friendly and executable. Otherwise, the given scheme is impractical and completely useless.
- **Adversaries:** They aim to compromise the security of the cryptographic scheme, and harm users' benefits by breaking confidentiality or integrity. We are concerned with adversaries because they are entities that create security threats for users. Roughly speaking, the given scheme should include features that make it difficult for adversaries to abuse.

In those key-related cryptographic primitives[2], users utilize secret keys in secure computing to receive protections, while adversaries, also known as unauthorized users or illegal users, attempt to do the same computing without possessing these keys to compromise security. For example, given a ciphertext, users can decrypt it and recover the plaintext with a valid secret key, while adversaries cannot do so without a valid secret key.

Drawing inspiration from Oded Goldreich in [26] (Page 1), we introduce the cryptography principle from our perspective. It states that

Cryptography Principle

A proposed cryptographic scheme/protocol must be easy for users to use and hard for adversaries to abuse.

An inherent question associated with cryptography that should be aware is:

? Question

How to define cryptographic primitives such that proposed constructions meeting definition imply meeting the cryptography principle?

---

[2] We say a cryptographic primitive is key-related if one of its cryptographic algorithms needs to use a secret key as the input. Most cryptographic primitives are secret-key related. The exception includes cryptographic hash function because it has no secret key.

5.2 Cryptography and Its Algorithms

The inherent question above can be seen as the main reason why we need to correctly comprehend cryptographic definitions. *Without accurate definitions, a proposed scheme that meets the definition could be insecure or impractical, or a scheme that does not fulfill the definition might actually be secure and practical.* However, the introduced cryptography principle could be too abstract for beginners making it difficult for beginners to grasp any clues on how to define primitives. In the next subsections, we will first introduce a case study and then parse the principle into a guideline for definitions.

5.2.3 Case Study: Key Generation Algorithm

The key generation algorithm in public-key cryptographic primitives, such as digital signatures and public-key encryption, is commonly defined as follows:

Example

- $(pk, sk) \leftarrow$ **KeyGen**(1^κ): Taking as input a security parameter κ, this key generation algorithm returns a key pair (pk, sk), where pk is a public key and sk is a secret key.

Given a scheme for this public-key cryptographic primitive, there could be more than a million users who will run this algorithm to generate key pairs to receive security protections. Suppose Alice is one of the users. When she generates a key pair (pk_A, sk_A), this key pair should protect her computing. That is, any user who runs this algorithm and uses his or her generated key pair should be protected.

At the same time, there could be thousands of adversaries who are trying to compromise this cryptographic scheme. From the perspective of adversaries,

- They can see all users' public keys $(pk_1, pk_2, pk_3, pk_4, \cdots, pk_{9527}, \cdots)$.
- They can also access the key generation algorithm and generate some key pairs by themselves. That is, they can obtain the secret keys corresponding to some public keys.
- They can even access and see how the key generation algorithm works inside, namely how an output is produced through operations on an input. This is because all algorithms and their operations are public.

If one of the adversaries can find one of the other users' secret keys, such as Alice's secret key, this adversary will be able to do what Alice can do. Then, Alice will no longer receive security protection from this cryptographic scheme.

5.2.4 Guideline for Definitions

Based on the key generation algorithm described above, it is now relatively easy for us to introduce the guideline for definitions about how to define cryptographic primitives to align with the cryptography principle. The guideline is based on two key aspects: usability and security.

Overview

$$\text{How to define cyptographic primitives} = \begin{cases} \text{Define Usability for Users.} \\ \text{Define Security against Adversaries.} \end{cases}$$

Usability ensures that a cryptographic primitive and its schemes are easy for users to use. Based on the above observation on the key generation algorithm, the definition guideline in terms of usability includes the following requirement.

Requirement 1: A scheme is deficient if one of its algorithm is not friendly for one user to use on one day.

For example, a key generation algorithm does not satisfy the usability if Alice runs the key generation algorithm many times but most of the returned key pairs do not work at all. Specifically, in public-key encryption, the secret key cannot correctly decrypt ciphertexts generated using their corresponding public keys.

Security ensures that it is hard for adversaries to abuse. We note that it is much more complex to achieve security than usability due to multiple factors. There is more than one cryptographic algorithm in a primitive and each cryptographic primitive usually has at least one algorithm with distinct security requirements. Based on our observations, the definition guideline for security has the following basic requirements:

Requirement 1: A scheme is useless if adversaries can compromise security protections by a cryptographic algorithm affecting one user in a single day.

Requirement 2: Adversaries could obtain maximum information to compromise security, such as compromising some users and obtaining their secret keys.

Requirement 3: Compromising security should not only be difficult for the most advanced adversary today, but also for an even smarter adversary in the future. Those future adversaries could invent new and more powerful approaches to break cryptographic schemes, but we do not yet know these approaches.

The above three security requirements are interrelated. For example, a million users have run the key generation algorithm to generate their key pairs, and an adversary aims to compute sk from pk for one of the key pairs, including Alice's key pair (pk_A, sk_A). The first security requirement is to protect security for all users, including Alice. Even if it is not easy for the adversary to compute sk_A from pk_A, the adversary might try to compromise another user, Bob, first and then attack Alice's secret key security with the help of sk_B (Bob's secret key). The second security requirement is to prevent this kind of attack by ensuring that compromising some users does not break the security of others. Even if the adversary cannot do so currently using all known methods, they might hire experts to find new ways to compromise key security. The third security requirement is to prevent future attacks.

5.2.5 Key Characteristic in Usability and Security: Algorithms

Overview

$$\text{Algorithms} = \begin{cases} \text{Cryptographic algorithms for operations run by users.} \\ \text{Attacking algorithms for breaking schemes run by adversaries.} \end{cases}$$

The key characteristic influencing both the usability and security of a cryptographic primitive and its constructions is its algorithms. If cryptographic algorithms within a primitive operate effectively and correctly, this primitive is user-friendly and easy to use. In cryptography, a key security concern is whether adversaries can compromise cryptographic security by discovering other algorithms and use these discovered algorithms. We refer to these other algorithms as attacking algorithms, which are designed to break cryptographic algorithms. For example, an attack algorithm can generate valid signatures using public keys and messages only. If adversaries cannot exploit such knowledge, we consider the cryptographic primitive difficult for adversaries to exploit.

Generally speaking, algorithms are used to solve computing problems or find y for a given x that satisfies $R(x, y) = 1$. However, users and adversaries execute different algorithms to solve distinct computing problems, although both parties engage in algorithmic computations.

- **Users:** They execute cryptographic algorithms aiming to perform and generate some outputs for security protections. Algorithms in this kind of computing are proposed for performing specific operations. Take the key generation algorithm as an example. Given input a security parameter $x = \kappa$, the cryptographic algorithm returns a key pair $y = (pk, sk)$.

- **Adversaries:** They seek attacking algorithms that differ from cryptographic algorithms and aim to compromise the security of cryptographic schemes. Algorithms in this kind of computing are proposed for breaking. Take the key generation algorithm as an example. Given input a public key $x = pk$ to be compromised, the attacking algorithm returns its secret key $y = sk$.

That is, algorithms serve users and adversaries with different purposes. For users, we refer to their computations as "operations" because they are provided with predefined cryptographic algorithms that are ready for use. In contrast, for adversaries, we term their computations as "breaking", meaning that adversaries must successfully find an attacking algorithm to achieve their goals.

5.2.6 Probabilistic Polynomial-Time Algorithms for Cryptography

In cryptography, users run cryptographic algorithms for protection, while adversaries find and execute attacking algorithms to compromise security. The key questions for defining usability and security are as follows.

? Questions

1. *How to define cryptographic algorithms to satisfy usability?*
2. *How to define attacking algorithms to satisfy security?*

The cryptology community has chosen

"probabilistic polynomial-time (PPT) algorithms"

from computational complexity theory to define both cryptographic algorithms and attacking algorithms. They are both PPT algorithms that satisfy certain properties. That is, it is not necessary to consider probabilistic mixed-time algorithms and probabilistic non-polynomial-time algorithms.

However, probabilistic polynomial-time algorithms required for usability and security are not exactly the same. Furthermore, defining security using PPT algorithms is not entirely accurate without considering quantum computers, quantum Turing machines, and quantum adversaries. The adopted PPT algorithms can be seen as a foundational requirement for defining security. We will further introduce PPT algorithms with different features for usability and security in the next two chapters separately.

5.3 Summary and Roadmap

This chapter has briefly reviewed key terms in computational complexity and ends with the term "probabilistic polynomial-time algorithms". We then explored cryptography. To help beginners gain a clear understanding of the cryptography principle, we provide a flowchart of key concepts in Figure 5.1. The grey fields have been introduced, whereas the white fields will be covered in the next two chapters.

5.3 Summary and Roadmap

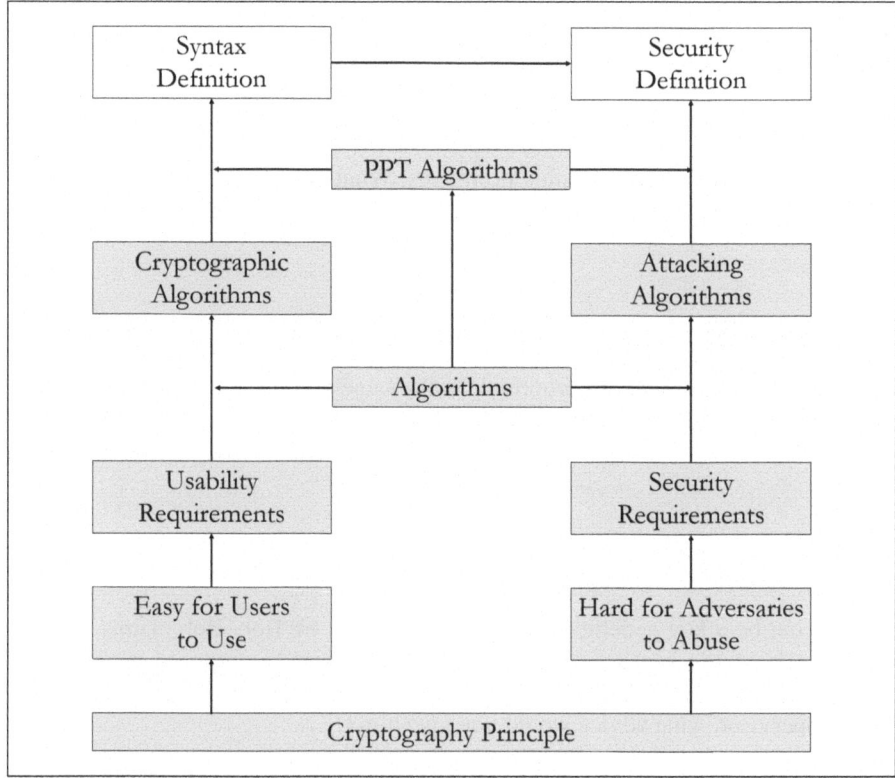

Fig. 5.1 Key concepts from the cryptography principle up to definitions

Cryptography aims to protect users against adversaries. Any cryptographic algorithms should be practical and easy for users to use, and also be impractical and hard for adversaries to abuse. We have interpreted "easy" as usability and "hard" as security, each with distinct requirements. In cryptography, regardless of whether it is used or abused, the key characteristic is the algorithm. Users execute cryptographic algorithms defined in cryptographic primitives for security protection, while adversaries explore the existence of attacking algorithms to compromise security. Although cryptographic and attacking algorithms serve different purposes for users and adversaries, both will be defined using probabilistic polynomial-time algorithms.

In the following two chapters, we will introduce how probabilistic polynomial-time algorithms are employed in the definitions of syntax and security for a cryptographic primitive. All cryptographic algorithms in a syntax definition must satisfy usability requirements, and all attacking algorithms in a security definition must satisfy security requirements. This completes the transition from computational complexity to cryptography.

5.4 Review Questions

> **? Question 25**

Let A and B be two cryptographic primitives. What are their main differences according to the concepts introduced in this book?

> **? Question 26**

Let A and B be two schemes proposed for the same cryptographic primitive. What are their main similarities and differences according to the concepts introduced in this book?

> **? Question 27**

Let *KeyGen* be a key generation algorithm proposed by Bob. Bob claims that the algorithm is secure because he has analyzed all currently proposed probabilistic polynomial-time (PPT) attacking algorithms and found that none could break it. As Bob's supervisor, what advice would you give him?

Chapter 6
Cryptographic Primitives: Syntax Definitions

Abstract A cryptographic primitive is a collection of predefined cryptographic algorithms designed to be executed by users, providing security protections within a specific application context. These algorithms, encapsulated within primitives, are merely syntax that define inputs and outputs. In this chapter, we summarize the characteristics of cryptographic algorithms for cryptographic primitives in the context of syntax definitions. We employ identity-based encryption and its variants as illustrative examples and classify four distinct categories of algorithms to help understand the role played by syntax definitions.

6.1 Role of Syntax Definition

Function, operation, and algorithm are three interrelated terms in cryptography. To secure a given application scenario through cryptography, users perform mathematical operations on input data. These operations can be abstracted as specific functions, denoted by f. Instead of manually executing operations to compute $f(\text{data})$, users employ cryptographic algorithms that can be executed by computing machines to automate these operations.

A set of cryptographic algorithms with predefined and fixed inputs and outputs for a cryptographic primitive is termed a syntax definition. The role of the syntax definition is to offer a formal framework that outlines the components and operations of a cryptographic primitive. This definition acts as a bridge between application scenarios and concrete constructions, such as schemes or protocols. On one hand, it suffices to understand how application scenarios can be secured using the algorithms defined in the syntax without the need to examine the details. On the other hand, the syntax definition serves as a blueprint for researchers to design corresponding constructions and operations within the algorithms.

Specifically, syntax definition serves several purposes:

- **Formal Specification:** It precisely defines the elements of cryptographic algorithms involved in the cryptographic primitive, ensuring that everyone has a common understanding of the notations, terms, and processes.
- **Standardization:** By providing a standardized description, the syntax definition allows researchers and developers to consistently implement and analyze constructed schemes and protocols.
- **Interoperability:** A well-defined syntax ensures that different cryptographic schemes and protocols can interoperate or be compared more effectively.

Although the syntax definition is crucial for a cryptographic primitive, it remains a subjective process, depending on the inventor's knowledge, experience, and understanding of the requirements of application scenarios. There is no universal standard for defining the syntax of a cryptographic primitive. This book will introduce some common guidelines for defining syntax.

6.2 Probabilistic Polynomial-Time Algorithms for Users

In the preceding chapter, we introduced the concept that *probabilistic polynomial-time (PPT)* algorithms are employed to define cryptographic algorithms. In this section, we explore the meaning of PPT algorithms for users and illustrate their roles in cryptography.

6.2.1 Randomized Operation, Efficiency, and Correctness

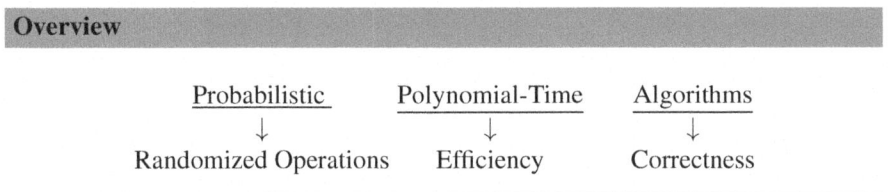

The implications of employing PPT algorithms in defining cryptographic algorithms encompass three fundamental components: *randomized operations*, *efficiency*, and *correctness*. These components are introduced in reverse order to enhance intuitive understanding.

Correctness. All defined algorithms within a cryptographic primitive must operate collaboratively and correctly to fulfill the usability requirement. For instance, in digital signatures, a key pair generated by the key generation algorithm must be capable of signing messages and verifying signatures correctly. To ensure this,

6.2 Probabilistic Polynomial-Time Algorithms for Users

a cryptographic primitive concludes with a correctness criterion, ensuring that all computed results returned by associated algorithms must be accurate and satisfy the specified requirements. In other words, correctness ensures that there are no errors when users "honestly" execute cryptographic algorithms.

To aid in understanding how correctness is described, we classify all cryptographic algorithms into two types: straight algorithms and forking algorithms. They are based on computational flow. A straight algorithm is linear and deterministic in its behavior, while a forking algorithm introduces conditional branching based on the input. They are described as follows:

- **Straight Algorithm:** *On input U and other elements, it computes and returns V.*
- **Forking Algorithm:** *On input W and other elements, it computes and returns X if and only if W fulfills the condition Y; otherwise, it returns Z.*

In those key-related cryptographic primitives, there should have one "forking" algorithm. For example, in digital signatures, if σ_m is a signature generated by the signing algorithm on input (sk, m) (i.e., condition Y), the verification algorithm (i.e., the forking algorithm) should return 1 (indicating valid signature). We will introduce how to formulate the probability for correctness in the next subsection.

> **! Attention**
>
> It is possible that the verification algorithm still returns 1 even if a signature σ_m fails to satisfy the condition Y (generated by the signing algorithm on input (sk, m)). The security definition introduced in the next chapter ensures that this event will not occur.

Efficiency. Cryptographic algorithms must be efficiently executable on computing machines. The cryptology community recognizes polynomial-time algorithms as computationally efficient. These cryptographic algorithms are computationally efficient if their computational cost for producing an output from any given input is polynomial in the input length and independent of its specific characteristics.

However, there is a distinction between efficiency and polynomial-time complexity. Even if cryptographic algorithms in a particular construction have polynomial-time complexity, this does not necessarily mean they are sufficiently efficient for practical use. Beginners should be aware of this gap and understand that polynomial-time complexity provides an appropriate framework for defining efficient computations within the field of complexity theory. The difference between efficiency and polynomial-time complexity comes from the nature of theoretical studies. We will further discuss the difference with examples in Section 8.1.

Randomized Operations. Cryptographic algorithms are inherently probabilistic algorithms that utilize random numbers to compute outputs. Importantly, these random numbers are not used to speed up computation but to introduce randomness into the output generation process. Consequently, when a probabilistic algorithm is executed multiple times with the same input, it may yield different computational results. Each of these outcomes must be valid and satisfy the usability requirement; otherwise, the algorithm would fail to satisfy the usability requirement.

Consider the encryption algorithm of the ElGamal scheme [22] as an example. Let $(\mathbb{G}, g, p)$ be a cyclic group, where $\mathbb{G}$ is the set of group elements, g is a generator, and p is the group order. Let $pk = h$ and $sk = \alpha \in \mathbb{Z}_p$ be a key pair where $h = g^\alpha$. The encryption algorithm is designed as follows:

Example

$CT \leftarrow Enc(pk, m)$: On input a public key pk and a message $m \in \mathbb{G}$, the encryption algorithm

- Chooses a random integer r from $\mathbb{Z}_p$,
- Computes $c_1 = g^r$ and $c_2 = h^r \cdot m$, and
- Returns the ciphertext $CT = (c_1, c_2)$.

In this probabilistic encryption algorithm, the returned ciphertext depends on the chosen integer r, and every produced ciphertext must be correctly decryptable.

It is worth noting that not all cryptographic algorithms are required to be probabilistic polynomial-time algorithms. For example, unique signatures [32] are a counterexample, defining the signing algorithm as a deterministic polynomial-time algorithm. Another example is the definition of the decryption algorithm within public-key encryption. Since a deterministic algorithm is a specific type of probabilistic algorithm, it remains valid to use probabilistic algorithms to define cryptographic algorithms. One solution is leveraging correctness to determine whether probabilistic or deterministic algorithms are required (as defined in the unique signature scheme [32] and the definition of public-key encryption in Section 6.4.1).

6.2.2 Formulating Probability for Correctness

Correctness ensures that all outcomes produced by the defined cryptographic algorithms are accurate and reliable. All forking algorithms must have correctness descriptions to ensure usability. In the syntax definition of a cryptographic primitive, correctness is formulated using probability.

In general, let Alg_1 be a PPT algorithm that generates W satisfying certain conditions, and let Alg_2 be a PPT forking algorithm that, on input W and other elements, returns X if W meets the specified conditions. Correctness can be formulated with probability using the following framework:

$$\forall W \leftarrow Alg_1(), \ \Pr[Alg_2(W, \cdots) = X] = 1.$$

6.2 Probabilistic Polynomial-Time Algorithms for Users

This states that the PPT forking algorithm Alg_2 will return X' and it is equal to X with probability 1 for any "instance" W generated by the PPT algorithm Alg_1.

Recall the definition of correctness within the syntax definition of digital signatures in Definition 1.1.1. We copy its correctness part as follows:

> The correctness of the above algorithms requires
>
> $$\Pr[\mathsf{Verify}(pk, m, \sigma_m) = 1] = 1$$
>
> for any key pair (pk, sk), any message to be signed from the message space $\mathcal{M}$, and any signature $\sigma_m \leftarrow \mathsf{Sign}(sk, m)$.

It is clear that the definition of correctness aligns with the above framework. In this framework, the verification algorithm is a forking algorithm. This correctness description is a bit more complicated than the introduced framework because we need to define all components in W, including key pairs, messages, and signatures.

There are two key points regarding the definition of correctness.

- First, correctness does not always need to be defined as holding true for all computational results with probability 1. It may also be defined with overwhelming probability, denoted by $1 - \epsilon(\kappa)$, where $\epsilon(\kappa)$ is a negligible function in κ (which will be introduced later).
- Second, the number of probability formulas for defining correctness depends on the number of forking algorithms within the cryptographic primitive, but they may be merged together in definition.

This completes the introduction to the first formula for cryptographic definitions. Two more probability formulas will appear within security definitions.

6.2.3 Why Randomized Operations Matter

> **Overview**
>
> $$\text{Why} = \begin{cases} \text{Because deterministic operations could not be secure.} \\ \text{Because deterministic operations could not achieve better security.} \end{cases}$$

In the previous subsection, we introduced the concept that cryptographic algorithms are probabilistic algorithms that perform randomized operations. Here, we briefly explain the importance of randomized operations through examples.

Firstly, only randomized operations can meet security requirements in some applications. Consider the key generation algorithm as an example. When different users run this algorithm with the same security parameter κ as input, it should return distinct key pairs (pk, sk) while maintaining the same key length. Notice that a deterministic key generation algorithm will always return the same key pair. Since this key generation algorithm is public, it is easy for an adversary to run it and steal users' secret keys. In the literature, many other cryptographic algorithms also rely on random integers during execution and become insecure if randomness is removed. A simple example is the encryption algorithm in the ElGamal scheme. Suppose r is fixed in all 100 ciphertexts generated by Alice. As long as an adversary knows a single plaintext-ciphertext pair (m, CT), they can extract h^r and use it to decrypt the other 99 ciphertexts generated by Alice.

Secondly, randomized operations can provide stronger security guarantees than deterministic operations. One example is the security definition of public-key encryption. There are two security notions, namely one-way security and indistinguishability. Informally speaking, the former states that given a ciphertext $CT \leftarrow Enc(pk, m)$, adversaries cannot recover the plaintext m from it. The latter states that given a ciphertext CT and two messages (m_0, m_1), adversaries cannot distinguish which of the two messages was encrypted. If the encryption algorithm is deterministic rather than probabilistic, it is impossible to achieve indistinguishability. This is because the adversary can run the encryption algorithm on their own to determine whether $CT = Enc(pk, m_0)$ or $CT = Enc(pk, m_1)$.

6.3 Inputs and Entities of Cryptographic Algorithms

In cryptology, each cryptographic algorithm is defined with some predefined elements (objects) as input and output. Each algorithm will be executed by at least one entity. This section further classifies the inputs and entities of cryptographic algorithms in general. This classification aims to help beginners gain a broad understanding of cryptographic algorithms.

6.3.1 What Can an Input Be?

Each cryptographic algorithm must be executed with certain elements as input. We categorize the input elements of most cryptographic algorithms into four main categories: data, identity, keys, and outputs from other algorithms.

Overview

$$\text{Input of Algorithms} = \begin{cases} \text{Data} & \begin{cases} \text{Parameters} \\ \text{Messages, Functions, Circuits} \end{cases} \\ \text{Identity} & \begin{cases} \text{IDs, Attributes} \\ \text{Indexes} \end{cases} \\ \text{Keys} & \begin{cases} \text{Public Keys} \\ \text{Secret Keys} \end{cases} \\ \text{Outputs} & \begin{cases} \text{Proof, Ciphertext, Token} \\ \text{Data, Identity, Keys} \end{cases} \end{cases}$$

The first category is data, which includes elements such as parameters, messages, functions, and circuits. Parameters, such as integers or random bit strings, are required in many algorithms, including key generation. These are referred to as parameters because they are not the protected objects. Instead, other types of data, such as messages, functions, and circuits, require protection for confidentiality or integrity. Here, messages include digital files that need to be secured. Functions and circuits are also considered data because users may wish to keep them confidential from others.

The second category is identity, which includes IDs (e.g., name, email address, and passport number), attributes (e.g., gender, career, and nationality), and indexes. Some identity information is associated with or embedded in cryptographic primitives. For example, an identity serves as part of the input in the key generation algorithm of identity-based encryption [11], while attributes are used as input in the key generation algorithm of attribute-based encryption [29]. In some cryptographic primitives, an index alone is sufficient to serve as an identity. This is because, in certain cases, a public table external to the cryptographic algorithms defines the mapping between public keys and indexes. As a result, an index can be used to represent the identity of a public key. One example of using an index is traitor-tracing identity-based encryption, which will be introduced in the next section.

The third category is about keys, including public keys and secret keys. In all key-related primitives, there must be at least two algorithms: one for generating keys and another that uses a key as part of its input. The definition of a secret key can vary. For example, in symmetric-key encryption, a secret key refers to a random bit string chosen from a key space. In public-key cryptography, a secret key is also a random bit string or integer selected from a key space, but it corresponds to a specific public key. In identity-based cryptography, a secret key may refer to a master secret key owned by a trusted third party or a private key associated with a user's identity.

The fourth category includes all elements derived from the output of other algorithms. In addition to data, identity, and keys, certain other elements are defined as outputs for confidentiality or integrity purposes. For example, in a zero-knowledge proof, a proof is generated to demonstrate knowledge of a particular value, while in encryption, a ciphertext is produced to protect the confidentiality of the input plaintext. If an output serves a purpose different from that of a proof or ciphertext, it is generally referred to as a token.

For each object in these four categories, a formal definition should also specify its space. For example, a message m is chosen from its space $\mathcal{M}$, and a parameter is selected from its space $\{0, 1\}^n$. While this set description is not essential in syntax definitions, it is useful for conveying the practicality of a proposed scheme. For instance, the encryption algorithm in the ElGamal encryption scheme only supports messages from the space $\mathbb{G}$. To encrypt a message outside this space, encoding is required before encryption, followed by decoding after decryption.

6.3.2 Who Can an Entity Be?

A cryptographic primitive consists of at least one algorithm. In this context, an entity refers to users executing the same algorithm. For instance, a user who executes the digital signature verification algorithm to verify a signature is called a verifier, while a user who uses the encryption algorithm to generate ciphertext is known as an encryptor or sender. Assigning an appropriate name to each entity clarifies the role of its users within the application scenario, outlining the concerns and responsibilities of different users. For example, a signer is primarily concerned with the integrity of the messages rather than their confidentiality.

We have categorized entities into three distinct groups: basic entities, issuers, and third parties. Each category is characterized as follows:

Overview

$$\text{Entities} = \begin{cases} \text{Basic Entities} & \begin{cases} \text{Signer, Verifier, Encryptor, Decryptor, Prover} \\ \text{Delegator, Client, Party} \\ \text{Data Owner, Data Receiver} \end{cases} \\ \text{Issuers} & \begin{cases} \text{Private-Key Generator} \\ \text{Trusted Third Party} \\ \text{Authority, Manager} \end{cases} \\ \text{Third Parties} & \begin{cases} \text{Proxy, Delegatee} \\ \text{(Cloud) Server, Auditor} \end{cases} \end{cases}$$

A basic entity encompasses a user type that requires security protections. Examples include a signer and a verifier in digital signatures, an encryptor and a decryptor in an encryption scheme, and a prover and a verifier in a zero-knowledge proof. In a scenario where an individual, such as Alice, delegates a computational task, she assumes the role of a delegator. A user who receives a service from a provider is referred to as a client, while one engaged in a collaborative computation within a cryptographic protocol, such as a multi-party computation, is termed a party. In a context like cloud computing, the terms data owner and data receiver indicate the ownership and utilization of data, respectively.

The issuers are entities responsible for tasks such as issuing secret keys or generating credentials for other entities. In general, users are required to trust the computations performed by issuers on their behalf. For instance, in identity-based encryption, the private-key generator issues private keys to users. A trusted third party is an entity that has complete trust from other users, while an authority (or manager) generates tokens like certificates for users. These entities have different names according to the tasks they are going to do.

The third parties refer to those entities who are involved in computing or communications helping basic entities. For example, proxy and delegatee are two entities trying to run computing for delegator, while server and auditor are entities trying to store and verify data for clients. Unlike issuers, these third parties are semi-honest or curious third parties. They might follow and run cryptographic algorithms but are also curious to learn more. They are therefore not fully trusted in computing. For instance, a cryptographic primitive called cloud auditing [6] was proposed to audit whether cloud servers have honestly stored clients' data without any damage.

In an application scenario secured by a cryptographic primitive, each entity communicates with at least one other entity if multiple entities are involved. For example, as introduced at the beginning of this subsection, digital signatures involve two entities responsible for signing and verification, respectively. It is also possible for a scenario to have only one entity while multiple users within that entity engage in communication. For instance, in cryptographic protocols such as key exchange and multi-party computation, communication between users (parties) may occur within the same entity.

6.4 Syntax Definition for a New Cryptographic Primitive

In the previous section, we have introduced the preliminaries of all cryptographic algorithms including the meaning of PPT algorithms, their input elements, and entities. Based on this knowledge, given a syntax definition of a cryptographic primitive, we should be able to analyze how cryptographic algorithms work. In this section, we will examine cryptographic algorithms within a primitive as a whole. That is, given a syntax definition, we should examine why cryptographic algorithms can work together to secure or benefit an application scenario. The introduction in this section aims to help beginners understand what to think of and how to validate a syntax definition new to them. Our observations are grounded in the syntax definitions for existing cryptographic primitives.

6.4.1 From Scenario to Proof of Concept

Overview

$$\text{5-Step Explanation} = \begin{cases} \text{Step 1: Scenario} \\ \text{Step 2: Concern} \\ \text{Step 3: Wish} \\ \text{Step 4: Definition} \\ \text{Step 5: Proof of Concept} \end{cases}$$

In cryptology, a syntax definition for a cryptographic primitive cannot be introduced without preliminary support; otherwise, it would be difficult to validate. In this book, we present a five-step framework for introducing or validating a new cryptographic primitive and its syntax definition. We will outline these steps and use public-key encryption as a case study to demonstrate their practical application.

Step 1: Scenario. In this step, an application scenario is presented which explains how entities operate and interact with each other. The scenario may lack either cryptographic protection or strong protections from existing cryptographic primitives. To ensure a smooth transition to the next step, the description should highlight the key elements that will be analyzed and addressed.

Example. Suppose Alice wants to send a sensitive message over an insecure network to Bob. They can use symmetric-key encryption to protect the confidentiality of the message. Alice (sender) encrypts the message into ciphertext using a secret key K, and Bob (decryptor) can then decrypt the ciphertext with the same secret key K to read the sensitive message.

Step 2: Concern. In this step, a concern is identified to highlight a concern that needs to be addressed. There are two types of concerns. The first type involves issues with confidentiality or integrity in the application scenario due to the absence of cryptographic protection. The second type examines the limitations of applying existing cryptographic primitives to this scenario, particularly when special events occur.

Continuing the Example. Symmetric-key encryption requires Alice and Bob to have a pre-shared secret key K before they can encrypt and decrypt messages[1]. However, this approach becomes problematic when Alice and Bob do not have a shared key or cannot establish one. For instance, if they do not know each other and are separated by great distances, such as living in different countries, this method is not feasible.

Expressing concerns is often referred to as identifying research motivations. We have observed that enhancing existing cryptographic primitives with new function-

---

[1] This concern addresses the pre-shared secret key; therefore, the previous scenario must introduce how the secret key K is used in encryption and decryption.

6.4 Syntax Definition for a New Cryptographic Primitive

alities is a key driving force behind the development of new cryptographic primitives. Beginners may refer to [33] for a summary of strategies used to explore research motivations. The main ideas from this work are illustrated in Figure 6.1.

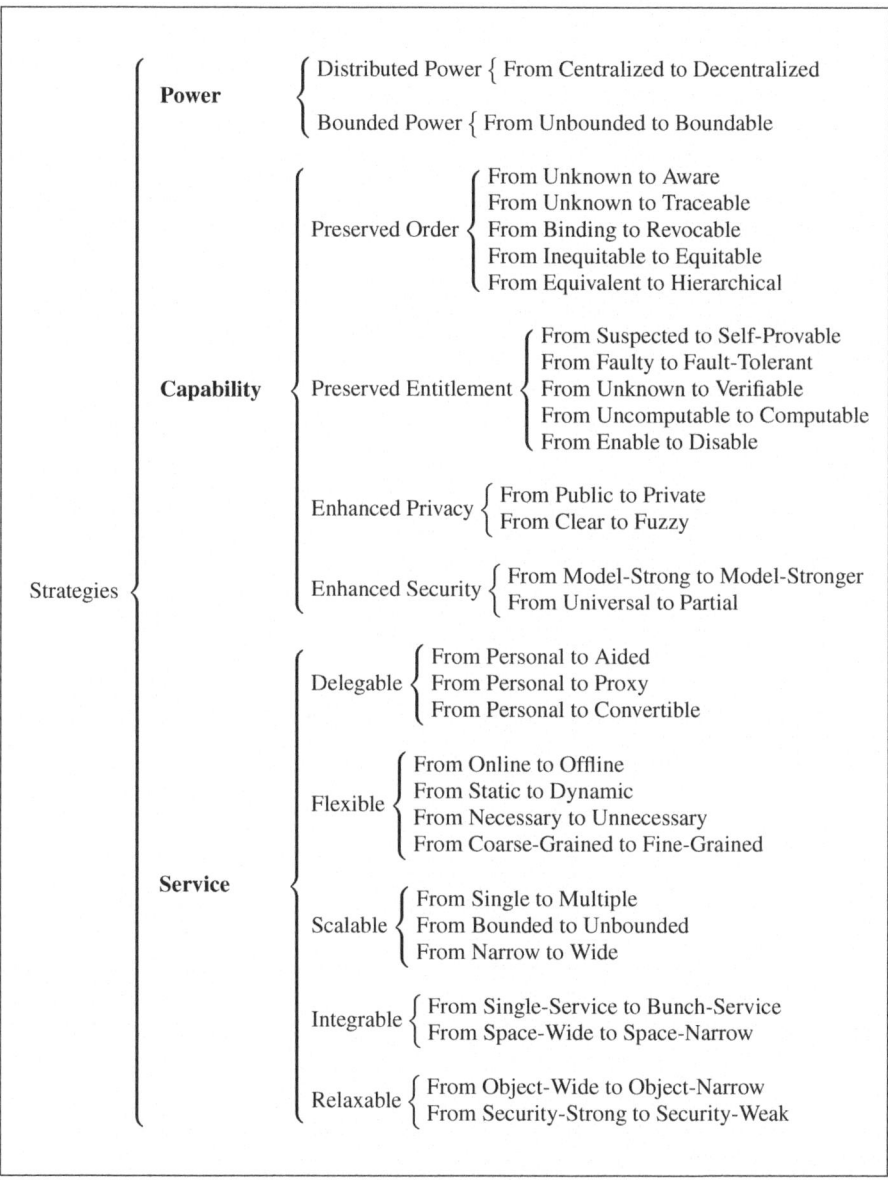

Fig. 6.1 Strategies for exploring new cryptographic primitives. The presentation structure "From A to B" indicates that current cryptographic primitives have characteristic A and it will be promoted to a robust cryptographic primitive with characteristic B.

Step 3: Wish. In this step, a wish or vision is proposed to address the identified concern. There may be multiple cryptographic primitives that can address this concern, and the described wish should align with the characteristics of the new cryptographic primitive to be proposed. For beginners, it is important to note that a new cryptographic primitive, along with its definition, is usually introduced first, followed by the five-step framework, rather than the reverse order.

Continuing the Example. Given the limitations of symmetric-key encryption, we wish for a new encryption primitive that allows Alice to securely send sensitive messages to Bob even if they do not share a secret key. In other words, any two users should be able to communicate confidentially without requiring a pre-shared secret key.

Step 4: Definition. In this step, a cryptographic primitive will be formally defined, including its syntax and security definitions.

Continuing the Example. A new cryptographic primitive called public-key encryption (PKE) has the syntax definition as follows.

> **Definition 6.4.1** (Public-Key Encryption). *A public-key encryption is composed of the following three probabilistic polynomial-time (PPT) algorithms fulfilling correctness.*
>
> - $\mathsf{KeyGen}(1^\kappa) \to (pk, sk)$: *The PPT key generation algorithm takes as input a security parameter κ, and returns a key pair denoted by (pk, sk), where pk denotes a public key and sk denotes a secret key.*
> - $\mathsf{Enc}(pk, m) \to CT$: *The PPT encryption algorithm takes as input a message $m \in \mathcal{M}$ and pk. It returns a ciphertext denoted by CT.*
> - $\mathsf{Dec}(CT, sk) \to m/\bot$: *The PPT decryption algorithm takes as input CT and sk. It returns m if CT is a valid ciphertext or a failure symbol $\bot$.*
>
> *The correctness of the above algorithms requires*
>
> $$\Pr[\mathsf{Dec}(CT, sk) = m] = 1$$
>
> *for any key pair (pk, sk), any message to be encrypted from the message space $\mathcal{M}$, and any ciphertext $CT \leftarrow \mathsf{Enc}(pk, m)$.*

Step 5: Proof of Concept. In this step, a proof of concept is proposed to demonstrate how the new cryptographic primitive addresses the identified concern and fulfills the stated wish. The proof of concept can be viewed as a high-level analysis. This step involves examining why the new primitive resolves the concerns raised in Step 2. It may be necessary to include both the cryptographic algorithms and the security properties (from the security definition) to explain why the wish can be achieved in the revised scenario using the new primitive.

Continuing the Example. Using public-key encryption, Alice can encrypt the sensitive message for Bob using his public key, provided that she believes the public key pk belongs to him. This approach eliminates the need for a shared secret key, addressing the limitation of symmetric-key encryption.

6.4 Syntax Definition for a New Cryptographic Primitive

The five-step explanation above can be viewed as an introduction by inventors proposing a new cryptographic primitive. On the other hand, readers or researchers typically assess the soundness of a syntax definition by reviewing the following components of a newly proposed primitive.

Summary

$$\text{Check} = \begin{cases} 1.\ \text{Assess the number of involved entities} \\ 2.\ \text{Comprehend the name and funtionality of each algorithm} \\ 3.\ \text{Verify the input and output of each algorithm} \end{cases}$$

Assessing the involved entities involves determining which additional entities need to be introduced to secure or enhance the application scenario. The name of each cryptographic algorithm should not be assigned arbitrarily, as it helps convey the function or purpose of the algorithm. Verifying the input and output ensures that the defined algorithms are both practical and secure in application. In this chapter, we will introduce how to define syntax and provide related exercises at the end.

6.4.2 Directions of Syntax Definition

A syntax definition for a cryptographic primitive formally specifies the involved cryptographic algorithms along with their respective inputs and outputs. While there is no universal standard for defining syntax, a robust syntax definition should take the following considerations into account:

Overview

$$\text{Directions} = \begin{cases} 1.\ \text{Minimum number of algorithms} \\ 2.\ \text{Minimum input to be easy in use} \\ 3.\ \text{Minimum management to be easy in use} \\ 4.\ \text{Powerful algorithm for wide-range applications} \end{cases}$$

The first consideration is minimizing the number of algorithms. A cryptographic primitive's syntax definition should include as few algorithms as possible. By minimizing the number of algorithms, the primitive becomes easier to analyze, implement, and verify, thus reducing the likelihood of errors or vulnerabilities due to complexity.

The second consideration is minimizing input. When an entity runs an algorithm, it needs to be aware of all its inputs. Intuitively, only essential objects (elements) should be included as inputs. Including non-essential objects forces users to be aware of these inputs before running the algorithm. For example, consider the encryption algorithm in public-key encryption (PKE), defined as $Enc(pk, m, i)$, where i represents the number of ciphertexts that the owner (Bob) of pk has successfully decrypted so far. The stateful syntax implies that using an incorrect value for i could lead to decryption failures. As a result, Alice, the encryptor, must know the value of i before generating a ciphertext for Bob, which may inconvenience encryptors.

The third consideration is minimizing management. This primarily concerns secret key owners. For example, consider the decryption algorithm in public-key encryption, defined as $Dec(CT, sk, i)$, where i denotes the count of ciphertexts successfully decrypted by the owner of pk. If an incorrect value for i is used, it could lead to decryption failures. Consequently, the decryptor, Bob, must keep track of and update a counter after each successful decryption, increasing management overhead.

The final consideration is how to make algorithms more powerful. When defining the inputs and outputs for an algorithm, they should be general enough to accommodate a wide range of cases and applications. This consideration cannot not be well illustrated by public-key encryption (PKE), but it is relevant to other cryptographic primitives introduced in the next section. It is important to note that some cryptographic primitives in the literature have evolved into more advanced syntax definitions, with the main improvement being the replacement of a weaker algorithm with a more powerful one. We will discuss some examples in the next section.

6.4.3 Limitations of Syntax Definition

We have discussed the approach to obtaining a robust syntax definition for a cryptographic primitive. In this section, we outline the limitations in syntax definitions encountered by the cryptology community so far. This introduction provides a high-level overview, with specific examples given in the next section.

Overview

$$\text{Limitations} = \begin{cases} 1.\ \text{Imperfect definition due to known constructions} \\ 2.\ \text{Gaps between syntax definitions and real-world applications} \\ 3.\ \text{Unclear benefits from the syntax definition} \\ 4.\ \text{Unclear guidance on how to use algorithms and outputs} \end{cases}$$

The first limitation is an imperfect definition influenced by existing constructions. Typically, a new cryptographic primitive is first introduced in an academic paper along with a proposed scheme. The proposed scheme might not align with the syntax definition if it follows principles such as minimizing the number of algorithms, input, and management, or ensuring powerful algorithms. To ensure consistency between the syntax definition and the proposed scheme, the syntax definition might need to be adjusted, either by adding additional algorithms, permitting additional inputs, enhancing management, or restricting algorithm functionality.

The second limitation is the gaps between syntax definitions and real-world applications caused by various factors. In short, addressing concerns in practical scenarios cannot rely solely on a new cryptographic primitive and its algorithms; it often requires support from additional solutions or assumptions. For example, to use public-key encryption effectively, Alice needs a method to verify that pk belongs to Bob. Additionally, encryption might only be feasible for messages within a certain space $\mathcal{M}$, necessitating other solutions for encrypting larger messages. Most proposed primitives cannot independently resolve these concerns, though they serve as crucial components in broader solutions.

The third limitation is the unclear benefits of the syntax definition. The revised application scenario in Step 5 (proof of concept) using the new cryptographic primitive should ideally demonstrate additional benefits compared to the original scenario, such as improved efficiency, enhanced security, or new functionalities. However, this is not always the case, as some newly proposed cryptographic primitives have trivial constructions (i.e., those that are easily constructed). Specifically, efficiency improvements from a new cryptographic primitive cannot be fully demonstrated by its syntax definition alone but also require an analysis of the proposed schemes.

The final limitation is the lack of clear guidance on the correct and secure use of algorithms and their outputs. For example, consider a (secret) token generated by an algorithm. It may be unclear how many times this token can be securely used by other algorithms. Reusing the token could introduce security vulnerabilities. This ambiguity in usage is more pronounced in protocols[2].

6.4.4 Subtle Differences of Syntax Definition

A cryptographic primitive is often defined in multiple references, but these definitions may have subtle differences. We have summarized key observations on subtle differences in the syntax definitions of the same cryptographic primitive across different authors. Such variations can be confusing for beginners and may hinder their understanding.

Overview

$$\text{Subtle Differences} = \begin{cases} 1.\ \text{No standard symbol/notation representation for objects} \\ 2.\ \text{Syntax order of input and output} \\ 3.\ \text{Inconsistent algorithms in syntax} \\ 4.\ \text{Incomplete syntax definition} \end{cases}$$

---

[2] We will discuss the distinction between schemes and protocols at the end of this chapter.

The first subtle difference is the representation of each object. There is no universally standardized notation for representing objects. For instance, in the syntax definition of public-key encryption, one author might use CT to denote ciphertext, while another might simply use the symbol C. Although any symbol can represent an object, it is crucial that the notation avoids confusion and effectively conveys its purpose, especially for beginners. For example, it is common to use pk for a public key and sk for a secret key, as these notations are abbreviations of their respective objects. Using pk for a secret key and sk for a public key could create significant comprehension challenges.

The second subtle difference is how input and output syntax is presented. There are two common ways to represent the input and output of each algorithm. For example, in the key generation algorithm, one might use either *KeyGen(1^κ)* $\to (pk, sk)$ or $(pk, sk) \leftarrow$ *KeyGen(1^κ)*. The first syntax shows a natural flow from input to output, while the second is consistent with the syntax $y \leftarrow A(x)$ used in distribution and sampling. In this book, we primarily use the first syntax.

The third subtle difference involves algorithms in syntax definition. The same primitive could be defined and consist of a different number of algorithms. One of the examples is the need for a setup algorithm in cryptographic primitives, such as digital signatures and public key encryption, which generates public parameters for key generation. Intuitively speaking, there is no need to include this algorithm to generate a key pair. However, when multiple users need to generate distinct key pairs, it is better to include it. This is because the setup algorithm can generate common parameters such as cyclic group in construction to be used by all users.

The final subtle difference is the incompleteness of syntax definitions, where certain non-essential details may be omitted. For instance, some public parameters might be included in one paper but not in another for the same cryptographic algorithm. For example, the input to the decryption algorithm *Dec(CT, sk)* might sometimes include pk and sometimes not. Additionally, definitions often omit the specification of object spaces, such as those for public keys, messages, and ciphertexts. Finally, it is often unclear which entity should run each algorithm according to the syntax definition. As a result, beginners may struggle to grasp the application of a cryptographic primitive without analyzing its application scenario or acquiring the 5-step explanations.

6.4.5 Classifications of Cryptographic Algorithms

All cryptographic algorithms are designed with users in mind. Proper classification of cryptographic algorithms aids in understanding syntax definitions and the rationale behind them. This book introduces three classifications, as shown in Figure 6.2. This overview will help in understanding the subsequent chapters of the book.

The first classification is based on computational flow. A cryptographic algorithm is categorized as either a straight or a forking algorithm. Straight algorithms offer direct mappings, whereas forking algorithms introduce decision points that alter

6.5 From Scenario to Proof of Concept: Examples

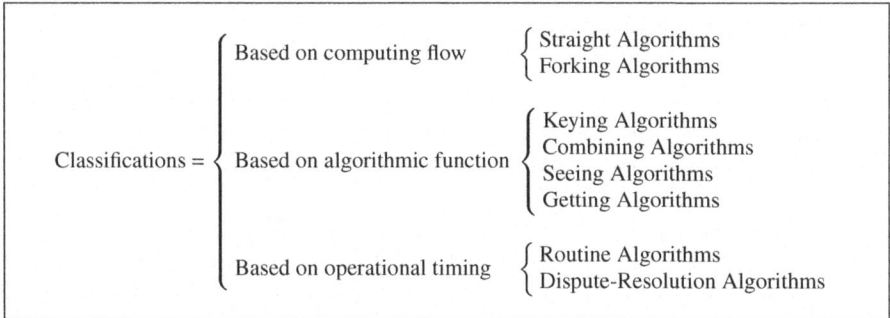

Fig. 6.2 Classifications of PPT Algorithms for Users

outcomes based on input conditions. At least one forking algorithm must be present in the syntax definition of a cryptographic primitive. This classification is essential for understanding what to consider when defining correctness.

The second classification is based on algorithmic function or purpose, as introduced in Section 6.6. In this classification, four categories distinguish the functions and purposes of cryptographic algorithms. This classification is crucial for understanding the role of cryptographic algorithms in security applications. Most cryptographic algorithms in the next section will fall into one of these four categories.

The third classification is based on the timing of a cryptographic algorithm's execution. Routine algorithms, such as those for key generation, signing, encryption, and verification, are executed by users for daily security protections. Dispute-resolution algorithms, such as judging, tracing, and opening, are used only when disputes or abuses arise and require resolution. For example, if a user with a secret key abuses cryptographic algorithms and their applications, a dispute-resolution algorithm is applied to identify the user. This section provides only an overview. Several examples (Syntax Definition 6.5.6 and Syntax Definition 6.5.19) will be provided to help readers understand this classification. It is important to note that most cryptographic algorithms are routine, and only a few cryptographic primitives include dispute-resolution algorithms.

6.5 From Scenario to Proof of Concept: Examples

In this section, we present syntax definitions for identity-based encryption (IBE) and its variants to further illustrate the concepts and observations outlined in the previous section. We have collected 19 variants from the literature (with minor modifications). These definitions will follow the 5-step framework, from scenario to proof of concept. Some primitives defined in this book have been slightly modified from their original literature descriptions, and their names may also be adjusted. These modifications aim to improve readability and maintain consistency.

6.5.1 Identity-Based Encryption

Scenario. With the help of public-key encryption, even if Alice and Bob do not share a secret key, Alice can still send sensitive messages to Bob. Alice encrypts messages with Bob's public key pk, and Bob can decrypt the ciphertext using his secret key sk known only to himself.

Concern. However, public-key encryption requires Alice to verify and obtain Bob's correct public key, since the public key pk is a pseudo-random string derived from Bob's secret key sk and other public parameters. The most practical solution is to use digital certificates, which require a complex certificate management system.

Wish. It would be ideal if Alice could use Bob's public information, such as his email address or name, as his public key for encryption. This would eliminate the complexity of certificate management.

Definition 6.5.1 (Identity-Based Encryption). *An identity-based encryption consists of the following four probabilistic polynomial-time (PPT) algorithms fulfilling correctness.*

- Setup(1^κ) → (mpk, msk): *The PPT setup algorithm takes as input a security parameter κ, and returns a key pair denoted by (mpk, msk), where mpk denotes a master public key and msk denotes a master secret key.*
- KeyGen(msk, ID) → d_{ID}: *The PPT key generation algorithm takes as input msk and an identity ID. It returns a private key of ID denoted by d_{ID}.*
- Enc(mpk, ID, m) → CT_{ID}: *The PPT encryption algorithm takes as input mpk, ID, and a message m. It returns a ciphertext for ID denoted by CT_{ID}.*
- Dec(mpk, CT_{ID}, d_{ID}) → $m/\bot$: *The PPT decryption algorithm takes as input mpk, CT_{ID}, and d_{ID}. It returns a plaintext m if CT_{ID} is a valid ciphertext or a failure symbol $\bot$.*

The correctness of the above algorithms requires

$$\Pr[\mathsf{Dec}(mpk, CT_{ID}, d_{ID}) = m] = 1$$

for any master key pair (mpk, msk), any identity ID, any message m, any ciphertext CT_{ID} generated from encryption algorithm on input (mpk, ID, m), and any private key d_{ID} generated from key generation algorithm on input (msk, ID).

Proof of Concept. Identity-based encryption enables arbitrary string to serve as a public key. This means Alice can use Bob's public information as his public key for encryption. As long as only the owner of the information ID obtains their private key from the trusted PKG, the sensitive message can be securely delivered to Bob.

This completes the syntax of identity-based encryption (see [11]). Compared to traditional public-key encryption (PKE), IBE introduces an additional entity and imposes trust assumptions. For instance, the PKG must be trusted, ensuring that only the owner of ID can obtain their private key d_{ID} from the trusted PKG.

6.5.2 Online/Offline Identity-Based Encryption

Scenario. Identity-based encryption enables a sender to encrypt sensitive messages for a receiver using the receiver's public information, such as an email address or name, as the public key. This approach significantly simplifies encryption for senders, eliminating the need to verify public keys.

Concern. However, all existing identity-based encryption (IBE) schemes incur high computational costs in encryption, which poses challenges for adopting this primitive in lightweight applications.

Wish. It would be ideal if the encryption algorithm should be made highly efficient and suitable for lightweight applications.

Definition 6.5.2 (Online/Offline Identity-Based Encryption). *An online offline identity-based encryption consists of the following five probabilistic polynomial-time (PPT) algorithms fulfilling correctness.*

- Setup(1^κ) $\to$ (mpk, msk): *The PPT setup algorithm takes as input a security parameter κ, and returns a key pair denoted by (mpk, msk), where mpk denotes a master public key and msk denotes a master secret key.*

- KeyGen(msk, ID) $\to$ d_{ID}: *The PPT key generation algorithm takes as input msk and an identity ID. It returns a private key of ID denoted by d_{ID}.*

- OffEnc(mpk) $\to$ IT: *The PPT offline encryption algorithm takes as input mpk and returns an intermediate ciphertext denoted by IT.*

- OnEnc(mpk, IT, ID, m) $\to$ CT_{ID}: *The PPT online encryption algorithm takes as input mpk, IT, ID, and a message m. It returns a ciphertext for ID denoted by CT_{ID}.*

- Dec(mpk, CT_{ID}, d_{ID}) $\to$ $m/\bot$: *The PPT decryption algorithm takes as input mpk, CT_{ID}, and d_{ID}. It returns a plaintext m if CT_{ID} is a valid ciphertext or a failure symbol $\bot$.*

The correctness of the above algorithms requires

$$\Pr[\mathsf{Dec}(mpk, CT_{ID}, d_{ID}) = m] = 1$$

for any master key pair (mpk, msk), any identity ID, any intermediate ciphertext IT generated from offline encryption algorithm on input mpk, any

> *message m, any ciphertext CT generated from online encryption algorithm on input (mpk, IT, ID, m), and any private key d_{ID} generated from key generation algorithm on input (msk, ID).*

Proof of Concept. Online/offline identity-based encryption is very suitable for lightweight applications when the online encryption algorithm is highly efficient. This approach runs the offline encryption algorithm on a more capable device, storing the intermediate result IT on a lightweight device to efficiently complete the remaining encryption. Thus, this primitive fulfills the stated wish.

This completes the syntax of online/offline identity-based encryption (see [31]). This syntax definition has unclear benefits, as it does not specify the efficiency of the online encryption algorithm. It is also unclear how many times the intermediate ciphertext IT can be reused. Existing schemes in the literature assume that IT must remain secret and be used only once.

6.5.3 Broadcast Identity-Based Encryption

Scenario. Identity-based encryption (IBE) enables a sender to encrypt sensitive messages for a receiver using the receiver's identity (ID) as the public key. The sender generates ciphertext using a master public key, the receiver's ID, and a message m.

Concern. However, when sending m to multiple receivers, the encryption algorithm must be executed separately for each receiver. This process is inefficient and computationally expensive.

Wish. It would be ideal if a message can be encrypted for a set of receivers in a single encryption operation, without affecting each receiver's ability to decrypt independently using their private key.

> **Definition 6.5.3** (Broadcast Identity-Based Encryption). *A broadcast identity-based encryption consists of the following four probabilistic polynomial-time (PPT) algorithms fulfilling correctness.*
>
> - Setup($1^\kappa, n$) → (mpk, msk): *The PPT setup algorithm takes as input a security parameter κ and a parameter n presenting the maximum number of receivers in one broadcasting. It returns a key pair denoted by (mpk, msk), where mpk denotes a master public key and msk denotes a master secret key.*
>
> - KeyGen(msk, ID) → d_{ID}: *The PPT key generation algorithm takes as input msk and an identity ID. It returns a private key of ID denoted by d_{ID}.*

- Enc($mpk, \mathbf{ID}, m$) → $CT_\mathbf{ID}$: *The PPT encryption algorithm takes as input mpk, a set of identities $\mathbf{ID} = \{ID_1, ID_2, \cdots, ID_t\}(1 \leq t \leq n)$, and a message m. It returns a ciphertext for $\mathbf{ID}$ denoted by $CT_\mathbf{ID}$.*
- Dec($mpk, \mathbf{ID}, CT_\mathbf{ID}, d_{ID}$) → $m/\perp$: *The PPT decryption algorithm takes as input mpk, $\mathbf{ID}$, $CT_\mathbf{ID}$, and d_{ID}. It returns a plaintext m if $CT_\mathbf{ID}$ is a valid ciphertext and $ID \in \mathbf{ID}$, or a failure symbol $\perp$.*

The correctness of the above algorithms requires

$$\Pr[ID \in \mathbf{ID} : \text{Dec}(mpk, \mathbf{ID}, CT_\mathbf{ID}, d_{ID}) = m] = 1$$

for any master key pair (mpk, msk), any identity ID, any message m, any $1 \leq t \leq n$, any identity set $\mathbf{ID} = \{ID_1, ID_2, \cdots, ID_t\}$, any ciphertext $CT_\mathbf{ID}$ generated from encryption algorithm on input $(mpk, \mathbf{ID}, m)$, and any private key d_{ID} generated from key generation algorithm on input (msk, ID).

Proof of Concept. Broadcast identity-based encryption enables encrypting messages for multiple users using their identities as public keys. Each receiver can then use their private key to independently decrypt the ciphertext. Thus, this primitive meets the stated requirement.

This completes the syntax of broadcast identity-based encryption (see [19]). This definition has two limitations. First, the setup algorithm requires an additional parameter n as input. Ideally, a perfect broadcast identity-based encryption scheme should accommodate any number of receivers in a single broadcast encryption. However, by setting a maximum number n in advance, the efficiency of the constructed schemes can be significantly improved. Many syntax definitions include this "imperfect" restriction. Second, decryption requires both the identity set $\mathbf{ID}$ and the ciphertext $CT_\mathbf{ID}$. Efficiency would improve if $\mathbf{ID}$ did not need to be broadcast, as the set $\mathbf{ID}$ could be very large, potentially involving thousands of receivers.

6.5.4 Fuzzy Identity-Based Encryption

Scenario. Identity-based encryption (IBE) enables a sender to encrypt sensitive messages for a receiver using the receiver's identity (ID) as the public key. The ciphertext can be decrypted only with the private key corresponding to ID.

Concern. In the real world, the sender could input ID' in encryption, which is biometric data that does not exactly match the ID associated with the receiver's private key. As a result, the receiver cannot use d_{ID} to decrypt the ciphertext, as IBE requires an exact match between the identity used for encryption and decryption.

Wish. It would be beneficial to have an encryption scheme that permits decryption with private keys of identities that do not exactly match the chosen identities for encryption. Instead, decryption should be possible if the identities are sufficiently similar based on a predefined fuzzy function. This feature would improve the usability and robustness of identity-based encryption in real-world scenarios where exact identity matches are not always feasible.

Definition 6.5.4 (Fuzzy Identity-Based Encryption). *A fuzzy identity-based encryption consists of the following four probabilistic polynomial-time (PPT) algorithms fulfilling correctness.*

- Setup(1^κ) → (mpk, msk): *The PPT setup algorithm takes as input a security parameter κ, and returns a key pair denoted by (mpk, msk), where mpk denotes a master public key and msk denotes a master secret key.*
- KeyGen(msk, ID) → d_{ID}: *The PPT key generation algorithm takes as input msk and an identity ID. It returns a private key of ID denoted by d_{ID}.*
- Enc(mpk, ID', m, F) → $CT_{ID'}^F$: *The PPT encryption algorithm takes as input mpk, ID', a message m, and a fuzzy function F. It returns a ciphertext for ID' denoted by $CT_{ID'}^F$.*
- Dec($mpk, CT_{ID'}^F, d_{ID}$) → $m/\bot$: *The PPT decryption algorithm takes as input mpk, $CT_{ID'}^F$, and d_{ID}. It returns a plaintext m if $CT_{ID'}^F$ is a valid ciphertext and $F(ID, ID') = 1$, or a failure symbol $\bot$.*

The correctness of the above algorithms requires

$$\Pr[F(ID, ID') = 1 : \mathsf{Dec}(mpk, CT_{ID'}^F, d_{ID}) = m] = 1$$

for any master key pair (mpk, msk), any identities ID, ID', any message m, any fuzzy function F, any ciphertext $CT_{ID'}^F$ generated from encryption algorithm on input (mpk, ID', m, F), and any private key d_{ID} generated from key generation algorithm on input (msk, ID).

Proof of Concept. Fuzzy identity-based encryption allows a message to be encrypted using an identity ID' and a fuzzy function F defined by the encryptor. A private key corresponding to an identity ID can decrypt the ciphertext if $F(ID, ID') = 1$. With an appropriately chosen fuzzy function, the identity ID' used in encryption does not need to perfectly match ID in the private key, making this primitive suitable for scenarios where exact identity matching is challenging.

This completes the syntax for fuzzy identity-based encryption (see [42]). Although this syntax definition ideally supports any fuzzy function, a specific fuzzy identity-based encryption scheme may only support a restricted class of fuzzy functions. For example, a scheme may be designed to support a fuzzy function $F(ID, ID') = 1$ only if the identity bit strings have the same length and differ by exactly one bit at the same position.

6.5.5 Functional Identity-Based Encryption

Scenario. Identity-based encryption (IBE) enables a sender to encrypt a sensitive message m for a receiver using the receiver's identity (ID) as the public key. The receiver can then decrypt the ciphertext using the private key corresponding to ID and recover the plaintext m.

Concern. IBE enables the receiver to decrypt the ciphertext and directly obtain the plaintext message. This direct decryption approach may reveal more information than necessary, potentially compromising message privacy.

Wish. It would be beneficial to have an encryption scheme where the decryption process produces a functionally transformed version of the plaintext denoted by $F(m)$, rather than the plaintext itself. Moreover, the result a receiver obtains depends on the provided private key. This capability enhances privacy by restricting receivers' access to information based on the function F specified during key generation, thereby enabling controlled access to encrypted data.

Definition 6.5.5 (Functional Identity-Based Encryption). *A functional identity-based encryption consists of the following four probabilistic polynomial-time (PPT) algorithms fulfilling correctness.*

- Setup(1^κ) $\to$ (mpk, msk): *The PPT setup algorithm takes as input a security parameter κ, and returns a key pair denoted by (mpk, msk), where mpk denotes a master public key and msk denotes a master secret key.*
- KeyGen(msk, ID, F) $\to d_{ID,F}$: *The PPT key generation algorithm takes as input msk, an identity ID, and a function F. It returns a private key of (ID, F) denoted by $d_{ID,F}$.*
- Enc(mpk, ID, m) $\to CT_{ID}$: *The PPT encryption algorithm takes as input mpk, ID, and a message m. It returns a ciphertext for ID denoted by CT_{ID}.*
- Dec($mpk, CT_{ID}, d_{ID,F}$) $\to F(m)/\bot$: *The PPT decryption algorithm takes as input mpk, CT_{ID}, and $d_{ID,F}$. It returns the functional plaintext $F(m)$ if CT_{ID} is a valid ciphertext or a failure symbol $\bot$.*

The correctness of the above algorithms requires

$$\Pr[\text{Dec}(mpk, CT_{ID}, d_{ID,F}) = F(m)] = 1$$

for any master key pair (mpk, msk), any identity ID, any function F, any message m, any ciphertext generated from encryption algorithm on input (mpk, ID, m), and any private key $d_{ID,F}$ generated from key generation algorithm on input (msk, ID, F).

Proof of Concept. Functional identity-based encryption enables the PKG to generate a private key associated with an identity ID and a function F. The user can then decrypt CT_{ID} to obtain $F(m)$, representing the function applied to the encrypted message m instead of revealing m itself. Thus, this primitive effectively meets the stated requirement.

This concludes the syntax definition for functional identity-based encryption (see [14]). Similar to fuzzy identity-based encryption, this syntax definition features a powerful key generation algorithm, making it well-suited for supporting any function in private key generation.

6.5.6 Traitor-Tracing Identity-Based Encryption

Scenario. Identity-based encryption (IBE) enables a sender to encrypt sensitive messages for a receiver using only the receiver's identity (ID) as the public key. The owner of the private key can decrypt the ciphertext and recover the plaintext using the private key associated with ID.

Concern. In some scenarios, a set of users may possess private keys corresponding to the same identity (ID). For example, these users may be assigned to collaboratively process privacy-preserving tasks encoded in m. If some of these users collude to construct a pirate decryption device for decrypting ciphertexts CT_{ID}, tracing the users involved in this illegal activity becomes challenging.

Wish. It would be beneficial to have an encryption scheme that enables the Private-Key Generator (PKG) to trace and identify at least one traitor who contributed to the creation of a pirate decryption device, even when the box is accessed as a black box. This capability enhances security by deterring users from engaging in illegal key-sharing activities and facilitating appropriate actions against traitors.

Definition 6.5.6 (Traitor-Tracing Identity-Based Encryption). *A traitor tracing identity-based encryption consists of the following five probabilistic polynomial-time (PPT) algorithms fulfilling correctness.*

- Setup($1^\kappa, n$) → (mpk, msk): *The PPT setup algorithm takes as input a security parameter κ and a parameter n presenting the maximum number of users having the private key of the same identity. It returns a key pair denoted by (mpk, msk), where mpk denotes a master public key and msk denotes a master secret key.*

- KeyGen(msk, ID, t) → ($d_{ID}^1, d_{ID}^2, \cdots, d_{ID}^t$): *The PPT key generation algorithm takes as input msk, an identity ID, and the number of users $1 \leq t \leq n$ to possess the private key of ID. It returns ($d_{ID}^1, d_{ID}^2, \cdots, d_{ID}^t$). In particular, the private key d_{ID}^i will be given to the i-th user.*

- Enc(mpk, ID, m) → CT_{ID}: *The PPT encryption algorithm takes as input mpk, ID, and a message m. It returns a ciphertext for ID denoted by CT_{ID}.*

- Dec(mpk, CT_{ID}, d_{ID}^i) → $m/\bot$: *The PPT decryption algorithm takes as input mpk, CT_{ID}, and d_{ID}^i. It returns a plaintext m if CT_{ID} is a valid ciphertext or a failure symbol $\bot$.*
- Trace$^{\mathcal{D}_{ID}}$(mpk, ID, msk) → i: *The PPT tracing algorithm takes as input mpk, ID, msk, and a decryption device $\mathcal{D}_{ID}$ that can decrypt ciphertexts for ID. It returns an index i whose private key is used in creating the decryption device.*

The correctness of the above algorithms requires

$$\Pr[\text{Dec}(mpk, CT_{ID}, d_{ID}^i) = m] = 1$$

$$\Pr[i \leftarrow \text{Trace}^{\mathcal{D}_{ID}}(mpk, ID, msk) : i \in S] = 1$$

for any master key pair (mpk, msk), any identity ID, any $1 \leq t \leq n$, any message m, any ciphertext CT_{ID} generated from encryption algorithm on input (mpk, ID, m), any $i \in [1, t]$, any private key d_{ID}^i generated from key generation algorithm on input (msk, ID, t), and any decryption device $\mathcal{D}_{ID}$ generated using private keys from the set of traitors denoted by $S \subset \{1, 2, \cdots, t\}$.

Proof of Concept. Traitor-tracing identity-based encryption enables the PKG to assign a unique index to each private key associated with the same identity ID. Each of these distinct private keys can decrypt any ciphertext intended for ID. Additionally, the PKG can trace the specific index associated with ID whose private key was used in the decryption process by analyzing the decryption device $\mathcal{D}_{ID}$. Thus, this primitive fulfills the stated requirement.

This completes the syntax for traitor-tracing identity-based encryption (see [2]). This syntax introduces a "hardware" component, referred to as a pirate decryption device, which is distinct from previous digital objects. It can be regarded as a tamper-proof hardware device with specific operational capabilities. Note that incorporating a hardware device in syntax definitions is not uncommon; other examples in the literature include [44]. On the other side, this syntax definition is imperfect due to the additional parameter n in the setup algorithm.

6.5.7 Revocable Identity-Based Encryption

Scenario. Identity-based encryption (IBE) enables a sender to encrypt sensitive messages for a receiver using only the receiver's identity (ID) as the public key. The receiver can always use the private key associated with ID to decrypt all ciphertexts intended for ID.

Concern. In IBE, once issued, a private key remains valid indefinitely, posing security risks if a user accidentally loses it or if it is compromised. IBE lacks a built-in mechanism to revoke private keys and prevent their use in decryption, potentially leading to unauthorized access to encrypted data.

Wish. It would be beneficial to have an encryption scheme that allows private keys to be revoked at any time, preventing them from decrypting ciphertexts. This feature would enable the Private-Key Generator (PKG) to manage users' private keys more flexibly, particularly when keys are lost or compromised, thereby improving the overall security and manageability of the encryption system.

Definition 6.5.7 (Revocable Identity-Based Encryption). *A revocable identity-based encryption consists of the following five probabilistic polynomial-time (PPT) algorithms fulfilling correctness.*

- Setup$(1^\kappa) \to (mpk, msk)$: *The PPT setup algorithm takes as input a security parameter κ, and returns a key pair denoted by (mpk, msk), where mpk denotes a master public key and msk denotes a master secret key. The initial mpk is set as mpk_0.*
- KeyGen$(msk, ID) \to d_{ID}$: *The PPT key generation algorithm takes as input msk and an identity ID. It returns a private key of ID denoted by d_{ID}.*
- Revoke$(ID, mpk_i, msk) \to mpk_{i+1}$: *The PPT revocation algorithm takes as input ID be to revoked, an old master public key mpk_i to be updated, and msk. It returns an updated master public key mpk_{i+1}.*
- Enc$(mpk_j, ID, m) \to CT_{ID}^{mpk_j}$: *The PPT encryption algorithm takes as input the latest updated master public key mpk_j, ID, and a message m. It returns a ciphertext for ID denoted by $CT_{ID}^{mpk_j}$.*
- Dec$(mpk_j, CT_{ID}^{mpk_j}, d_{ID}) \to m/\bot$: *The PPT decryption algorithm takes as input $mpk_j, CT_{ID}^{mpk_j}$, and d_{ID}. It returns m if $CT_{ID}^{mpk_j}$ is a valid ciphertext and ID has not yet been revoked, or a failure symbol $\bot$.*

The correctness of the above algorithms requires

$$\Pr\left[ID \notin mpk_i, i \in [1,j] : \mathsf{Dec}(mpk_j, CT_{ID}^{mpk_j}, d_{ID}) = m\right] = 1$$

for any master key pair (mpk, msk), any identity ID, any message m, any updated master public key mpk_j, any ciphertext $CT_{ID}^{mpk_j}$ generated from encryption algorithm on input (mpk_j, ID, m), and any private key d_{ID} generated from key generation algorithm on input (msk, ID).

Proof of Concept. Revocable identity-based encryption allows the PKG to revoke a user's private key by updating the master public key (mpk) used for encryption. If an identity ID is revoked and this revocation is recorded in the updated master public key (mpk), any message encrypted for ID under the updated mpk cannot be decrypted with the private key d_{ID} of the revoked identity. Thus, this primitive fulfills the stated requirement.

This completes the syntax for revocable identity-based encryption (see [43]). This syntax definition has two primary limitations. First, without a defined security model, the correctness of the revocation process remains unclear. Second, the revocation process requires encryptors to use the most recent mpk for encryption. As a result, ciphertexts encrypted under an outdated mpk for ID remain decryptable with the corresponding private key, even if ID has been revoked in the latest master public key mpk.

6.5.8 Hierarchical Identity-Based Encryption

Scenario. Identity-based encryption (IBE) enables a sender to encrypt sensitive messages for a receiver using the receiver's identity (ID) as the public key. A trusted third party, called the Private-Key Generator (PKG), is responsible for issuing private keys to all users.

Concern. In traditional IBE, the PKG alone is responsible for issuing and generating individual private keys for all receivers. This responsibility can become overwhelming in large-scale systems with many users, significantly increasing the PKG's workload.

Wish. It would be advantageous to have an encryption scheme that allows both the PKG and users to issue private keys. In a hierarchical structure, a top-level private key should be capable of generating private keys for descendant identities at lower levels. This hierarchical approach streamlines key management, reduces the PKG's workload, and improves the scalability and efficiency of the encryption system.

> **Definition 6.5.8** (Hierarchical Identity-Based Encryption). *A hierarchical identity-based encryption consists of the following four probabilistic polynomial-time (PPT) algorithms fulfilling correctness.*
>
> - Setup($1^\kappa, n$) $\to$ (mpk, msk): *The PPT setup algorithm takes as input a security parameter κ and a parameter n presenting the maximum length of identity. It returns a key pair denoted by (mpk, msk), where mpk denotes a master public key and msk denotes a master secret key.*
> - KeyGen($d_{\mathbf{ID}_{[i-1]}}, \mathbf{ID}_{[i]}$) $\to d_{\mathbf{ID}_{[i]}}$: *The PPT key generation algorithm takes as input a private key $d_{\mathbf{ID}_{[i-1]}}$ of identity $\mathbf{ID}_{[i-1]} = ID_1 \| ID_2 \| \cdots \| ID_{i-1}$, and an identity $\mathbf{ID}_{[i]} = \mathbf{ID}_{[i-1]} \| ID_i$ ($1 \leq i \leq n$). It returns a private key of $\mathbf{ID}_{[i]}$ denoted by $d_{\mathbf{ID}_{[i]}}$. In particular, if $i = 1$, the private key $d_{\mathbf{ID}_{[i-1]}}$ refers to the master secret key.*
> - Enc($mpk, \mathbf{ID}_{[i]}, m$) $\to CT_{\mathbf{ID}_{[i]}}$: *The PPT encryption algorithm takes as input mpk, $\mathbf{ID}_{[i]}$, and a message m. It returns a ciphertext for $\mathbf{ID}_{[i]}$ denoted by $CT_{\mathbf{ID}_{[i]}}$.*

- Dec($mpk, CT_{\mathbf{ID}_{[i]}}, d_{\mathbf{ID}_{[j]}}$) → $m/\bot$: *The PPT decryption algorithm takes as input mpk, $CT_{\mathbf{ID}_{[i]}}$, and $d_{\mathbf{ID}_{[j]}}$. It returns a plaintext m if $CT_{\mathbf{ID}_{[i]}}$ is a valid ciphertext or a failure symbol $\bot$.*

The correctness of the above algorithms requires

$$\Pr[\text{Dec}(mpk, CT_{\mathbf{ID}_{[i]}}, d_{\mathbf{ID}_{[j]}}) = m] = 1$$

for any master key pair (mpk, msk), any $\mathbf{ID}_{[i]} = ID_1 \| ID_2 \| \cdots \| ID_i$, any level $1 \le j \le i \le n$ satisfying $\mathbf{ID}_{[i]} = \mathbf{ID}_{[j]} \| ID_{j+1} \| \cdots \| ID_i$, any message m, any ciphertext $CT_{\mathbf{ID}_{[i]}}$ generated from encryption algorithm on input $(mpk, \mathbf{ID}_{[i]}, m)$, and any private key $d_{\mathbf{ID}_{[j]}}$ generated from key generation algorithm on input $(d_{\mathbf{ID}_{[j-1]}}, \mathbf{ID}_{[j]})$.

Proof of Concept. Hierarchical identity-based encryption enables a private key associated with an identity $\mathbf{ID}_{[i]} = ID_1 \| ID_2 \| \cdots \| ID_i$ to generate a private key for an extended identity $\mathbf{ID}_{[i+1]} = ID_1 \| ID_2 \| \cdots \| ID_i \| ID_{i+1}$ by appending the additional identity information ID_{i+1}. When an identity $\mathbf{ID}_{[i]}$ represents a user's identity, this primitive effectively supports hierarchical key generation and management, thereby fulfilling the stated requirement.

This completes the syntax for hierarchical identity-based encryption (see [10]). The setup algorithm is imperfect due to the inclusion of an extra parameter n. Additionally, the proper execution of decryption remains undefined. For example, it is unclear how a private key associated with an identity $ID_1 \| ID_2 \| ID_3$ at level 3 can be used to decrypt a ciphertext intended for $ID_1 \| ID_2 \| ID_3 \| ID_4 \| ID_5 \| ID_6$ at level 6.

6.5.9 Server-Aided Identity-Based Encryption

Scenario. Identity-based encryption (IBE) enables a sender to encrypt sensitive messages for a receiver using the receiver's identity (ID) as the public key. The receiver decrypts the ciphertext using the private key associated with ID, which is generated by the PKG.

Concern. In IBE, decryption is performed solely by the decryptor using their private key, making it computationally intensive, particularly for resource-constrained devices. This high computational cost may reduce the practicality of IBE in scenarios requiring fast or lightweight decryption.

Wish. It would be beneficial to have an encryption scheme that allows a third party (such as a server) to assist in decryption, thereby reducing the computational burden on the decryptor. Moreover, the encrypted message must remain confidential from the third party's perspective.

6.5 From Scenario to Proof of Concept: Examples

Definition 6.5.9 (Server-Aided Identity-Based Encryption). *A server-aided identity-based encryption consists of the following six probabilistic polynomial-time (PPT) algorithms fulfilling correctness.*

- Setup(1^κ) $\to$ (mpk, msk): *The PPT setup algorithm takes as input a security parameter κ, and returns a key pair denoted by (mpk, msk), where mpk denotes a master public key and msk denotes a master secret key.*
- KeyGen(msk, ID) $\to$ d_{ID}: *The PPT key generation algorithm takes as input msk and an identity ID. It returns a private key of ID denoted by d_{ID}.*
- DKeyGen(mpk, ID, d_{ID}) $\to$ dd_{ID}: *The PPT delegated key generation algorithm takes as input mpk, ID, and d_{ID}. It returns a delegated private key for ID denoted by dd_{ID}.*
- Enc(mpk, ID, m) $\to$ CT_{ID}: *The PPT encryption algorithm takes as input mpk, ID, and a message m. It returns a ciphertext for ID denoted by CT_{ID}.*
- DDec(mpk, CT_{ID}, dd_{ID}) $\to$ IT_{ID}: *The PPT delegated decryption algorithm takes as input mpk, CT_{ID}, and dd_{ID}. It returns an intermediate ciphertext IT_{ID}.*
- Dec(mpk, IT_{ID}, d_{ID}) $\to$ $m/\perp$: *The PPT decryption algorithm takes as input mpk, IT_{ID}, and d_{ID}. It returns a plaintext m if IT_{ID} is a valid intermediate ciphertext or a failure symbol $\perp$.*

The correctness of the above algorithms requires

$$\Pr[\text{Dec}(mpk, IT_{ID}, d_{ID}) = m] = 1$$

for any master key pair (mpk, msk), any identity ID, any private key d_{ID} generated from key generation algorithm on input (msk, ID), any delegated private key dd_{ID} generated from delegated algorithm on input (mpk, ID, d_{ID}), any message m, any ciphertext CT_{ID} generated from encryption algorithm on input (mpk, ID, m), and any intermediate ciphertext IT_{ID} generated from delegated decryption algorithm on input (mpk, CT_{ID}, dd_{ID}).

Proof of Concept. Server-aided identity-based encryption splits decryption into two phases. In the first phase, a delegated private key dd_{ID} decrypts the ciphertext CT_{ID} to produce an intermediate ciphertext IT_{ID}. In the second phase, the private key d_{ID} decrypts IT_{ID} to obtain the plaintext. If the decryption cost in the second phase is significantly reduced while IT_{ID} preserves the confidentiality of the plaintext, this primitive effectively meets the stated requirement.

This completes the syntax for server-aided identity-based encryption (see [38]). Compared to identity-based encryption (IBE), this syntax definition does not explicitly demonstrate its benefits, as the efficiency of the decryption algorithm remains uncertain until a specific scheme is implemented.

6.5.10 Threshold Identity-Based Encryption

Scenario. Identity-based encryption (IBE) enables a sender to encrypt sensitive messages using an identity (ID) as the public key. A user possessing the private key d_{ID} can decrypt the ciphertext to recover the plaintext.

Concern. In IBE, the private key d_{ID} is held by a single user. If ID represents a group, granting decryption capability to a single user poses a significant risk, as they might misuse this power without detection.

Wish. It would be advantageous to have an encryption scheme that allows a private key for an identity to be shared among a set of users. Decryption should only be possible when a threshold number of these users collaborate to decrypt a ciphertext, thereby preventing misuse.

Definition 6.5.10 (Threshold Identity-Based Encryption). *A threshold identity-based encryption consists of the following five probabilistic polynomial-time (PPT) algorithms fulfilling correctness.*

- Setup$(1^\kappa, N) \to (mpk, msk)$: *The PPT setup algorithm takes as input a security parameter κ and a parameter N presenting the maximum number of users having the shared private key of one identity. It returns a key pair denoted by (mpk, msk), where mpk denotes a master public key and msk denotes a master secret key.*
- KeyGen$(msk, ID, n, t) \to (d_{ID}^1, d_{ID}^2, \cdots, d_{ID}^n)$: *The PPT key generation algorithm takes as input msk, an identity ID, a number of shares n, and a threshold number t. It returns n shares of private keys of ID denoted by $(d_{ID}^1, d_{ID}^2, \cdots, d_{ID}^n)$.*
- Enc$(mpk, ID, m) \to CT_{ID}$: *The PPT encryption algorithm takes as input mpk, ID, and a message m. It returns a ciphertext for ID denoted by CT_{ID}.*
- SDec$(mpk, CT_{ID}, d_{ID}^i) \to S_m^i / \bot$: *The PPT shared decryption algorithm takes as input mpk, CT_{ID}, and a shared private key d_{ID}^i. It returns a shared plaintext S_m^i if CT_{ID} is a valid ciphertext or a failure symbol $\bot$.*
- Combine$(mpk, \{S_m^i\}_{i \in T}) \to m / \bot$: *The PPT combination algorithm takes as input mpk and a set of shared plaintexts $\{S_m^i\}_{i \in T}$ where T is a subset of $\{1, 2, \cdots, n\}$. It returns a plaintext m if S_m^i is a valid shared plaintext and $|T| = t$, or a failure symbol $\bot$.*

The correctness of the above algorithms requires

$$\Pr\left[\begin{array}{l}|T| = t \\ S_m^i \leftarrow \mathsf{SDec}(mpk, CT_{ID}, d_{ID}^i)\end{array} : \mathsf{Combine}(mpk, \{S_m^i\}_{i \in T}) = m\right] = 1$$

for any master key pair (mpk, msk), any identity ID, any parameters (n, t), any private key shares $(d_{ID}^1, d_{ID}^2, \cdots, d_{ID}^n)$ generated from key generation al-

gorithm on input (msk, ID, n, t), any message m, any ciphertext CT_{ID} generated from encryption algorithm on input (mpk, ID, m), any index $1 \leq i \leq n$, and any shared plaintext S_m^i generated from shared decryption algorithm on input (mpk, CT_{ID}, d_{ID}^i).

Proof of Concept. Threshold identity-based encryption consists of two steps for decrypting a ciphertext. First, a share of the private key is used to decrypt the ciphertext, yielding a partial plaintext. Next, the partial plaintexts are combined to reconstruct the original plaintext. As long as successful combination requires a threshold number of partial plaintexts generated by distinct key shares, this primitive effectively meets the stated requirement.

This completes the syntax for threshold identity-based encryption (see [7]). The setup algorithm is not perfect due to the inclusion of an extra parameter N. This syntax defines a simplified decryption process in which users do not need to interact when computing shared plaintexts. A simpler syntax for threshold identity-based encryption can define a decryption algorithm that, given at least t shared private keys and the ciphertext, outputs the plaintext. However, this definition is less practical because it remains unclear who should securely execute the decryption algorithm.

6.5.11 Key-Aggregate Identity-Based Encryption

Scenario. Identity-based encryption (IBE) enables a sender to encrypt sensitive messages using an identity (ID) as the public key. A user possessing the private key d_{ID} can decrypt the ciphertext to recover the plaintext.

Concern. In applications where a MAC address is used as the identity for encryption, a user managing multiple devices faces key management challenges. The user must handle numerous private keys for different identities, increasing the complexity of secure storage and key management.

Wish. It would be beneficial to have an encryption scheme that aggregates multiple private keys for different identities into a single private key. The aggregated private key should retain the ability to decrypt ciphertexts as effectively as the individual private keys before aggregation.

Definition 6.5.11 (Key-Aggregate Identity-Based Encryption).
A key aggregate identity-based encryption consists of the following six probabilistic polynomial-time (PPT) algorithms fulfilling correctness.

- Setup($1^\kappa, n$) $\to$ (mpk, msk): *The PPT setup algorithm takes as input a security parameter κ and a parameter n presenting the maximum number of private keys in one aggregation. It returns a key pair denoted by (mpk, msk), where mpk denotes a master public key and msk denotes a master secret key.*

- KeyGen(msk, ID) → d_{ID}: *The PPT key generation algorithm takes as input msk and an identity ID. It returns a private key of ID denoted by d_{ID}.*
- Enc(mpk, ID, m) → CT_{ID}: *The PPT encryption algorithm takes as input mpk, ID, and a message m. It returns a ciphertext for ID denoted by CT_{ID}.*
- Dec(mpk, CT_{ID}, d_{ID}) → $m/\bot$: *The PPT decryption algorithm takes as input mpk, CT_{ID}, and d_{ID}. It returns a plaintext m if CT_{ID} is a valid ciphertext or a failure symbol $\bot$.*
- AggKeyGen($ID_1, d_{ID_1}, ID_2, d_{ID_2}, \cdots, ID_t, d_{ID_t}$) → $d_{\mathbf{ID}}$: *The PPT key aggregation algorithm takes as input a set of identities and their private keys denoted by $(ID_1, d_{ID_1}, ID_2, d_{ID_2}, \cdots, ID_t, d_{ID_t})$ where $2 \leq t \leq n$. It returns an aggregated private key denoted by $d_{\mathbf{ID}}$ for $\mathbf{ID} = \{ID_1, ID_2, \cdots, ID_t\}$.*
- AggDec($mpk, CT_{ID}, \mathbf{ID}, d_{\mathbf{ID}}$) → $m/\bot$: *The PPT aggregate decryption algorithm takes as input mpk, CT_{ID}, $\mathbf{ID}$, and $d_{\mathbf{ID}}$. It returns a plaintext m if CT_{ID} is a valid ciphertext and $ID \in \mathbf{ID}$, or a failure symbol $\bot$.*

The correctness of the above algorithms requires

$$\Pr[\text{Dec}(mpk, CT_{ID}, d_{ID}) = m] = 1$$

$$\Pr[ID \in \mathbf{ID} : \text{AggDec}(mpk, CT_{ID}, \mathbf{ID}, d_{\mathbf{ID}}) = m] = 1$$

for any master key pair (mpk, msk), any identity ID, any private key d_{ID} generated from key generation algorithm on input (msk, ID), any message m, any identity set $\mathbf{ID}$, any ciphertext CT_{ID} generated from encryption algorithm on input (mpk, ID, m), any $2 \leq t \leq n$, and any aggregated private key $d_{\mathbf{ID}}$ generated from key aggregation algorithm on input $(ID_1, d_{ID_1}, \cdots, ID_t, d_{ID_t})$.

Proof of Concept. Key-aggregate identity-based encryption extends IBE by introducing two additional algorithms. These algorithms enable a user to aggregate multiple private keys into a single private key. The aggregated private key can decrypt ciphertexts for any ID, provided that the private key for ID was included in the aggregation. Thus, this primitive fulfills the stated requirement.

This completes the syntax for key-aggregate identity-based encryption (see [27]). On one hand, this syntax definition minimizes input requirements for the encryption algorithm, as it does not require knowledge of the identities whose private keys have been aggregated. On the other hand, the setup algorithm requires an additional parameter n, and the aggregate decryption algorithm takes an extra identity set as input. Moreover, the benefits of this syntax definition remain unclear, as the size of the aggregated private key is unknown until a specific scheme is implemented. For instance, a trivial scheme could merely concatenate all input private keys, providing no actual size reduction.

6.5.12 Re-Encryptable Identity-Based Encryption

Scenario. Identity-based encryption (IBE) enables a sender to encrypt sensitive messages using an identity (ID) as the public key. A ciphertext for ID can only be decrypted by a receiver possessing the private key d_{ID}.

Concern. Consider a scenario where Bob, the intended receiver, is on leave. In this case, all messages directed to him remain unprocessed because only Bob can decrypt ciphertexts intended for him. Although Bob could delegate this task to a third party, the only available method is to share his private key, which introduces a security risk.

Wish. It would be beneficial to have an encryption scheme that enables a ciphertext for one identity (ID) to be re-encrypted into a ciphertext for another identity (ID'). The transformed ciphertext should be decryptable with the private key associated with ID'. Importantly, the re-encryption process should not require decryption capabilities.

Definition 6.5.12 (Re-Encryptable Identity-Based Encryption).
A re-encryptable identity-based encryption consists of the following six probabilistic polynomial-time (PPT) algorithms fulfilling correctness.

- Setup(1^κ) $\to$ (mpk, msk): *The PPT setup algorithm takes as input a security parameter κ, and returns a key pair denoted by (mpk, msk), where mpk denotes a master public key and msk denotes a master secret key.*
- KeyGen(msk, ID) $\to$ d_{ID}: *The PPT key generation algorithm takes as input msk and an identity ID. It returns a private key of ID denoted by d_{ID}.*
- RKeyGen(ID, d_{ID}, ID') $\to$ $d_{ID \Rightarrow ID'}$: *The PPT re-encryption key generation algorithm takes as input ID, d_{ID}, and another identity ID'. It returns a re-encryption key denoted by $d_{ID \Rightarrow ID'}$.*
- Enc(mpk, ID, m) $\to$ CT_{ID}: *The PPT encryption algorithm takes as input mpk, ID, and a message m. It returns a ciphertext for ID denoted by CT_{ID}.*
- Re-Encrypt($mpk, CT_{ID}, d_{ID \Rightarrow ID'}$) $\to$ $CT_{ID'}$: *The PPT re-encryption algorithm takes as input mpk, CT_{ID}, and $d_{ID \Rightarrow ID'}$. It returns a ciphertext for ID' denoted by $CT_{ID'}$.*
- Dec($mpk, CT_{ID'}, d_{ID'}$) $\to$ $m/\bot$: *The PPT decryption algorithm takes as input mpk, $CT_{ID'}$, and $d_{ID'}$. It returns a plaintext m if $CT_{ID'}$ is a valid ciphertext generated using (mpk, ID', m) or transformed using ($mpk, CT_{ID}, d_{ID \Rightarrow ID'}$), or a failure symbol $\bot$.*

The correctness of the above algorithms requires

$$\Pr[\mathsf{Dec}(mpk, CT_{ID'}, d_{ID'}) = m] = 1$$

for any master key pair (mpk, msk), any identities ID, ID', any private keys $d_{ID}, d_{ID'}$ generated from key generation algorithm on input (msk, ID), (msk, ID'), any re-encryption key $d_{ID \Rightarrow ID'}$ generated from re-encryption key generation algorithm on input (ID, d_{ID}, ID'), any message m, and any ciphertext $CT_{ID'}$ generated from either encryption algorithm on input (mpk, ID', m) or re-encryption algorithm on input $(mpk, CT_{ID}, d_{ID \Rightarrow ID'})$, where CT_{ID} is any ciphertext generated from encryption algorithm on input (mpk, ID, m).

Proof of Concept. Re-encryptable identity-based encryption enables the owner of a private key d_{ID} to generate a re-encryption key $d_{ID \Rightarrow ID'}$. This re-encryption key converts ciphertexts intended for ID into ciphertexts for ID', which can subsequently be decrypted with the private key $d_{ID'}$. If the re-encryption key is restricted to re-encryption and lacks decryption capabilities, this primitive effectively meets the stated requirement.

This completes the syntax for re-encryptable identity-based encryption (see [30]). This syntax definition offers two advantages. First, the re-encryption key generation algorithm requires minimal input and does not need interaction with the user ID'. Second, ciphertexts can be decrypted using the same algorithm, regardless of whether they were encrypted directly or re-encrypted. However, some constructed schemes may require a separate decryption algorithm for transformed ciphertexts. On the other hand, this syntax does not specify who is responsible for executing the re-encryption algorithm.

6.5.13 Homomorphic Identity-Based Encryption

Scenario. Identity-based encryption (IBE) enables a sender to encrypt sensitive data using an identity (ID) as the public key. A user possessing the private key d_{ID} can decrypt the ciphertext to recover the plaintext.

Concern. Once data are encrypted and sent to Bob, IBE does not permit Bob to delegate computations on the encrypted data to a third party. The only available solution is to share the private key with this third party, allowing them to access the encrypted data and perform operations on the decrypted data. However, this approach compromises Bob's private key and exposes all encrypted data intended for him.

Wish. It would be advantageous to have an encryption scheme that enables arbitrary evaluation of encrypted messages within a set of ciphertexts for an identity (ID) into a new ciphertext for the same identity (ID), without requiring the private key d_{ID}. Decrypting this new ciphertext should return the evaluated result derived from the original encrypted messages.

6.5 From Scenario to Proof of Concept: Examples

Definition 6.5.13 (Homomorphic Identity-Based Encryption).
A homomorphic identity-based encryption consists of the following five probabilistic polynomial-time (PPT) algorithms fulfilling correctness.

- **Setup**$(1^\kappa) \to (mpk, msk)$: *The PPT setup algorithm takes as input a security parameter κ, and returns a key pair denoted by (mpk, msk), where mpk denotes a master public key and msk denotes a master secret key.*
- **KeyGen**$(msk, ID) \to d_{ID}$: *The PPT key generation algorithm takes as input msk and an identity ID. It returns a private key of ID denoted by d_{ID}.*
- **Enc**$(mpk, ID, m) \to CT_{ID}$: *The PPT encryption algorithm takes as input mpk, ID, and a message m. It returns a ciphertext for ID denoted by CT_{ID}.*
- **Evaluate**$(mpk, \mathcal{C}, CT_{ID}^1, CT_{ID}^2, \cdots, CT_{ID}^t) \to CT_{ID}^\mathcal{C}$: *The PPT evaluation algorithm takes as input mpk, a circuit $\mathcal{C}$ that accepts t inputs, and t number of ciphertexts for ID where CT_{ID}^i is an encryption on m_i. It returns a ciphertext after evaluation denoted by $CT_{ID}^\mathcal{C}$.*
- **Dec**$(mpk, CT_{ID}^\mathcal{C}, d_{ID}) \to \mathcal{C}(m_1, m_2, \cdots, m_t)/\bot$: *The PPT decryption algorithm takes as input mpk, $CT_{ID}^\mathcal{C}$, and d_{ID}. It returns a plaintext $\mathcal{C}(m_1, m_2, \cdots, m_t)$ if $CT_{ID}^\mathcal{C}$ is a valid ciphertext or a failure symbol $\bot$.*

The correctness of the above algorithms requires

$$\Pr[\text{Dec}(mpk, CT_{ID}^\mathcal{C}, d_{ID}) = \mathcal{C}(m_1, m_2, \cdots, m_t)] = 1$$

for any master key pair (mpk, msk), any identity ID, any $1 \leq i \leq t$, any message m_i, any ciphertext CT_{ID}^i generated from encryption algorithm on input (mpk, ID, m_i), any circuit $\mathcal{C}$, any evaluated ciphertext $CT_{ID}^\mathcal{C}$ generated from evaluation algorithm on input $(mpk, \mathcal{C}, CT_{ID}^1, CT_{ID}^2, \cdots, CT_{ID}^t)$, and any private key d_{ID} generated from key generation algorithm on input (msk, ID).

Proof of Concept. Homomorphic identity-based encryption incorporates an evaluation algorithm that processes encrypted messages $(m_1, m_2, \cdots, m_t)$, each in a separate ciphertext for the same identity ID, and generates a ciphertext for the evaluated result without requiring any private key. The resulting ciphertext remains decryptable with the private key associated with ID. Thus, this primitive fulfills the stated requirement.

This completes the syntax for homomorphic identity-based encryption (see [25]). The evaluation algorithm in this syntax definition is sufficiently powerful to handle most functions representable by circuits. This is because any function, including Boolean and computational functions, can be expressed and implemented as a digital circuit using appropriate combinations of logic gates.

6.5.14 Searchable Identity-Based Encryption

Scenario. Identity-based encryption (IBE) enables a sender to encrypt sensitive messages using an identity (ID) as the public key. No user can access the encrypted message without possessing the private key d_{ID}.

Concern. Consider a scenario in which all emails are encrypted using IBE. Clients cannot delegate the task of searching for emails containing specific content to the email server without revealing their private keys. However, sharing the private key with a third party would compromise security, as all sensitive information would be exposed to the server.

Wish. It would be advantageous to have an encryption scheme that allows an authorized third party to search for ciphertexts containing specific content without requiring access to private keys.

Definition 6.5.14 (Searchable Identity-Based Encryption).
A searchable identity based encryption consists of the following six probabilistic polynomial-time (PPT) algorithms fulfilling correctness.

- Setup(1^κ) $\to$ (mpk, msk): *The PPT setup algorithm takes as input a security parameter κ, and returns a key pair denoted by (mpk, msk), where mpk denotes a master public key and msk denotes a master secret key.*

- KeyGen(msk, ID) $\to$ d_{ID}: *The PPT key generation algorithm takes as input msk and an identity ID. It returns a private key of ID denoted by d_{ID}.*

- Enc(mpk, ID, m, w) $\to$ CT_{ID}^w: *The PPT encryption algorithm takes as input mpk, ID, a message m, and a keyword w. It returns a ciphertext for ID with w denoted by CT_{ID}^w.*

- TokenGen($mpk, ID', d_{ID'}, w'$) $\to$ $T_{ID'}^{w'}$: *The PPT token generation algorithm takes as input ID', $d_{ID'}$, and w'. It returns a search token denoted by $T_{ID'}^{w'}$.*

- Search($mpk, CT_{ID}^w, T_{ID'}^{w'}$) $\to$ $1/0$: *The PPT search algorithm takes as input mpk, C_{ID}^w, and $T_{ID'}^{w'}$. It returns 1 if $(ID, w) = (ID', w')$ or 0.*

- Dec(mpk, CT_{ID}^w, d_{ID}) $\to$ $m/\bot$: *The PPT decryption algorithm takes as input mpk, CT_{ID}^w, and d_{ID}. It returns a plaintext m if CT_{ID} is a valid ciphertext or a failure symbol $\bot$.*

The correctness of the above algorithms requires

$$\Pr[(ID, w) = (ID', w') : \mathsf{Search}(mpk, CT_{ID}^w, T_{ID'}^{w'}) = 1] = 1$$

$$\Pr[\mathsf{Dec}(mpk, CT_{ID}^w, d_{ID}) = m] = 1$$

for any master key pair (mpk, msk), any identity ID, any private key d_{ID} generated from key generation algorithm on input (msk, ID), any message m, any keyword w, any ciphertext CT_{ID}^w generated from encryption algorithm on input (mpk, ID, m, w), and any token $T_{ID'}^{w'}$ generated from token generation algorithm on input $(mpk, ID', d_{ID'}, w')$.

Proof of Concept. Searchable identity-based encryption enables a client to specify a keyword and generate a corresponding search token. The email server can then apply a search algorithm to determine whether (ID, w) in a ciphertext matches (ID', w') in the token. If they match, the server sends the corresponding ciphertext to the client. The search algorithm operates solely on the ciphertext and token, and the token cannot be generated without the private key. This allows an authorized third party to conduct searches without knowing the actual keywords. Thus, this primitive effectively meets the stated requirement.

This completes the syntax for searchable identity-based encryption (see [1]). However, this syntax definition has certain limitations, particularly regarding the search algorithm, which lacks sufficient flexibility. The sender must specify an exact keyword when encrypting a message, and the search process strictly depends on this keyword. For instance, the search keyword cannot be a substring of the encrypted message m; it must exactly match the keyword embedded in the ciphertext.

6.5.15 Testable Identity-Based Encryption

Scenario. Identity-based encryption (IBE) enables a sender to encrypt sensitive messages using an identity (ID) as the public key. No third party can access the encrypted message without possessing the private key d_{ID}.

Concern. Consider an application scenario where IBE is used to encrypt short and sensitive news messages. A receiver is likely to receive a large number of encrypted messages from the server, some of which may be identical. This results in wasted resources for the receiver, as they must download and decrypt different ciphertexts only to obtain the same plaintext message. However, providing the private key to the server, which stores all received ciphertexts for the receivers, is impractical.

Wish. It would be beneficial to have an encryption scheme that allows the server to determine whether two ciphertexts for the same identity encrypt the same message. This would enable the server to filter redundant ciphertexts for the receivers.

Definition 6.5.15 (Testable Identity-Based Encryption). *A testable identity-based encryption consists of the following five probabilistic polynomial-time (PPT) algorithms fulfilling correctness.*

- **Setup**(1^κ) → (mpk, msk): *The PPT setup algorithm takes as input a security parameter κ, and returns a key pair denoted by (mpk, msk), where mpk denotes a master public key and msk denotes a master secret key.*
- **KeyGen**(msk, ID) → d_{ID}: *The PPT key generation algorithm takes as input msk and an identity ID. It returns a private key of ID denoted by d_{ID}.*
- **Enc**(mpk, ID, m) → CT_{ID}: *The PPT encryption algorithm takes as input mpk, ID, and a message m. It returns a ciphertext for ID denoted by CT_{ID}.*
- **Test**($mpk, ID, CT_{ID}^1, CT_{ID}^2$) → $1/0$: *The PPT testing algorithm takes as input mpk, ID, and two ciphertexts CT_{ID}^1, CT_{ID}^2. It returns 1 if the two input ciphertexts have identical plaintext for ID or 0.*
- **Dec**(mpk, CT_{ID}, d_{ID}) → $m/\bot$: *The PPT decryption algorithm takes as input mpk, CT_{ID}, and d_{ID}. It returns a plaintext m if CT_{ID} is a valid ciphertext or a failure symbol $\bot$.*

The correctness of the above algorithms requires

$$\Pr[m_1 = m_2 : \mathsf{Test}(mpk, ID, CT_{ID}^1, CT_{ID}^2) = 1] = 1$$

$$\Pr[\mathsf{Dec}(mpk, CT_{ID}, d_{ID}) = m] = 1$$

for any master key pair (mpk, msk), any identity ID, any private key d_{ID} generated from key generation algorithm on input (msk, ID), any messages m, m_1, m_2, and any ciphertexts $CT_{ID}, CT_{ID}^1, CT_{ID}^2$ generated from encryption algorithms on input (mpk, ID, m), (mpk, ID, m_1) and (mpk, ID, m_2) respectively.

Proof of Concept. Testable identity-based encryption enables a third party (server) to execute a testing algorithm to determine whether two ciphertexts for the same receiver encrypt the same plaintext. This testing algorithm operates without requiring access to a private key. As a result, receivers can securely delegate the task of comparing and filtering redundant ciphertexts to a third party. Thus, this primitive effectively meets the stated requirement.

This completes the syntax for testable identity-based encryption (see [39]). The syntax defines that the testing algorithm applies only to ciphertexts associated with the same identity. Although it could be extended to test ciphertexts associated with different identities that encrypt the same message, this enhancement is unnecessary for the given application scenario.

6.5.16 Membership Identity-Based Encryption

Scenario. Identity-based encryption (IBE) enables a sender to encrypt sensitive messages using an identity (ID) as the public key. Given a ciphertext for ID, no user can determine its encrypted content without possessing the private key d_{ID}.

Concern. Suppose Bob needs to prove to a third party that the encrypted message in a received ciphertext belongs to a predefined set of authorized messages. Bob would typically need to reveal his private key to the third party for verification. However, this compromises Bob's key privacy.

Wish. It would be advantageous to have an encryption scheme that allows Bob to prove to a third party that the encrypted message belongs to a predefined public message set without revealing its actual content. The verification process should not require a private key as input.

Definition 6.5.16 (Membership Identity-Based Encryption). *A membership identity-based encryption consists of the following six probabilistic polynomial-time (PPT) algorithms fulfilling correctness.*

- Setup(1^κ) $\to$ (mpk, msk): *The PPT setup algorithm takes as input a security parameter κ, and returns a key pair denoted by (mpk, msk), where mpk denotes a master public key and msk denotes a master secret key.*
- KeyGen(msk, ID) $\to d_{ID}$: *The PPT key generation algorithm takes as input msk and an identity ID. It returns a private key of ID denoted by d_{ID}.*
- Enc(mpk, ID, m) $\to CT_{ID}$: *The PPT encryption algorithm takes as input mpk, ID, and a message m. It returns a ciphertext for ID denoted by CT_{ID}.*
- Dec(mpk, CT_{ID}, d_{ID}) $\to m/\bot$: *The PPT decryption algorithm takes as input mpk, CT_{ID}, and d_{ID}. It returns a plaintext m if CT_{ID} is a valid ciphertext or a failure symbol $\bot$.*
- Prove($mpk, CT_{ID}, ID, m, d_{ID}, \mathbf{M}$) $\to \Sigma$: *The PPT proof algorithm takes as input mpk, CT_{ID}, ID, m, d_{ID}, and a set of message $\mathbf{M}$ satisfying $m \in \mathbf{M}$. It returns a proof Σ for proving membership $m \in \mathbf{M}$.*
- Verify($mpk, CT_{ID}, ID, \Sigma, \mathbf{M}$) $\to 1/0$: *The PPT verification algorithm takes as input mpk, CT_{ID}, ID, Σ, and $\mathbf{M}$. It returns 1 if CT_{ID} is a valid ciphertext encrypting a message from $\mathbf{M}$ or 0 otherwise.*

The correctness of the above algorithms requires

$$\Pr[\mathsf{Dec}(mpk, CT_{ID}, d_{ID}) = m] = 1$$

$$\Pr\left[\begin{array}{l}\mathsf{Dec}(mpk, CT_{ID}, d_{ID}) = m \\ m \in \mathbf{M}\end{array} : \mathsf{Verify}(mpk, CT_{ID}, ID, \Sigma, \mathbf{M}) = 1\right] = 1$$

for any master key pair (mpk, msk), any identity ID, any private key d_{ID} generated from key generation algorithm on input (msk, ID), any message m, any message set $\mathbf{M}$, any ciphertext CT_{ID} generated from encryption algorithm on input (mpk, ID, m), and any proof Σ generated from proof algorithm on input $(mpk, CT_{ID}, ID, m, d_{ID}, \mathbf{M})$.

Proof of Concept. Membership identity-based encryption incorporates two new algorithms: *Prove* and *Verify*. The proof algorithm allows the receiver to prove that an encrypted message belongs to a predefined set, while the verification algorithm enables verifiers to check the proof using the ciphertext and a predefined message set, without requiring access to the private key. Thus, this primitive effectively meets the stated requirement.

This completes the syntax for membership identity-based encryption (Note: this primitive does not appear in the existing literature but only a similar primitive). The syntax is well-defined; however, it remains unclear who is responsible for defining $\mathbf{M}$ and how this set should be established in real-world applications.

6.5.17 Escrow-Free Identity-Based Encryption

Scenario. Public-key encryption (PKE) enables a sender to securely transmit a sensitive message to a receiver using the receiver's public key, which corresponds to a secret key generated by the receiver. Identity-based encryption (IBE), by contrast, enables a sender to securely transmit sensitive messages to a receiver using the receiver's identity (ID) as the public key, with the private key generated by a trusted Private-Key Generator (PKG).

Concern. In PKE, each public key is a random string, and its owner must obtain a certificate to prove ownership of pk. Otherwise, senders would not know which public key to use for encryption. In IBE, certificates are unnecessary since public keys correspond directly to the receivers' identities. However, a major drawback of IBE is that a curious PKG can compute all private keys and decrypt ciphertexts, exposing sensitive messages.

Wish. It would be ideal to have an encryption scheme that eliminates the need for certificates, as in IBE, while also preventing the key escrow problem inherent in IBE.

Definition 6.5.17 (Escrow-Free Identity-Based Encryption). *An escrow-free identity-based encryption consists of the following five probabilistic polynomial-time (PPT) algorithms fulfilling correctness.*

- Setup(1^κ) $\to$ (mpk, msk): *The PPT setup algorithm takes as input a security parameter κ, and returns a key pair denoted by (mpk, msk), where mpk denotes a master public key and msk denotes a master secret key.*

- **PKeyGen**$(msk, ID) \to d_{ID}$: *The PPT key generation algorithm takes as input msk and an identity ID. It returns a private key of ID denoted by d_{ID}.*
- **UKeyGen**$(mpk) \to (pk, sk)$: *The PPT user key generation algorithm takes as input mpk. It returns a key pair denoted by (pk, sk), where pk denotes a public key and sk denotes a secret key.*
- **Enc**$(mpk, ID, pk, m) \to CT_{ID,pk}$: *The PPT encryption algorithm takes as input mpk, ID, pk, and a message m. It returns a ciphertext for (ID, pk) denoted by $CT_{ID,pk}$.*
- **Dec**$(mpk, CT_{ID,pk}, d_{ID}, sk) \to m/\bot$: *The PPT decryption algorithm takes as input mpk, $CT_{ID,pk}$, d_{ID}, and sk. It returns a plaintext m if $CT_{ID,pk}$ is a valid ciphertext or a failure symbol $\bot$.*

The correctness of the above algorithms requires

$$\Pr[\mathsf{Dec}(mpk, CT_{ID,pk}, d_{ID}, sk) = m] = 1$$

for any master key pair (mpk, msk), any identity ID, any message m, any key pair (pk, sk) generated from user key generation algorithm on input mpk, any private key d_{ID} generated from key generation algorithm on input (msk, ID), and any ciphertext $CT_{ID,pk}$ generated from encryption algorithm on input (mpk, ID, pk, m).

Proof of Concept. Escrow-free identity-based encryption introduces a dual-public-key mechanism. One public key is derived from the identity in IBE, while the other corresponds to a conventional PKE public key. Crucially, decryption requires both the private key associated with ID and the secret key corresponding to pk. On one hand, no certificate is required for pk because decrypting $CT_{ID,pk}$ is only possible for the user associated with ID using d_{ID} or the PKG. On the other hand, unless the curious PKG replaces pk with pk^* (a key it generates), the ciphertext remains indecipherable to the PKG. Thus, only a user possessing both d_{ID} and sk can decrypt the ciphertext.

This completes the syntax for escrow-free identity-based encryption (see [3]). This syntax definition is less flexible than IBE, as encryption additionally requires a public key. If an incorrect public key is provided, decryption becomes impossible.

6.5.18 Decentralized Identity-Based Encryption

Scenario. Identity-based encryption (IBE) enables a sender to transmit a sensitive message to a receiver using the receiver's identity (ID) as the public key. The sender obtains the private key for ID from a trusted Private-Key Generator (PKG), which has the capability to compute and access all users' private keys.

Concern. In IBE, the trusted Private-Key Generator (PKG) serves as the sole entity responsible for issuing private keys to all users, resulting in a centralized point of trust and potential vulnerability. Such centralization poses challenges, as it forces users to depend on a single PKG for security, which may not always be desirable or practical.

Wish. It would be beneficial to have an encryption scheme that allows anyone to act as a PKG and issue private keys to users. When sending a message to an identity (ID), the sender can select which PKGs to involve, and decryption should rely on private keys issued by these PKGs.

Definition 6.5.18 (Decentralized Identity-Based Encryption). *A decentralized identity-based encryption consists of the following five probabilistic polynomial-time (PPT) algorithms fulfilling correctness.*

- Setup(1^κ) $\to$ $Params$: *The PPT setup algorithm takes as input a security parameter κ, and returns public parameters denoted by $Params$.*
- MKeyGen($Params$) $\to$ (mpk_i, msk_i): *The PPT master key generation algorithm takes as input $Params$, and returns a key pair denoted by (mpk_i, msk_i), where mpk_i denotes a master public key and msk_i denotes a master secret key.*
- IDKeyGen(msk_i, ID) $\to$ $d_{ID}^{msk_i}$: *The PPT identity key generation algorithm takes as input msk_i and an identity ID. It returns a private key of ID denoted by $d_{ID}^{msk_i}$.*
- Enc($\{mpk_i\}_{i \in S}, t, ID, m$) $\to$ $CT_{ID}^{S,t}$: *The PPT encryption algorithm takes as input a set of master public keys $\{mpk_i\}_{i \in S}$, a threshold number t satisfying $(1 \leq t \leq |S|)$, ID, and a message m. It returns a ciphertext for ID denoted by $CT_{ID}^{S,t}$.*
- Dec($\{mpk_i\}_{i \in S}, CT_{ID}^{S,t}, \{d_{ID}^{msk_i}\}_{i \in T}$) $\to$ $m/\bot$: *The PPT decryption algorithm takes as input $\{mpk_i\}_{i \in S}$, $CT_{ID}^{S,t}$, and a set of private keys $\{d_{ID}^{msk_i}\}_{i \in T}$. It returns a plaintext m if $CT_{ID}^{S,t}$ is a valid ciphertext and $|T| = t$, or a failure symbol $\bot$.*

The correctness of the above algorithms requires

$$\Pr\left[T \subseteq S, |T| = t : \mathsf{Dec}(\{mpk_i\}_{i \in S}, CT_{ID}^{S,t}, \{d_{ID}^{msk_i}\}_{i \in T}) = m\right] = 1$$

for any master key pair (mpk_i, msk_i) generated from master key generation algorithm, any set S, any threshold number $1 \leq t \leq |S|$, any identity ID, any set T, any message m, any ciphertext $CT_{ID}^{S,t}$ generated from encryption algorithm on input $(\{mpk_i\}_{i \in S}, t, ID, m)$, and any private key $d_{ID}^{msk_i}$ generated from identity key generation algorithm on input (msk_i, ID).

Proof of Concept. Decentralized identity-based encryption leverages public parameters to generate multiple master key pairs. Each master key pair is capable of issuing private keys, and the encryption algorithm enables encryptors to specify which PKGs to involve. As a result, decryption necessitates private keys issued by the selected PKGs. Thus, this primitive effectively meets the stated requirement.

This completes the syntax for decentralized identity-based encryption (see [35]). This syntax definition is more powerful than initially expected, as decryption requires private keys from only a threshold number of involved PKGs rather than all of them. However, the advantages of this syntax remain unclear without analyzing specific schemes, as trivial constructions do exist. For instance, a basic IBE can achieve similar functionality by splitting m into secret shares and encrypting each share separately using a standard IBE under different PKGs, thereby producing multiple ciphertexts. Thus, any non-trivial scheme proposed for this primitive must ensure that the resulting ciphertext is shorter than the combined length of multiple ciphertexts.

6.5.19 Accountable Identity-Based Encryption

Scenario. Identity-based encryption (IBE) enables a sender to encrypt sensitive messages using an identity (ID) as the public key. The private key d_{ID} used for decrypting ciphertexts is generated by a Private-Key Generator (PKG) and is thus known to the PKG.

Concern. However, if a PKG were to leak or misuse the private key d_{ID}, the user would have no means to prove the PKG's misconduct, as the private key is known to both the PKG and the user. A user could engage in the same misconduct. This would undermine trust in the system and pose a significant security risk.

Wish. It would be beneficial to have an encryption scheme that allows users to obtain their private keys from the PKG in a blind approach, such that if the PKG (or user) leaks or misuses a private key, the other party can prove their responsibility.

Definition 6.5.19 (Accountable Identity-Based Encryption). *An accountable identity-based encryption consists of the following five probabilistic polynomial-time (PPT) algorithms fulfilling correctness.*

- Setup(1^κ) → (mpk, msk): *The PPT setup algorithm takes as input a security parameter κ, and returns a key pair denoted by (mpk, msk), where mpk denotes a master public key and msk denotes a master secret key.*
- KeyGen(msk, mpk, ID) → d_{ID}: *The PPT key generation interactive algorithm takes as input msk and an identity ID by the PKG, and also takes as input mpk and ID by a user. It returns a private key of ID denoted by d_{ID} to the user.*

- Enc(mpk, ID, m) → CT_{ID}: *The PPT encryption algorithm takes as input mpk, ID, and a message m. It returns a ciphertext for ID denoted by CT_{ID}.*
- Dec(mpk, CT_{ID}, d_{ID}) → $m/\bot$: *The PPT decryption algorithm takes as input mpk, CT_{ID}, and d_{ID}. It returns a plaintext m if CT_{ID} is a valid ciphertext or a failure symbol $\bot$.*
- Account$^{\mathcal{D}_{ID}}$(mpk, ID, d_{ID}) → $1/0$: *The PPT accounting algorithm takes as input mpk, ID, d_{ID}, and a decryption device $\mathcal{D}_{ID}$ that can decrypt ciphertexts for ID. It returns 1 if it is created using d_{ID} or 0 otherwise.*

The correctness of the above algorithms requires

$$\Pr[\text{Dec}(mpk, CT_{ID}, d_{ID}) = m] = 1$$

$$\Pr[d_{ID} \notin \mathcal{D}_{ID} : \text{Account}^{\mathcal{D}_{ID}}(mpk, ID, d_{ID}) = 0] = 1$$

$$\Pr[d_{ID} \in \mathcal{D}_{ID} : \text{Account}^{\mathcal{D}_{ID}}(mpk, ID, d_{ID}) = 1] = 1$$

for any master key pair (mpk, msk), any identity ID, any message m, any private key d_{ID} generated from key generation interactive algorithm on input (msk, mpk, ID), any ciphertext CT_{ID} generated from encryption algorithm on input (mpk, ID, m), and any decryption device $\mathcal{D}_{ID}$ created using a private key of ID that can always decrypt valid ciphertexts for ID.

Proof of Concept. Accountable identity-based encryption enables private key generation in a blind manner, ensuring that the PKG remains unaware of the specific private key d_{ID} received by the user. If the PKG constructs a decryption device, it must do so without knowledge of the private key d_{ID}, instead using a different private key associated with ID. If the user constructs the decryption device, they must use the received private key d_{ID}. The accounting algorithm then outputs 1 or 0 to determine whether the receiver or the PKG should be held accountable for the decryption device. Thus, this primitive effectively meets the stated requirement.

This completes the syntax for accountable identity-based encryption (see [28]). This syntax definition incorporates a powerful accounting algorithm that does not require access to the private key within the decryption device but instead relies on its decryption results. A weaker variant of this definition compares the private key generated by the PKG with the private key received by the user. If they differ, the PKG is held accountable; otherwise, the receiver bears responsibility. This syntax definition does not specify who is responsible for executing the accounting algorithm. Ideally, a fully trusted third party should execute this role, as it will have access to the receiver's private key d_{ID}. Additionally, the key generation algorithm in this syntax is interactive, differing from previous key generation algorithms. The concept of interactive algorithms will be elaborated on in the next section.

6.5.20 Registered Identity-Based Encryption

Scenario. Identity-based encryption (IBE) enables a sender to encrypt sensitive messages using an identity (ID) as the public key. The private key d_{ID} used for decrypting ciphertexts is generated by a Private-Key Generator (PKG) and is thus known to the PKG.

Concern. The PKG generates private keys and inherently possesses the capability to decrypt any ciphertext encrypted for a user's identity. This centralization presents a significant security risk, as compromising the PKG would expose all secret communications.

Wish. It would be advantageous to have an encryption scheme in which the PKG no longer generates private keys, thereby eliminating its ability to decrypt users' ciphertexts.

Definition 6.5.20 (Registered Identity-Based Encryption). *A registered identity-based encryption consists of the following five probabilistic polynomial-time (PPT) algorithms fulfilling correctness.*

- Setup($1^\kappa, n$) $\to Params$: *The PPT setup algorithm takes as input a security parameter κ and a parameter n presenting the maximum number of users in IBE. It returns a public parameter $Params$ (including an initial master public key mpk_0) to be used by other algorithms*

- KeyGen($Params$) $\to (pk, sk)$: *The PPT key generation algorithm takes as input $Params$ and returns a key pair denoted by (pk, sk), where pk denotes a public key and sk denotes a secret key.*

- Register($Params, mpk_i, ID, pk$) $\to mpk_{i+1}$: *The PPT key registration algorithm takes as input $Params$, a master public key mpk_i after i-th time update, ID, and pk. It returns an updated master public key mpk_{i+1}.*

- Enc($Params, mpk_j, ID, m$) $\to CT_{ID}^{mpk_j}$: *The PPT encryption algorithm takes as input $Params$, mpk_j, ID, and a message m. It returns a ciphertext for ID denoted by $CT_{ID}^{mpk_j}$.*

- Dec($Params, mpk_j, CT_{ID}^{mpk_j}, sk$) $\to m/\bot$: *The PPT decryption algorithm takes as input $Params$, mpk_j, $CT_{ID}^{mpk_j}$, and sk. It returns a plaintext m if $CT_{ID}^{mpk_j}$ is a valid ciphertext and (ID, pk) has been registered into mpk_j, or a failure symbol $\bot$.*

The correctness of the above algorithms requires

$$\Pr\left[\begin{array}{l}(ID, pk) \in mpk_i \\ i \in [1, j]\end{array} : \mathsf{Dec}(Params, mpk_j, CT_{ID}^{mpk_j}, sk) = m\right] = 1$$

for any $Params$, any key pair (pk, sk) generated from key generation algorithm on input $Params$, any integers $i < j$, any identity ID, any message m, *any update mpk_{i+1} from key registration algorithm on input $(Params, mpk_i, ID, pk)$, and any ciphertext $CT_{ID}^{mpk_j}$ generated from encryption algorithm on input $(Params, mpk_j, ID, m)$.*

Proof of Concept. Registered identity-based encryption permits the registration of any identity and public key pair (ID, pk) into the master public key mpk. The encryption process remains unchanged from standard IBE and does not require additional information. The decryption condition has changed significantly: it now requires both the secret key sk and the pair (ID, pk) to be registered in mpk. Thus, as long as the PKG manages mpk honestly, this primitive effectively meets the stated requirement.

This syntax definition appears powerful, as the decryption mechanism is fully developed and does not rely on a private key known to the PKG. However, trivial schemes for this primitive exist, where all (ID, pk) pairs are simply concatenated into mpk. In such schemes, the encryption algorithm takes (mpk, ID, m) as input, selects pk for ID from mpk, and then applies a standard public-key encryption algorithm using (pk, m) as input. This guarantees that only an entity possessing the corresponding sk can decrypt the message. The practical benefits of this syntax remain unclear until specific constructions are examined, but they likely depend on the feasibility of mpk size and encryption efficiency.

6.6 Algorithmic Functions and Explanations

Overview

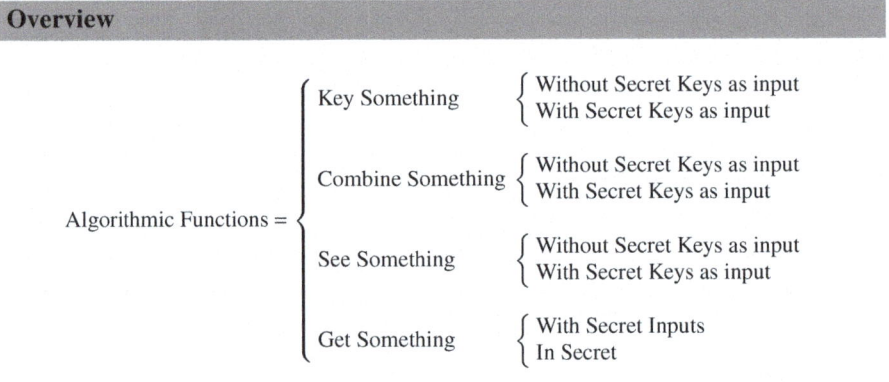

Considering all cryptographic algorithms across primitives, we classify them into four main categories based on their functions. The four categories are described as follows:

6.6 Algorithmic Functions and Explanations

- **Key Something:** The operation is to generate keys to be used.
- **Combine Something:** The operation is to combine multiple inputs together.
- **See Something:** The operation is to see something inside an input element.
- **Get Something:** The operation is to get something from the input elements.

In the first three categories, operations can be further classified as either requiring secret keys or operating without them, depending on the application scenarios and operational purposes. The last category follows a slightly different classification approach, which will be explained separately. In this section, we provide justifications and examples to facilitate a clearer understanding of these four categories for beginners.

We note that a specific type of cryptographic algorithm is excluded from the above classifications. This type uses a security parameter as input to generate public parameters for other algorithms. For example, the setup algorithm in decentralized IBE (Section 6.5.18) and registered IBE (Section 6.5.20) falls into this category. These algorithms are not included in our classifications since they do not directly execute cryptographic operations within application contexts.

6.6.1 Algorithms for Keying Something

The algorithms for keying something are responsible for producing secret objects, such as secret keys. Their inputs may or may not include secret keys, depending on their purposes. In the following, we present six examples of such algorithms.

Overview

$$\text{Key Something} = \begin{cases} \text{Without Secret Keys} \begin{cases} \text{Key Generation with Security Parameter} \\ \text{Key Generation with Public Parameters} \\ \text{Offline Encryption Algorithm} \end{cases} \\ \text{With Secret Keys} \begin{cases} \text{Key Extraction} \\ \text{Delegation} \\ \text{Aggregation} \end{cases} \end{cases}$$

The first example is a key generation algorithm that takes a security parameter as input. Given a security parameter κ, the algorithm outputs a key pair, such as (pk, sk) in public-key cryptography, or a secret key in symmetric-key cryptography. It is important to note that all key-related cryptographic primitives must include this algorithm to allow users to generate secret keys.

The second example is a key generation algorithm that takes public parameters as input. Given these parameters, the algorithm outputs such as a key pair (pk, sk) or just a secret key. Unlike the first example, this approach generates keys that share common public parameters. For instance, in decentralized IBE (Section 6.5.18), master key pairs are derived from the same public parameters $Params$, ensuring that all generated keys can be used as inputs to an encryption algorithm.

The third example is the offline encryption algorithm in online/offline IBE (Section 6.5.2). Given a master public key as input, this algorithm outputs an intermediate ciphertext IT that should be kept secret. This is because IT contains some secret information ensuring that online encryption can be executed efficiently. We note that this example is only partially true, as a trivial construction could set IT to be empty (thus containing no secret) and require the online encryption process to execute the entire encryption procedure, identical to the encryption algorithm in IBE.

The fourth example involves deriving a private key for a specific user. Given a secret key and relevant public information, this algorithm returns a private key corresponding to the input public information. For instance, in identity-based encryption (IBE) (Section 6.5.1), the key extraction algorithm derives a private key d_{ID} associated with the input identity ID.

The fifth example involves deriving a delegated private key. Given a secret key and other public information, this algorithm generates a delegation key linked to both the secret and public information. For example, in server-aided IBE (Section 6.5.9), a user can use their private key d_{ID} to generate a delegated private key dd_{ID} for partial decryption. Similarly, re-encryptable IBE (Section 6.5.12) provides a mechanism for generating re-encryption keys.

The last example involves deriving an aggregate key. Given a set of secret keys, this algorithm returns a single aggregate key that represents all input keys while preserving the functionality of each individual key. One example is the key aggregation algorithm used in key-aggregate IBE (Section 6.5.11).

6.6.2 Algorithms for Combining Something

Algorithms for combining something are designed to merge multiple inputs into one or more public objects, which can then be used by other algorithms. These combinations serve purposes such as confidentiality, integrity, or predefined operations. Depending on their purposes, these algorithms may or may not involve secret keys. In the following, we present six examples of such algorithms.

Overview

$$\text{Combine Something} = \begin{cases} \text{Without Secret Keys} \begin{cases} \text{Encryption} \\ \text{Homomorphic} \\ \text{Aggregation} \end{cases} \\ \text{With Secret Keys} \begin{cases} \text{Signing} \\ \text{Proof} \\ \text{Transformation} \end{cases} \end{cases}$$

6.6 Algorithmic Functions and Explanations

The first example is the encryption algorithm used in identity-based encryption (IBE) and its variants (Section 6.5.1). Given a master public key, an identity, and a message, the encryption algorithm combines these inputs into a ciphertext. The resulting ciphertext can later be decrypted to recover the original message.

The second example is the evaluation algorithm in homomorphic IBE (Section 6.5.13). Given a set of ciphertexts for identity ID, corresponding to messages $(m_1, m_2, \cdots, m_t)$, and a circuit $\mathcal{C}$, the evaluation algorithm combines these ciphertexts into a new ciphertext representing the result of $\mathcal{C}(m_1, m_2, \cdots, m_t)$ for identity ID. The new ciphertext can later be decrypted to obtain the evaluation result.

The third example is the registration algorithm in registered IBE (Section 6.5.20). Given a master public key and a pair (ID, pk), this algorithm combines them into an updated master public key. This process can be viewed as an aggregation that results in a shorter mpk, which is then used for encryption. Another example, outside of IBE variants, is aggregate signatures [12], where multiple signatures are combined into a single aggregate signature. Later, this aggregate signature is verified to determine the set of signed messages. Another similar example is the revocation algorithm $Revoke(ID, mpk_i, msk) \rightarrow mpk_{i+1}$ in revocable IBE (Section 6.5.7), but it needs a secret key as an input.

The fourth example is the signing algorithm in digital signatures (Section 1.1.1). Given a secret key and a message, this algorithm combines them into a signature. Later, the signature is verified using a verification algorithm to determine which message has been signed. It is worth noting that all digital signatures and their variants include this type of algorithm.

The fifth example is the proof algorithm in membership IBE (Section 6.5.16). Given $(CT_{ID}, ID, m, d_{ID}, \mathbf{M})$, the proof algorithm combines these inputs into a proof. Later, this proof is verified to check whether the plaintext inside a ciphertext is in the message set $\mathbf{M}$.

The last example is the re-encryption algorithm in re-encryptable IBE (Section 6.5.12). Given a ciphertext encrypted under ID and a re-encryption key $d_{ID \Rightarrow ID'}$, this algorithm combines them into a new ciphertext under ID'. Later, this new ciphertext is decrypted using the private key $d_{ID'}$ to recover the original plaintext.

We found that algorithms for combining inputs typically produce outputs with reserved structures and are not the final step in ensuring security. Subsequent algorithms, such as verification and decryption algorithms, are needed to interpret the results produced by these combination algorithms.

6.6.3 Algorithms for Seeing Something

Given as an input D from other algorithms and other elements, algorithms for seeing something are designed to determine what is included within D, with or without the use of secret keys. We introduce five examples of such algorithms.

Overview

$$\text{See Something} = \begin{cases} \text{Without Secret Keys} \begin{cases} \text{Verification} \\ \text{Equality Test} \\ \text{Search} \end{cases} \\ \text{With Secret Keys} \begin{cases} \text{Decryption} \\ \text{Tracing (Opening)} \end{cases} \end{cases}$$

The first example is the verification algorithm in digital signatures (Section 1.1.1). Given a public key pk, a message m, and a signature σ_m, this algorithm sees whether the signature σ_m was indeed combined using the secret key sk corresponding to pk and the message m. The algorithm returns true or false to indicate the result of this verification.

The second example is the testing algorithm in testable IBE (Section 6.5.15). Given two ciphertexts, this algorithm sees whether the encrypted messages within two ciphertexts for the same identity are identical or not, without requiring the private key d_{ID}. The algorithm returns true or false to indicate whether the messages are identical.

The third example is the search algorithm in searchable IBE (Section 6.5.14). Given a ciphertext for (ID, w) and a (secret) token for (ID', w'), this algorithm sees whether the identity and keyword within the ciphertext and the token match, without needing to know the keyword or private key. That is, running this seeing algorithm does not require private keys as input.

The fourth example is the decryption algorithm in identity-based encryption (Section 6.5.1). Given a ciphertext CT for ID and a private key d_{ID}, this algorithm can see the encrypted message within CT. All variants of IBE include this type of algorithm.

The last example is the tracing algorithm in traitor-tracing IBE (Section 6.5.6). Given a pirate decryption device $\mathcal{D}_{ID}$ for ID and the master secret key, this algorithm sees at least one traitor's identity if the pirate device $\mathcal{D}_{ID}$ is created with traitors' private keys. Similar algorithms outside IBE variants include the opening algorithm in group signatures [8]. On input a group signature and a secret key from group manager, the opening algorithm will return the identity of group user who generated the input group signature.

! Attention

Generally speaking, a cryptographic primitive is ended with a seeing algorithm in definition. All seeing algorithms are forking algorithms, and thus each seeing algorithm should have a correctness in syntax definition.

6.6.4 Algorithms for Getting Something

In the previous three categories of algorithms, all operations are conducted independently by an entity or user without interactions. In contrast, the algorithms for getting something are interactive and require more than one party (an entity or a user) to work together. In an interactive algorithm, each party could have individual secrets as input, and interactions build upon previous ones to achieve a common goal. These algorithms complete and return outputs only after the interaction process is finished. We introduce four examples of this type of algorithms.

Overview

$$\text{Get Something} = \begin{cases} \text{With Secret Inputs} \begin{cases} \text{Multi-Party Computations} \\ \text{Key Exchange} \end{cases} \\ \text{In Secret} \begin{cases} \text{Obvious Transfer} \\ \text{Key Generation in Accountable IBE} \end{cases} \end{cases}$$

The first example is multi-party computations (MPC) [36]. For instance, consider two-party computations (2PC). In 2PC, given a secret input x_1 from the first party and a secret input x_2 from the second party, along with some public parameters and two predefined functions f_1 and f_2, the interactive algorithm allows the first party to get $f_1(x_1, x_2)$ and the second party to get $f_2(x_1, x_2)$ after the interaction is complete. MPC can be viewed as a generalized form of interactive algorithms where each party aims to obtain specific outputs based on their individual inputs.

The second example is key exchange [34]. In this scenario, let (pk_1, sk_1) and (pk_2, sk_2) represent the key pairs generated by the first and second parties, respectively. On input (sk_1, pk_2) from the first party and (pk_1, sk_2) from the second party, the interactive algorithm enables both parties to derive a shared secret value. Specifically, the first party computes $f_1(sk_1, pk_2)$, and the second party computes $f_2(pk_1, sk_2)$, with the property that both computations yield the same secret value, namely $K = f_1(sk_1, pk_2) = f_2(pk_1, sk_2)$.

The third example is oblivious transfer [5]. Consider the 1-out-of-n oblivious transfer as an example. In this primitive, the first party holds $x_1 = (m_1, m_2, \cdots, m_n)$, a set of n different messages. The second party provides a secret index $x_2 = i \in [1, n]$ as the input. After the interactive algorithm completes, the first party learns nothing, i.e., $f_1(x_1, x_2) = \varnothing$, while the second party obtains only the selected message m_i, i.e., $f_2(x_1, x_2) = m_i$.

The last example is the key generation algorithm in accountable IBE (Section 6.5.19). In this primitive, the PKG inputs (msk, ID) and the user inputs (mpk, ID). After interaction between PKG and user, the PKG receives no information, i.e., $f_1(msk, ID, mpk, ID) = \varnothing$, while the user receives the private key d_{ID}, i.e., $f_2(msk, ID, mpk, ID) = d_{ID}$.

6.7 How to Define Syntax for a New Cryptographic Primitive

In Section 6.4.1, we have introduced how to parse or understand a new cryptographic primitive with 5-step explanations. However, this introduction is not enough for beginners who are trying to define syntax for newly proposed cryptographic primitives, especially when it consists of many algorithms. In this section, we introduce some tricks and processes for defining a correct syntax, which will be useful for beginners in validating their proposed syntax definitions.

The syntax definition for a new cryptographic primitive is a spiral process. Initially, a very basic definition is proposed. Then, it is fixed, modified, or improved until the syntax definition is correct and secure. The definition process is divided into three phases: the Prototype Phase, the Polishing Phase, and the Validating Phase.

Prototype Phase. In this phase, we should focus on proposing a basic syntax definition that meets the essential requirements derived from the following three questions.

1. **How many entities are involved in this new cryptographic primitive?**
2. **How to define** *an entity's operation* **into an algorithm?**
3. **Which elements does each entity know?**

The syntax definition starts with identifying the total number of entities in the new cryptographic primitive. Besides basic entities, the new primitive could require honest issuers like a trusted third party or a semi-honest third party. Each entity participates in at least one algorithm and must be capable of performing specific actions through it. An entity's capabilities within an algorithm are defined by its inputs, outputs, and associated elements.

Notably, the most common "do" operations in cryptography include encryption, decryption, signing, verification, proving, commitment, opening, extraction, tracing, revocation, distribution, searching, and other property-preserving computations. Each operation follows a specific pattern for its inputs and outputs, which can be derived from similar operations in existing primitives. The first two questions help clarify the number of involved algorithms in a syntax definition.

Lastly, summarizing the elements known to each entity is crucial for ensuring a smooth transition to the next two phases. If a non-interactive algorithm is executed by an entity, that entity must know all its input and output elements. Thus, a single key generation algorithm cannot be defined for all entities, such as the PKG, cloud server, and cloud users, as it would be unclear who executes the algorithm. However, a key generation algorithm *KeyGen*$(1^\kappa) \to (pk, sk)$ can be defined for all entities to run independently, allowing each to generate its own key pair.

Polishing Phase. In this phase, we should concentrate on checking completeness and soundness of syntax definition as follows.

4. **Check the completeness and soundness of each element.**
5. **Check the soundness of each algorithm.**
6. **Check the correctness in definition.**

6.7 How to Define Syntax for a New Cryptographic Primitive

The syntax definition after the first phase is usually incomplete or unsound and should be refined in this phase. Each element should be defined as a variable within a well-defined space rather than a fixed value. Furthermore, any element produced as the output of an algorithm must be utilized by other algorithms; otherwise, it is redundant.

Next, each algorithm's name should be checked to ensure clarity and avoid misleading interpretations. It is also important to verify whether any required input elements are missing. For example, the provided inputs might be insufficient in the decryption algorithm of hierarchical IBE (Section 6.5.8) using $d_{\mathbf{ID}_{[j]}}$ if the ciphertext $CT_{\mathbf{ID}_{[i]}}$ does not contain the encryption identity $\mathbf{ID}_{[i]}$.

Lastly, for any forking algorithms, there must be precise conditions defining the possible outputs. Each forking algorithm should include a correctness description at the end of the syntax definition, though multiple descriptions can be merged into a single correctness description.

Validating Phase. In this phase, we concentrate on security part as follows:

7. **Can any entity or adversary abuse the application of this cryptographic primitive by running its algorithms?**

The last and most complex phase is validating that no entity or adversary can abuse the primitive to compromise its security applications. In particular, we should double-check whether an entity can use the elements they know and provided cryptographic algorithms to exploit applications. If insecurity arises, we may need to return to the prototype phase to revise it until no security flaw remains. It is important to note that security requirements only address concerns outlined in the five-step explanation and are usually not comprehensive. For instance, when defining the syntax for identity-based encryption (IBE), we do not address concerns such as *"what if the PKG is curious and attempts to learn plaintexts by generating decryption keys"*, since this is not considered as a security concern.

In summary, defining syntax is a complex process that requires multiple rounds of refinement and revision. Here, we focus on defining a correct syntax rather than a robust one. Methods for further improving syntax definitions to robust definitions have already been discussed in Section 6.4.2.

> ❗ **Attention**
>
> We classify cryptographic algorithms as internal algorithms and attacking algorithms as external algorithms. In syntax definition, what (elements) each entity or adversary knows must be carefully designed and specified. Otherwise, an entity or adversary may exploit internal algorithms to misuse cryptographic primitives in applications, rendering any construction insecure. On the other hand, the security definition introduced in the next chapter ensures that no entity or adversary can exploit a cryptographic primitive's application using any algorithm, whether internal or external. We hope this clarification helps beginners understand the relationship between the validation phase and the security definition.

6.8 Scheme or Protocol?

Earlier, we discussed cryptographic schemes and protocols as implementations of cryptographic primitives, without distinguishing between them. In this section, we clarify their distinctions. Although the terms "scheme" and "protocol" are often used interchangeably, using precise terminology highlights differences in syntax and security definitions, since their definitional approaches differ.

6.8.1 Differences

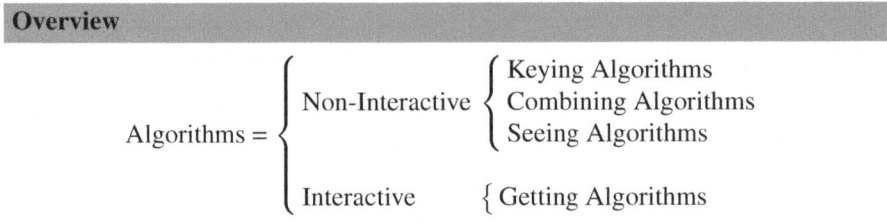

We categorized cryptographic algorithms into four categories: keying algorithms, combining algorithms, seeing algorithms, and getting algorithms. While the first three types operate in a non-interactive manner, the last type involves interaction.

The difference between a scheme and a protocol mainly lies in whether getting algorithms play a central role in the syntax definition. In this book, we classify an implementation of a cryptographic primitive as:

- **Scheme** if the primitive includes at least one seeing (forking) algorithm, regardless of whether it also has getting algorithms, or
- **Protocol** if the primitive does not include any seeing algorithms, but has getting algorithms along with keying algorithms if needed.

However, the above classification may require revision. A cryptographic primitive A might evolve into or be studied as a variant primitive B. If the construction for A is referred to as a scheme (protocol), then the construction for primitive B is also referred to as a scheme (protocol), even if the syntax definition for B does not strictly follow the above classification. We will provide some examples in Section 6.8.3.

A syntax definition is proposed for a cryptographic primitive. In cryptology, a syntax definition can also describe the algorithms in schemes or protocols proposed for a cryptographic primitive. These interpretations are considered equivalent but represent different ways of presenting a syntax definition. For instance, when defining the syntax for IBE, we may write "*An identity-based encryption consists of the following four PPT algorithms*" (syntax definition for a primitive) or "*An identity-based encryption scheme consists of the following four PPT algorithms*" (syntax definition for a scheme).

6.8 Scheme or Protocol?

> **! Attention**
>
> For two different constructions of the same non-interactive algorithm, the efficiency comparison primarily focuses on computation efficiency of operations and size efficiency of outputs. However, measuring the efficiency of interactive algorithms is significantly more complex. For interactive algorithms, two additional characteristics, namely communication efficiency, also play a crucial role in efficiency comparison. The first characteristic concerns the number of rounds or moves among parties before terminating and producing outputs. The second characteristic concerns the total communication cost, which includes intermediate data exchanged among parties before the final outputs are generated. Beginners should pay attention to this difference as it is related to security definition.

6.8.2 Syntax Definitions for Protocols

Defining a protocol-type cryptographic primitive is more flexible, particularly when it includes only a single interactive algorithm, such as a getting algorithm. The syntax definitions for protocols involve two key modifications:

- First, the term "probabilistic polynomial-time algorithm" is no longer needed and it has been replaced with the relaxed term "protocol", while maintaining explicit input and output specifications for each participating party.
- Second, a separate correctness description may not be required because the outputs of the protocol have been clearly defined, or it may be inherently included in the protocol's security definition (see [17]).

For example, the protocols of two-party computation and oblivious transfer are defined as follows:

> **Definition 6.8.1** (Two-Party Computation). *In a two-party computation protocol, party A has (x_1, f_1, f_2) and party B has (x_2, f_1, f_2), where f_1, f_2 are two functions and x_1, x_2 are part of function inputs. At the end of the protocol, party A outputs $f_1(x_1, x_2)$ and party B outputs $f_2(x_1, x_2)$.*

> **Definition 6.8.2** (Oblivious Transfer). *In a 1-out-of-n oblivious transfer protocol, party A has $(m_1, m_2, \cdots, m_n)$ and party B has $i \in [1, n]$, where each m is a piece of data message and i is an index of choice. At the end of the protocol, party A outputs nothing and party B outputs m_i.*

The above syntax definitions are concise, as each primitive contains only a single algorithm. When additional algorithms, such as a key generation algorithm, must be incorporated, the definition needs to be presented in a format similar to that of a scheme. We provide several examples in the next subsection.

6.8.3 Mixture of Scheme and Protocol

It is quite common for a cryptographic primitive to be composed of a combination of a getting algorithm and other types of algorithms. This complexity can make it challenging for beginners to distinguish between schemes and protocols. Here, we provide a set of mixed syntax definitions for three cryptographic primitives, presented either as schemes or protocols.

The first cryptographic primitive is blind signatures [21]. In this primitive, the signing algorithm in digital signatures is replaced by a signing protocol between signer and receiver, where the message being signed is unknown to the signer.

Definition 6.8.3 (Blind Signatures). *A blind signature scheme consists of the following three probabilistic polynomial-time (PPT) algorithms fulfilling correctness.*

- KeyGen(1^κ) $\to$ (pk, sk): *The PPT key generation algorithm takes as input a security parameter κ, and returns a key pair denoted by (pk, sk), where pk denotes a public key and sk denotes a secret key.*
- Sign(sk, pk, m) $\to \sigma_m$: *The PPT signing interactive algorithm takes as input sk from a signer and (pk, m) from a receiver. It returns a signature on m denoted by σ_m to the receiver.*
- Verify(m, σ_m, pk) $\to 1/0$: *The PPT verification algorithm takes as input (m, σ_m) and pk. It returns 1 if σ_m is a valid signature on m signed by the secret key of pk. Otherwise, it returns 0.*

The correctness of the above algorithms requires

$$\Pr[\mathsf{Verify}(pk, m, \sigma_m) = 1] = 1$$

for any key pair (pk, sk), any message m to be signed from the message space $\mathcal{M}$, and any signature σ_m generated from the signing algorithm on input sk from signer and (pk, m) from receiver.

Although the syntax definition of blind signatures includes an interactive signing algorithm, this primitive and its constructions are still referred to as schemes rather than protocols.

The second cryptographic primitive is authenticated key exchange (AKE). In this primitive, two parties establish a secure shared secret key only when both parties are authenticated. The implementation of AKE is referred to as a protocol rather than a scheme, as there is no seeing algorithm.

Definition 6.8.4 (Authenticated Key Exchange). *An authenticated key exchange protocol consists of the following three probabilistic polynomial-time (PPT) algorithms fulfilling correctness.*

6.8 Scheme or Protocol?

- Setup(1^κ) → $Params$: *The PPT setup algorithm takes as input a security parameter κ. It returns a public parameter $Params$.*
- KeyGen($Params$) → (pk, sk): *The PPT key generation algorithm takes as input $Params$ and returns a key pair denoted by (pk, sk), where pk denotes a public key and sk denotes a secret key.*
- AKE(sk_i, pk_j, sk_j, pk_i) → K: *The PPT authenticated key exchange interactive algorithm takes as input (sk_i, pk_j) from one party and (sk_j, pk_i) from another party. At the end of the protocol, both parties return a secret key K.*

The correctness of the above algorithms requires that for any key pair (pk, sk), two honest parties should return same output when running the protocol.

The third cryptographic primitive is two-move authenticated key exchange. In this primitive, an authenticated key exchange is completed between two parties in two moves. Since the number of rounds is fixed, the authenticated key exchange protocol (interactive algorithm) can be divided and predefined with three sub-algorithms. These non-interactive sub-algorithms can be seen as keying algorithms, combining algorithms, or seeing algorithms, and they are executed at each move or interaction. That is, a getting algorithm is decomposed into keying algorithms, combining algorithms, and seeing algorithms.

Definition 6.8.5 (Two-Move Authenticated Key Exchange). *A two-move authenticated key exchange protocol consists of the following three probabilistic polynomial-time (PPT) algorithms fulfilling correctness.*

- Setup(1^κ) → $Params$: *The PPT setup algorithm takes as input a security parameter κ. It returns a public parameter $Params$.*
- KeyGen($Params$) → (pk, sk): *The PPT key generation algorithm takes as input $Params$ and returns a key pair denoted by (pk, sk), where pk denotes a public key and sk denotes a secret key.*
- Init(pk_i, sk_i, pk_j) → (I, st): *The PPT initiation algorithm takes as input (pk_i, sk_i) and another public key pk_j for key exchange. It returns a message I and a state st.*
- Respond(sk_j, pk_i, I) → (R, K): *The PPT response algorithm takes as input sk_j and (pk_j, I) from another party for key exchange. It returns a response message R and a secret key K.*
- Der(sk_i, st, pk_j, R) → K: *The PPT derivation algorithm takes as input (sk_i, st) and (pk_j, R) from another party. It returns a secret key K.*

The correctness of the above algorithms requires that for any key pair (pk, sk), two honest parties should return same output when running the protocol.

The syntax described above is slightly modified from [34]. It is referred to as a protocol because it is a variant of the authenticated key exchange protocol. We note that it is quite common to define a protocol similarly to a scheme when the number of moves is fixed. Another well-known example is the Fiat-Shamir identification protocol [20], which is structured into three sub-algorithms: commitment, challenge, and response.

Additionally, understanding the syntax definition of fixed-move protocols could be challenging without further explanation, as it involves interactions among different parties and specifies what should be sent to each party. For example, in the syntax definition provided above, the symbols (I, R, st, K) represent generated data, (I, R, st) are intermediate data, and K is the final output. Only I and R will be sent to another party.

6.9 Practice Makes Perfect: Exercises

? Question 28

In public-key encryption, any user has a key pair (pk, sk) where pk is used for encryption and sk is used for decryption. This cryptographic primitive can be applied to a scenario where pk belongs to a group and each group user has a secret key to decrypt ciphertexts generated using pk. However, sharing the same secret key with all group users makes revoking users difficult. The following primitive has been defined to address this issue and also allows any user to dynamically join or leave the group as managed by a group manager.

Definition 6.9.1 (Threshold-Group Public-Key Encryption). *A threshold-group public-key encryption with dynamic revocation is composed of the following five probabilistic polynomial-time (PPT) algorithms fulfilling correctness.*

- KeyGen(1^κ) $\to$ (gpk, gsk, L_0, t): *The PPT key generation algorithm takes as input a security parameter κ. It returns a key pair denoted by (gpk, gsk), an initial revoked list L_0, and a threshold number t. Here, gpk denotes a group public key and gsk denotes a group secret key.*
- UKeyGen(ID, gsk) $\to$ sk_{ID}: *The PPT user key generation algorithm takes as input a user identity ID and gsk. It returns a secret key sk_{ID}.*
- Enc(m, gpk) $\to$ CT: *The PPT encryption algorithm takes as input a message $m \in \mathcal{M}$ and gpk. It returns a ciphertext denoted by CT.*
- Revoke(ID, gsk, L_{j-1}) $\to$ L_j: *The PPT revocation algorithm takes as input ID to be revoked, gsk, and the old revocation list denoted by L_{j-1}. It returns a new revocation list L_j included revoked identity ID.*
- Dec($CT, \{ID_1, sk_{ID_1}, ID_2, sk_{ID_2}, \cdots, ID_t, sk_{ID_t}\}, L_j$) $\to$ $m/\bot$: *The PPT decryption algorithm takes as input CT, t number of secret keys sk_{ID_i} for ID_i, and the latest revocation list L_j. It returns decryption result if any*

6.9 Practice Makes Perfect: Exercises

> ID_i has not yet been revoked in L_j or $\perp$ otherwise. Here, this algorithm will be run by each user who is involved in decryption.

Besides providing the correctness part, can you identify three main issues in the above syntax definition?

? Question 29

Read the following introductions and requirements.

- **Scenario.** In the applications of IBE, messages are encrypted using a meaningful string, namely ID, as the encryption key. Ciphertexts will be decrypted using the private key d_{ID}, which is generated by the PKG for ID.
- **Concern.** When IBE is adopted by an organization, the manager requires that all data generated by an employee (Alice) be sent to the client Bob using ID =Bob@uow.edu.au as the encryption key. However, when Alice encrypts data using this ID, she knows who the receiver is. Furthermore, the manager cannot audit the encrypted data.
- **Wish.** It would be ideal if any encryption key ID in IBE can be locked into a lock $L(ID)$ by an entity (manager). No one can retrieve ID from the lock. Ciphertexts encrypted using $L(ID)$ can still be decrypted with d_{ID} as long as the lock is also attached. Furthermore, the entity who created the lock $L(ID)$ can also decrypt the ciphertexts.

Propose a new cryptographic primitive called *Lockable Identity-Based Encryption* with syntax definition to satisfy the above requirements.

? Question 30

Read the following introductions and requirements.

- **Scenario.** In applications of IBE, any message to be sent to a person (e.g., Bob) can simply be encrypted using ID = Bob as the encryption key. Then, Bob can decrypt these ciphertexts using the private key d_{ID} generated by the PKG.
- **Concern.** One day, the encryptor Alice needs to send a particularly sensitive message to Bob and requires that this message cannot be decrypted by Bob unless he belongs to an organization "UOW". There are two straightforward solutions. In the first solution, Alice simply runs IBE using "UOW.Bob" as the encryption key. If Bob belongs to this organization, he can obtain the private key from the PKG after successfully proving his identity and affiliation with UOW. However, this solution may be inefficient in the real world. In the second solution, Alice can use HIBE and encrypt the message using the two-level identity "UOW‖Bob".

This solution is more practical than the first one because Bob only needs to obtain the private key from the "UOW" organization. However, Alice has privacy concerns about using HIBE because the manager of "UOW" knows the private key associated with "UOW∥Bob", which allows them to see the message.
- **Wish.** It would be ideal if Bob does not need to obtain any new private keys from the PKG and Alice could be assured that the message can only be decrypted by "Bob" who belongs to the organization "UOW".

Propose a new cryptographic primitive called *Relationship Identity-Based Encryption* with syntax definition to satisfy the above requirements.

? Question 31

Read the following introductions and requirements.

- **Scenario.** Registered IBE is a variant of IBE where users can register their identities and self-generated public keys with the PKG, who publishes and manages a master public key. Encryption and decryption use the same inputs as IBE. The benefit of registered IBE is that the key escrow issue is completely solved because there is no longer a master secret key, and the PKG cannot decrypt any ciphertexts for any registered identities.
- **Concern.** However, in the current registered IBE, when a new user registers, the master public key must be updated accordingly. This is becoming impractical when new users register every day, similar to the registration of new Gmail users.
- **Wish.** It would be ideal if a hierarchical approach is available in registered IBE. In particular, when ID_1 has been registered with the PKG, the owner of ID_1 can use his/her secret key to generate private keys for $ID_1\|ID_2$ for the second level of users ID_2, without registering ID_2 with the PKG again. For example, if $ID_1 =$ UOW represents an organization, it can issue private keys for its employees, such as $ID_1\|ID_2 =$ UOW∥Bob. Encryption and decryption should be similar to hierarchical IBE without the need for additional information.

Propose a new cryptographic primitive called *Registered Hierarchical Identity-Based Encryption* with syntax definition to satisfy the above requirements.

? Question 32

Read the following introductions and requirements.

- **Scenario.** Accountable IBE is a variant of IBE where users can obtain their private keys from the PKG in such a way that the PKG does not know which private key has been generated for each identity ID. If a private key for ID is leaked, a security mechanism exists to trace whether the PKG or the user is responsible for the leak.

6.9 Practice Makes Perfect: Exercises

- **Concern.** However, accountable IBE cannot prevent a curious PKG from accessing ciphertexts for any identity, as the PKG can still compute valid private keys for any identity.
- **Wish.** Ideally, accountable IBE could be enhanced so that the PKG will consider the risks before attempting decryption. This is because the owner of the private key d_{ID} can create a honeypot ciphertext for ID. If the PKG tries to decrypt it using a private key different from d_{ID} and the decryption result is revealed to the user, the user will be able to extract the PKG's master secret key.

Propose a new cryptographic primitive called *Honeypot Identity-Based Encryption* with syntax definition to satisfy the above requirements.

? Question 33

Read the following introductions and requirements.

- **Scenario.** Re-Encryptable IBE is a variant of IBE where any message that is encrypted for ID can be transformed into a ciphertext for ID' with a re-encryption key $d_{ID \Rightarrow ID'}$ generated using the private key d_{ID}.
- **Concern.** However, the re-encryption key in this primitive is too powerful. Any ciphertext for ID can be transformed into a ciphertext for ID' with $d_{ID \Rightarrow ID'}$. This could stop the owner of ID from using this mechanism because it would leak too many messages to ID'.
- **Wish.** It would be ideal if only a part of the ciphertexts can be transformed with the help of a keyword-based approach. More specifically, a ciphertext for ID is created using m and a keyword w. A re-encryption key from ID to ID' is restricted to the keyword w' only, denoted by $d_{ID|w' \Rightarrow ID'}$. That is, a ciphertext associated with (m, w) for ID can be transformed into a ciphertext for ID' using $d_{ID|w' \Rightarrow ID'}$ if and only if $w = w'$.

Propose a new cryptographic primitive called *Partially Re-Encryptable Identity-Based Encryption* with syntax definition to satisfy the above requirements.

? Question 34

Read the following introductions and requirements.

- **Scenario.** Testable IBE is a variant of IBE where messages that are encrypted for the same identity ID can be tested to determine whether they are identical based on their ciphertexts, without requiring the private key d_{ID}. This primitive could be useful in cloud-related applications where some encrypted messages are identical, allowing the cloud server to classify messages for the receiver ID, thereby enhancing data storage and access services.

- **Concern.** However, testable IBE can only determine whether messages within ciphertexts are identical. This type of classification is neither powerful nor compact enough, leading to a large number of classes, as they depend on the number of distinct messages.
- **Wish.** Ideally, the user of ID can authorize the cloud server to perform a broad classification. Specifically, the user of ID could use their private key to issue a token associated with a classification function F and generate a root ciphertext CT^* for a selected message m^*. The cloud server could then test any received ciphertext CT, which encrypts a message m, against the root ciphertext CT^* using the token. The ciphertext CT would be assigned to the same class as CT^* if $F(m^*, m) = 1$. With this primitive, all ciphertexts will be grouped into a small number of classes defined by the user of ID.

Propose a new cryptographic primitive called *Classifiable Identity-Based Encryption* with syntax definition to satisfy the above requirements.

? Question 35

Read the following introductions and requirements.

- **Scenario.** IBE is an encryption mechanism in which anyone can encrypt messages for the receiver ID. On receiving a ciphertext for ID, the receiver ID can decrypt it immediately using the private key d_{ID} generated by the PKG.
- **Concern.** Consider a scenario in which Alice and Bob both encrypt messages for the receiver Kevin. The messages m_a, m_b sent by Alice and Bob are related, and message m_b could cause trouble for the receiver Kevin if he has not yet received the message m_a.
- **Wish.** It would be ideal if senders could specify that ciphertexts be decrypted sequentially in a specific order. Let CT_a be the ciphertext generated by Alice. Bob can create CT_b using CT_a as an additional input such that CT_b cannot be decrypted before the receiver first sees m_a.

Propose a new cryptographic primitive called *Order-Preserving Identity-Based Encryption* with syntax definition to satisfy the above requirements.

Chapter 7
Cryptographic Primitives: Security Definitions

Abstract Security definitions are significantly more complex than syntax definitions. In this chapter, we introduce security definitions step by step. We begin by explaining how these definitions have evolved into a general framework applicable to all cryptographic primitives. Next, we describe security models and highlight their central role in security definitions. We then discuss how security is defined for an algorithm. Finally, we gradually extend this discussion to defining security for cryptographic primitives.

7.1 Role of Security Definition

In cryptology, security ensures that adversaries cannot exploit cryptographic constructions. The role of security definitions is to formally specify what it means for a cryptographic primitive to be secure. They provide a structured framework for analyzing the security of all proposed schemes and protocols. A scheme or protocol designed for a given cryptographic primitive is considered secure if it meets the criteria established by its security definition within this framework. To better understand what a security definition entails, we highlight three of its key characteristics.

The relationship between a security definition and security against specific attacks is akin to a set and its elements. Specific attacks include such as eavesdropping attacks, phishing attacks, replay attacks, and man-in-the-middle attacks. A security definition is a set that could contain an infinite number of elements, representing security resistance to specific attacks. When a proposed scheme or protocol meets a security definition, it is secure against all specific attacks covered by that definition. Intuitively, a scheme or protocol that satisfies a comprehensive security definition is more secure than one that only protects against a predefined list of specific attacks. However, each security definition has its limitations and cannot capture all possible attacks. Without a proper security definition, a scheme or protocol that satisfies the security definition of a cryptographic primitive might not be secure in the real world.

There is no universal security definition for all cryptographic primitives. Security definitions for different cryptographic primitives are usually distinct. This is because each cryptographic primitive consists of at least one unique algorithm requiring a specific security protection. Security definitions for cryptographic primitives change whenever the input or output of one of its algorithms changes. We will introduce various security definitions and explain the reasons behind them.

Security definitions must be rigorous. In general, a security definition for any cryptographic primitive consists of three key components: (1) Who the adversaries are, (2) What the adversaries know (or can do), and (3) The conditions under which the adversaries successfully break security. A rigorous security definition should encompass the following two aspects:

- The answers to these three questions must be general and universal enough to apply to all proposed schemes or protocols for that cryptographic primitive. Since a security definition is intended for a cryptographic primitive (not for a specific construction), it should only involve the syntax of cryptographic algorithms. A specific building-block definition should not be included in a security definition, as not all schemes or protocols will utilize that building block. For example, a cryptographic hash function or a cyclic group should not appear in the security definition for a primitive.

- The answers to these three questions must be clearly defined without ambiguity. The security of a scheme or protocol depends significantly on what the adversaries know. Consider an identity-based encryption scheme as an example. If the adversaries do not know the master public key or the specifics of how the cryptographic algorithms operate, they are unlikely to determine the plaintext from a given ciphertext. However, if the adversary can corrupt the PKG and obtain the master secret key along with all cryptographic algorithms, they can easily derive the plaintext from any ciphertext CT_{ID} by running the key generation algorithm to compute d_{ID} and then executing the decryption algorithm.

It is common in the literature for a basic security definition to be initially established for a cryptographic primitive, which is later refined into a more complex definition due to newly discovered attacks. Consequently, a cryptographic primitive may have multiple security definitions that account for different attacks in various applications. In short, a rigorous security definition helps researchers and readers assess the security strength of a cryptographic primitive and its proposed constructions.

7.2 Defining Security for It: In General

In this section, we introduce the general security definition for all cryptographic primitives as a whole. We call it "general" because the definition does not take any specific characteristics of a cryptographic primitive into account. Many terms and concepts will be combined to generate this general security definition. We present this general security definition progressively through six attempts.

7.2.1 1st Attempt at Definition: Initial

In general, any cryptographic primitive is defined using algorithms from four categories: keying algorithms, combining algorithms, seeing algorithms, and getting algorithms. Our initial attempt at defining security involves encapsulating all these primitives and algorithms into a single object called "**It**" in Figure 7.1.

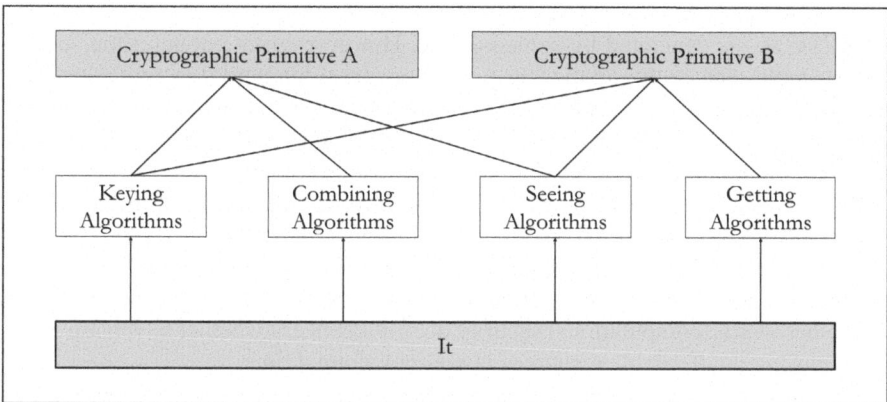

Fig. 7.1 Components behind "**It**"

To define that adversaries cannot abuse it, the first attempt at the definition starts with a very compact statement presented as follows:

Statement

1st Attempt at Definition
No adversary can break it.

This approach is explained in two parts.

- In this definition, "break it" means "abuse it". In this general security definition, we focus on rigorously defining what it means in the context of "break" and "adversary".
- In this definition, an adversary is an algorithm that can break it, rather than "an adversary who knows an algorithm that can break it". The adversary is not a person or an entity but an algorithm. This interpretation aligns closely with security definitions, which focus on defining security against algorithms.

In this security definition, no adversary can break it, meaning that all adversaries cannot break it, and therefore, it is secure.

7.2.2 2nd Attempt at Definition: PPT Adversaries

In modern cryptography, cryptographic schemes and protocols are designed in a way that adversaries could theoretically break them, but doing so would require an impractical amount of computational resources. This type of security is known as computational security. Consider the key generation algorithm in public-key encryption schemes. This algorithm computes a random key pair (pk, sk) from a very large but finite space. Security requires that an adversary cannot derive sk from pk when (pk, sk) is generated by someone else. However, given enough time, an adversary could repeatedly run the key generation algorithm until they find a key pair (pk', sk') such that $pk' = pk$ and $sk' = sk$. At this point, the adversary would have compromised the security of the key generation algorithm. Thus, stating "no adversary" in the initial security definition is not appropriate.

Recall that the length of public keys generated by a key generation algorithm is associated with the security parameter κ. Let the computational resources (time cost) required to break the security of this algorithm be $f_{\mathcal{A}}(\kappa)$. The cryptology community considers $f_{\mathcal{A}}(\kappa)$ to be unaffordable for adversaries if it is non-polynomial in κ. In other words, computational security does not concern whether adversaries can break it using unaffordable resources in non-polynomial time.

In Section 5.1.4, we categorized probabilistic algorithms into three types: probabilistic polynomial-time (PPT) algorithms, probabilistic mixed-time algorithms, and probabilistic non-polynomial-time algorithms. Building on the discussions above, the second attempt at defining security, after refining our understanding of adversaries, is presented as follows:

Statement

2nd Attempt at Definition
No probabilistic polynomial-time adversary can break it.

Security must account for all real-world adversaries who could potentially exploit the entirety of available computational resources to break it.

- On one hand, one might wonder why "probabilistic mixed-time algorithms" are not considered in the security definition. The reality is that ruling out probabilistic polynomial-time (PPT) adversaries naturally rules out probabilistic mixed-time adversaries too. We will revisit and explain the reason after we thoroughly introduce the general security definition.
- On the other hand, one might worry whether PPT algorithms are powerful enough. It is essential to realize that PPT adversaries represent the baseline set of adversaries that should be considered for security. Depending on the specific primitives, security goals, and constructions being studied, PPT adversaries

7.2 Defining Security for It: In General

might need to be enhanced to non-uniform PPT adversaries as seen in many security definitions for MPC protocols, or to quantum polynomial-time (QPT) adversaries especially in post-quantum cryptography.

It is important to note that security against adversaries and usability for users are trade-offs in constructions. Specifically, an enhanced but unnecessary security definition will likely reduce the efficiency of constructed schemes and protocols for users, and also narrow down the choice of building blocks in constructions. For example, a cyclic group cannot be used as a building block to construct schemes or protocols secure against QPT adversaries.

7.2.3 3rd Attempt at Definition: Non-Negligible

So far, both algorithms in cryptographic primitives and security definitions are defined using probabilistic polynomial-time (PPT) algorithms. For users and usability, "probabilistic" is desired for randomized operations, and all outputs from such algorithms should be correct with overwhelming probability close to 1. However, there are some differences in how adversaries interpret "probabilistic".

- Firstly, "probabilistic" is not only used for a randomized output but also to represent powerful adversaries. This is because probabilistic adversaries are more powerful than deterministic ones. Adopting "probabilistic" helps capture all types of adversaries that might be encountered in the real world.
- Secondly, security should not only exclude probabilistic polynomial-time adversaries who can break it with probability 1, but also those adversaries who can break it with a small probability. For example, given a public key pk of a public-key encryption scheme, a PPT adversary might successfully compute its secret key sk with probability $\frac{1}{95279527}$, which is significantly smaller than 1. Such a scheme is not secure in use as it still has a high chance of being broken.

Therefore, the second attempt at defining security is inaccurate, as it does not account for the probability of a successful attack.

Intuitively, the success probability of breaking it should be bounded by a small probability, so a successful attack will not occur during an adversary's lifetime. The third attempt at defining security addresses this concern and is stated as follows:

Statement

3rd Attempt at Definition

No probabilistic polynomial-time adversary can break it with non-negligible probability.

In the above definition, a new term called non-negligible has been used to bound probability. The definitions of negligible and non-negligible are presented as follows:

Definition 7.1 A function $\epsilon(n)$ in n is

- **Negligible** if $\forall c, \exists n_0 \in \mathbb{N}$ such that $\forall n > n_0$, we have $\epsilon(n) \leq \frac{1}{n^c}$.
- **Non-Negligible** if $\exists c$, there exist infinitely many $n \in \mathbb{N}$ such that $\epsilon(n) \geq \frac{1}{n^c}$.

It is important to note that the non-negligible function defined using "*infinitely many $n \in \mathbb{N}$*" has a wider range than "$\forall n_0 \in \mathbb{N}, \exists c$ *such that* $\forall n > n_0$, *we have* $\epsilon(n) \geq \frac{1}{n^c}$". This is because "non-negligible" should be defined to capture all functions that do not belong to the class of negligible functions. For example, a function $f(n)$ that is negligible for even numbers n and $f(n) = 1$ for all odd numbers n is considered a non-negligible function according to this definition.

The above security definition has further narrowed down the meaning of security. Given a secure scheme generated with security parameter κ, such a scheme allows probabilistic non-polynomial-time adversaries to break it with probability 1. It also allows probabilistic polynomial-time adversaries to break it with negligible probability in κ. Both of these allowances do not contradict the meaning of security in cryptology. For beginners, it is interesting to note that this security definition will classify a scheme as insecure even if all probabilistic polynomial-time adversaries cannot break it when generated with security parameter κ, provided that κ is even.

7.2.4 4th Attempt at Definition: Sampling

In the previous attempt at defining security, the term "non-negligible" was used to bound probability. But how is the probability calculated in cryptology? Let $\epsilon(\kappa)$ denote the probability that a PPT adversary breaks a scheme (protocol) generated with security parameter κ. In this section, we introduce how probability measurement is considered in security definitions.

In general, let P be a computing problem represented as a relation function R, let (x, y) be an instance-solution pair of this computing problem, and let $\mathbb{S}_P^\kappa$ be the set of instances generated using security parameter κ. Let $\mathcal{A}$ be a probabilistic algorithm for solving the computing problem P. The general probability measurement for solving this computing problem is defined as

$$\epsilon(\kappa) = \sum_{x \in \mathbb{S}_P^\kappa} \Pr[x = x_i] \cdot \Pr[y_i \leftarrow \mathcal{A}(x_i) : R(x_i, y_i) = 1].$$

This formula represents the success probability of solving the computing problem P, where x is the instance (variable) sampled from the entire instance set $\mathbb{S}_P^\kappa$.

If each instance is randomly sampled from the instance set $\mathbb{S}_P^\kappa$ with the same probability, the success probability $\epsilon(\kappa)$ can be rewritten as

7.2 Defining Security for It: In General

$$\epsilon(\kappa) = \sum_{x \leftarrow_U \mathbb{S}_P^\kappa} \Pr[x = x_i] \cdot \Pr[y_i \leftarrow \mathcal{A}(x_i) : R(x_i, y_i) = 1]$$

$$= \frac{1}{|\mathbb{S}_P^\kappa|} \cdot \left(\sum_{x_i \leftarrow_U \mathbb{S}_P^\kappa} \Pr[y_i \leftarrow \mathcal{A}(x_i) : R(x_i, y_i) = 1] \right).$$

However, the success probability calculated using random sampling is not suitable for cryptography. Here, we provide an example to explain why it is not accurate. Let $(\mathbb{G}, g, p)$ be a cyclic group, where $\mathbb{G}$ represents the set of group elements, g is a group generator, and p is the group order equal to 13. Suppose that a key generation algorithm in a scheme generates a key pair by first choosing a 4-bit random string w and then computing $pk = g^w$. The value w is randomly chosen from the integer set $\{0, 1, 2, 3, 4, 5, 6, 7, 8, 9, 10, 11, 12, 13, 14, 15\}$ with equal probability. Thus, we have

$$\Pr[(pk, sk) \leftarrow KeyGen(\kappa) : pk = g^2] = \frac{2}{16}.$$

This key generation algorithm will return $pk = g^2$ if and only if $w = 2$ or $w = 15$. On the other hand,

$$\Pr[(pk, sk) \leftarrow KeyGen(\kappa) : pk = g^7] = \frac{1}{16}.$$

This is because $pk = g^7$ if and only if $w = 7$ is chosen. In short, instances in cryptographic schemes are generated by an algorithm and are not necessarily uniformly distributed within their spaces.

In general, let $\mathcal{B}$ be a probabilistic polynomial-time cryptographic algorithm for generating an instance x. The probability of breaking it should be revised as

$$\epsilon(\kappa) = \sum_{x \in \mathbb{S}_P^\kappa} \Pr[x \leftarrow \mathcal{B}(\kappa, \cdot) : x = x_i] \cdot \Pr[y_i \leftarrow \mathcal{A}(x_i) : R(x_i, y_i) = 1].$$

Here, $\Pr[x \leftarrow \mathcal{B}(\kappa, \cdot) : x = x_i]$ defines that the variable x is not randomly sampled from its set but according to the algorithm $\mathcal{B}$.

Therefore, the previous attempt at defining security is not precise without properly defining the probability measurement. The fourth attempt is presented as follows:

Statement

4th Attempt at Definition

No probabilistic polynomial-time adversary can break it with non-negligible probability, where the probability is taken over all internal coin tosses of related algorithms.

In the above definition, it has been emphasized that probability is calculated based on instances generated by related (cryptographic) algorithms and the outcomes of the random coins tossed by these probabilistic algorithms.

Probability Ensemble. The term probability ensemble is an important concept that generalizes $\mathcal{B}(\kappa, \cdot)$ in the above probability formula. Firstly, each instance sampled from the algorithm (experiment) $\mathcal{B}(\kappa, \cdot)$ is abstracted as a probability distribution. Secondly, the probability distribution might not be identical and could be influenced by the size of the security parameter κ. Therefore, $\mathcal{B}(\kappa, \cdot)$ is equivalent to a probability distribution X_κ associated with κ.

A probability ensemble is a collection of probability distributions denoted by

$$X = \{X_1, X_2, X_3, \cdots, X_i, \cdots\}_{i \in \mathbb{N}},$$

where $\mathbb{N}$ is the set of positive integers $\{1, 2, 3, \cdots\}$. Here are some explanations of probability ensemble:

- It is a collection of the same type of probability distributions. For example, the probability ensemble can be seen as the collection of problem instances generated by a cryptographic algorithm. All instances of the same length are grouped into one distribution X_i. The probability distribution X_i also defines the probability of choosing each instance. The probability distributions X_i and X_j could therefore have different numbers of possible outcomes and different probabilities.
- The probability distribution X_i in the ensemble can be seen as a distribution for a variable whose length is associated with i. It is incorrect to understand i as the output length of the random variable in X_i, because the random variable in X_i could have i bits or $2i$ bits.

When a computing problem R is defined using a probability ensemble, the probability of solving it by a probabilistic algorithm $\mathcal{A}$ is denoted by

$$\epsilon(\kappa) = \sum_{x \in X_\kappa} \Pr[x = x_i] \cdot \Pr[y_i \leftarrow \mathcal{A}(x_i) : R(x_i, y_i) = 1],$$

where x is sampled from probability distribution X_κ in its probability ensemble. The probability $\Pr[x = x_i]$ is specified by the probability distribution X_κ. Therefore, a probability ensemble defines a computing problem more precisely by including all outcomes and their sampling probabilities. This approach is more suitable for cryptography since instances are generated using algorithms and the probability distribution is associated with algorithms and security parameter.

7.2.5 5th Attempt at Definition: Security Model

Cryptography aims to protect the confidentiality and/or integrity of "**It**" on something. The term "break it" specifically refers to breaking the confidentiality or in-

7.2 Defining Security for It: In General

tegrity of it, such that the related cryptographic primitive has failed to ensure security. For example,

- In an application scenario using digital signatures, Alice publishes a message m by signing it using her secret key sk. On input m and its signature, Bob is able to verify the integrity of the message published by Alice using her public key pk. However, given a badly-designed signature scheme, an adversary is able to break the integrity of it by inputting (pk, m) and outputting a valid signature σ_m on m.
- In an application scenario using public-key encryption, Bob can send a sensitive message to Alice. On input a public key pk belonging to Alice and message m, Bob runs the encryption algorithm to obtain a ciphertext CT, which is sent to Alice. Upon receiving this ciphertext, Alice can decrypt it using her secret key sk. However, given a badly-designed encryption scheme, an adversary is able to break the confidentiality of it by inputting (pk, CT) and outputting m, which is the plaintext of CT.

Based on the above examples, the term "break it" comprises input and output, like a computing problem to be solved.

A formalization of "break it" is called a security model, which is a formal framework used to define breaking it. The framework of a security model has three components:

- **Input** (a.k.a., what the adversary knows),
- **Output** and **Success Condition** (a.k.a., what the adversary should return indicating that the adversary has successfully broken it).

For example, the input is x, the output is y, and the success condition is $R_B(x, y) = 1$, where R_B is a relation function abstracted from breaking it. What kind of relation function R_B should be defined in a security model is associated with the cryptographic primitive and its security requirements or protections.

Security models show different levels of difficulty in breaking a cryptographic primitive. Consider two simple security models for digital signatures. In the first security model, an adversary given as input (pk, m) is to compute a valid signature σ_m on m. Here, "valid signature" is the success condition. In the second security model, an adversary given as input (pk, sk, m) is to compute a valid signature σ_m on m. It is clear that the adversary in the second security model can break it more easily than in the first security model because the adversary can simply run the signing algorithm to compute σ_m in the second security model. In other words, whether it is secure or insecure depends on the security model. Therefore, the fourth attempt at security definition without formally modelling "break it" is not formal or precise enough.

Based on the above explanations and discussions, the fifth attempt at security definition is presented as follows. In this definition attempt, "in a security model" has been added. The security model has formally defined "break it" like "solve a computing problem". We will revisit security model in the next section.

Statement

5th Attempt at Definition

No probabilistic polynomial-time adversary can break it in a security model with non-negligible probability, where the probability is taken over all internal coin tosses of related algorithms.

7.2.6 6th Attempt at Definition: Advantage

In the previous attempt at defining security, a proposed scheme is considered secure if PPT adversaries can break it only with negligible probability. In other words, if a PPT adversary can break it with a probability such as $1/2$, this scheme would be treated as insecure.

However, this security definition is not universal for all cryptographic primitives and their security requirements. Consider the security of public-key encryption as an example. Suppose Alice wants to tell a secret answer (Yes or No) to Bob and encrypts the answer using Bob's public key. Alice encrypts the bit 1 if she wants to tell Bob "Yes" or encrypts the bit 0 if the answer is "No". Let the ciphertext be $CT \leftarrow Enc(pk, b)$, where $b \in \{0, 1\}$ is the answer. Given this ciphertext, an adversary tries to correctly guess the answer b to break the security. Since the message is either 1 or 0, it is clear that an adversary can guess b correctly with probability $1/2$ even without seeing the ciphertext, simply by guessing randomly. Therefore, defining security using "negligible probability" is not suitable for all cryptographic primitives.

The sixth attempt at security definition is revised and presented as follows:

Statement

6th Attempt at Definition

No probabilistic polynomial-time adversary can break it in a security model with non-negligible advantage, where the probability is taken over all internal coin tosses of related algorithms.

The above definition is exactly the same as the previous definition except that "probability" is replaced with a new term "advantage". This definition will be accepted and used as the general security definition.

Advantage. In cryptology, advantage is a measure of how successfully an adversary can break it in a security model by distinguishing it from breaking it in an

7.2 Defining Security for It: In General

idealized security model. Here, idealized security model can be simply understood as a model in which the scheme to be attacked is contained in a black box and the adversary has no access to any internal elements.

Let $\Pr_{\mathcal{A}}$ be the probability of breaking it in a security model and $\Pr_I$ be the corresponding probability in the idealized security model. In the cryptology community, the advantage of the adversary in successfully breaking it is defined as

$$\mathbf{Adv}_{\mathcal{A}} = \epsilon(\kappa) = \begin{cases} \Pr_{\mathcal{A}} - \Pr_I & \text{if } \Pr_I \text{ is non-negligible,} \\ \Pr_{\mathcal{A}} & \text{if } \Pr_I \text{ is negligible.} \end{cases}$$

In the definition above, $\Pr_{\mathcal{A}}$ refers to the maximum probability returned by all PPT adversaries. In the next section, we will present the general formula for defining the success probability $\Pr_{\mathcal{A}}$.

We note that some researchers define the advantage with $|\Pr_{\mathcal{A}} - \Pr_I|$ including an absolute value. The purpose is to account for a naughty adversary that deliberately breaks it with probability less than $\Pr_I$. For instance, the adversary might return $1 - b$ when guessing the encrypted message b in $Enc(pk, b)$, and the success probability is $\Pr_{\mathcal{A}} = 0$. It is important to note that the advantage definition might have some variants in different references (especially for encryption). When $\Pr_I = 1/2$, the advantage $\mathbf{Adv}_{\mathcal{A}}$ has been defined with either $\Pr_{\mathcal{A}} - 1/2$ or $2(\Pr_{\mathcal{A}} - 1/2)$. One reason for using the second definition is to keep the advantage range the same as the probability range, between $[0, 1]$. However, this is not fundamentally important since security definition only considers two kinds of results: negligible advantage (meaning secure) and non-negligible advantage (meaning insecure). Whether the maximum advantage is 1 or $1/2$, both are considered non-negligible.

7.2.7 PPT Adversaries, Revisited

We have one remaining question about the use of probabilistic polynomial-time (PPT) adversaries in the general security definitions. It asks whether we should include probabilistic mixed-time (PMT) adversaries in the general security definitions. The answer is that it is not necessary.

Consider the key generation algorithm as an example. Given a PMT adversary that can compute secret key from its public key, we can classify all key pairs into three categories:

- In the first category, for each public key, the adversary stops in polynomial time and returns its correct secret key with non-negligible probability.
- In the second category, for each public key, the adversary stops in polynomial time but returns its correct secret key with negligible probability.
- In the third category, for each public key, the adversary will stop in non-polynomial time, regardless of whether the returned output is correct or not.

If this PMT adversary can break this key generation algorithm and cause damage to users, it means that at least one key pair generated by some user will fall into the first category with non-negligible probability.

Given the above PMT adversary, we can construct a PPT adversary by forcing the PMT adversary to stop in polynomial time for any public key. The only change is that all public keys in the third category will either remain unsolved or be solved only with negligible probability. Consequently, this constructed PPT adversary will also break the key generation algorithm and compute one of the users' secret keys with non-negligible probability. Therefore, a PMT adversary that can break it with non-negligible probability should not exist if no PPT adversary can do so.

This concludes our introduction to the general security definition of "breaking it", where all cryptographic algorithms and primitives are folded together. In the cryptology community, security definitions are typically framed within the context of the sixth attempt at defining security. Each specific security definition of a cryptographic primitive will elaborate on the term "breaking it" in various ways (namely security models) and with greater detail. In the following sections, after revisiting security models, we will begin to refine "break it" into "break an algorithm" and ultimately "break a cryptographic primitive".

7.3 Security Model, Revisited

Previously, we have briefly introduced what a security model and its framework are in the general security definition. Due to the importance and complexity of the security model, in this section, we further expand on the security model to help beginners understand how to deal with this term.

7.3.1 Role of Security Model

The security model plays a core role in defining the security of a cryptographic primitive. Most cryptographic primitives will have their security defined using the same general security description from the previous section, with slight differences (such as using QPT instead of PPT adversaries). The primary differences among security definitions for cryptographic primitives lie in their adopted security models. In other words, when defining security for a cryptographic primitive, the main focus is on defining a security model for that primitive.

The relationship between a security definition and security against specific attacks is similar to that of a set and its elements, as briefly outlined at the beginning of this chapter. A security model, within a security definition, defines an abstract relationship between input and output, while a specific attack details how an output is derived from an input through concrete operational steps. If this specific attack can be abstracted or captured by the relationship defined in the security model, it

7.3 Security Model, Revisited

means that the security model accounts for this specific attack. In other words, if no PPT adversary can break it within this security model, it implies that no PPT adversary can successfully carry out this specific attack on it. Consequently, proving the security of a scheme (or protocol) within a security model demonstrates that the scheme is secure against all attacks captured by that security model.

7.3.2 Adversaries from Entities

Overview

$$\begin{cases} \text{Adversaries} \begin{cases} \text{Entities in Syntax Definition excluding TTP} \\ \text{Outsider} \end{cases} \\ \text{Entity} \begin{cases} \text{Single-User Entity} \\ \text{Multi-User Entity} \end{cases} \end{cases}$$

In Section 6.3.2, we introduced the entities involved in syntax definitions, including Signer, Verifier, Encryptor, Decryptor, Prover, Delegator, Client, Party, Data Owner, Data Receiver, Private-Key Generator, Trusted Third Party (TTP), Authority, Manager, Proxy, Delegatee, (Cloud) Server, and Auditor. All these entities participate in executing one of the cryptographic algorithms. Except for TTP, all other entities could potentially act as adversaries attempting to compromise security protections for other entities.

In security models, another entity called outsider plays a significant role as an additional adversary. The outsider (adversary) is assumed to know all public information, such as the public key of each user. Including this entity will be sound for security modelling to be introduced in this book

An entity in a cryptographic primitive can be either a single-user entity or a multi-user entity. For example, the PKG in IBE is a single-user entity, while the encryptor in IBE is a multi-user entity because multiple users can send encrypted messages to the same receiver. Similarly, the decryptor in IBE is also a multi-user entity. A cryptographic primitive may require a minimum number of users in a multi-user entity to execute correctly. For example, an encryptor and a decryptor can operate with a single user. However, in threshold IBE, the decryptor consists of n users, each possessing a different share of the private key.

Clearly defining all entities and the number of users within them is essential for effectively conveying the security modelling of cryptographic primitives introduced in Section 7.5.

7.3.3 Input, Output, and Success Condition

The framework of a security model consists of three components: input, output, and success condition. We introduce these three components in the following framework as an initial entry point for understanding security models, though the presentation will be restructured later.

Security Model

Input: x
Output: y satisfying that

- The success condition $R_B(x, y) = 1$.

Firstly, the input encompasses all information that PPT adversaries could obtain when a cryptographic primitive is employed for security protections. The input may include data (e.g., parameters, messages, functions, circuits), identity (e.g., IDs, attributes, indices), keys (e.g., public and secret keys), and outputs (e.g., proofs, ciphertexts, tokens). The input also includes all cryptographic algorithms associated with the primitive, in accordance with the widely recognized Kerckhoffs' principle[1]. In this book, cryptographic algorithms are considered default input and will not be explicitly displayed as part of the input.

Secondly, the output, which signifies a successful security break, depends heavily on what the cryptographic primitive is designed to protect. For example, the output could be a signature where an adversary aims to forge one signature, or a plaintext where an adversary aims to extract the encrypted message from a given ciphertext. We will further elaborate on the output in the next subsection.

Finally, the success condition specifies under what circumstances the output y to be generated by adversaries indicates that the cryptographic primitive is broken. For example, y is a valid signature on a new message whose signature is not given in x, or y is the valid encrypted message in a ciphertext in x.

Any security model should be defined in the way that no PPT adversary can compute the output from the input that satisfies the success condition, ensuring no trivial breaking or trivial attack. Here, trivial breaking refers to the output y being computable from the input x by simply executing the defined cryptographic algorithms. If a security model has trivial breaking, it means all constructions for this primitive are insecure in this security model. The fundamental goal of cryptography is to design solutions that remain secure under a given security model.

---

[1] This principle, a cornerstone of modern cryptographic design, asserts that a cryptosystem should remain secure even if everything about it, except the key, is known to an adversary.

7.3.4 Characteristics of Outputs: Hidden Target or Learn Nothing

In the general framework of a security model, given x, an adversary aims to compute an output y such that $R_B(x, y) = 1$. The value y returned by the adversary serves as evidence that the cryptographic primitive has been broken. In the cryptology community, there are two types of outputs that the adversary aims to compute.

- **Hidden Target.** The output y refers to a specific piece of information or structure, known as the target, which should be intentionally uncomputable by an adversary. In cryptographic terms, the target could be an element like a signature, a key, or a plaintext within a ciphertext. We say a security model has hidden-target security if a well-defined information structure y cannot be computed from x.
- **Learn Nothing.** The output y refers to any additional information that the adversary should not know beyond what it already knows. The term "secret" is used to denote this additional information. Typically, the set of potential secrets is infinite, encompassing anything that the adversary is unable to learn through the computation process. We say a security model has learn-nothing security if any secret y cannot be computed from x.

Clearly, learn-nothing security is stronger and more comprehensive than hidden-target security. The latter only prevents the adversary from computing a specific target with a well-defined structure, whereas the former ensures that the adversary cannot gain any additional information. However, learn-nothing security is not always necessary in all application scenarios involving cryptographic primitives.

Consider the BLS signature scheme [13] as an example. In this scheme, the key pair is defined as $(pk, sk) = (h, \alpha)$, where $h = g^\alpha$, g is a generator of a pairing group, and $\alpha \in \mathbb{Z}_p$. A signature on a message m is represented as $H(m)^\alpha$, where $H : \{0, 1\}^* \to \mathbb{G}$ is a cryptographic hash function. The two security goals based on this example are explained as follows:

- **Hidden-target security** requires that the adversary cannot forge a valid signature (therefore a piece of structure) on a new message m^* denoted by $H(m^*)^\alpha$. Even if the adversary could compute the group element g^{α^2} from pk, the scheme remains secure because g^{α^2} is not a valid signature for any message.
- **Learn-nothing security** requires that the adversary cannot obtain any secret beyond what it already knows. In the cryptology community, g^{α^2} is considered a secret that PPT adversaries cannot compute from (g, h). If g^{α^2} were computable from pk, the BLS scheme would fail to achieve learn-nothing security.

We observe that security for schemes is primarily defined by hidden-target security, whereas security for protocols is primarily defined by learn-nothing security. This distinction likely arises because schemes consider an output y from the adversary as a threat if and only if it can pass some algorithmic check, thus requiring the structure of y. However, this observation is not entirely accurate. We will provide examples of this distinction when introducing security models for algorithms and primitives.

7.3.5 Characteristics of Inputs: The Need of Oracles

The framework of a security model we introduced is very similar to a computing problem in complexity theory, consisting of input and output. However, security models exhibit certain unusual characteristics, particularly regarding input.

- First, the input x is not randomly chosen or sampled from a space; rather, it is generated by PPT cryptographic algorithms. For example, a PPT adversary, given a public key pk as input, is tasked with computing the corresponding secret key. In this example, pk is not randomly chosen from the key space but is generated by the key generation algorithm.
- Second, the input could be partially from the adversary. For example, in digital signatures, the PPT adversary is tasked with forging a valid signature on message m^* and is allowed to know a signature on any message m different from m^* before the forgery. In this case, the input is (pk, m, σ_m), but m is chosen by the adversary. It is important to note that m may not be uniformly selected from the message space by the adversary.

In summary, the input x in a security model is either generated by cryptographic algorithms or chosen by the adversary. Most importantly, it is not randomly chosen from its space.

To simplify input components, the cryptology community has introduced the term "Oracle" to represent parts of the input provided by the adversary. More precisely, an oracle is a theoretical black box or a hypothetical entity that responds to queries according to predefined operational rules.

$$\xrightarrow{\text{Query}} \quad \mathcal{O} \text{ (Oracle)} \quad \xleftarrow{\text{Response}}$$

Most importantly, adversaries cannot observe any secret values or internal operations of the black box. When an adversary makes a query to the oracle, the oracle will honestly return a response following the definition of operation. An oracle is defined to model the behaviour of an adversary with specific capabilities. For example, a signing oracle is given as input to the adversary, who can query any message m to the signing oracle. The signing oracle, which knows sk, runs the signing algorithm to sign m and returns the signature to the adversary.

Generally speaking, oracles serve as powerful tools for adversaries to expand their input x. However, queries to oracles must be restricted; otherwise, trivial attacks may arise. For example, if an adversary is tasked with forging a valid signature for a message m^*, the query on m^* to the signing oracle must be prohibited. Without this restriction, the adversary could simply use the oracle's response to produce the forgery directly. The description of oracle restriction can be specified within the oracle definition or as part of the success condition.

7.3 Security Model, Revisited 169

This book will present a security model in a framework as follows when the input has included at least one oracle.

Security Model

Input: $(x, \mathcal{O})$
Output: y satisfying that

- The success condition $R_B(x, y) = 1$.

Oracle $\mathcal{O}$: The description of how to respond to each query.

To emphasize once again, there are multiple ways to present a security model. The above framework is beginner-friendly as it resembles the structure of computing problems. We will introduce the presentation methods that are commonly used in the cryptology community.

7.3.6 Directions of Modelling

When giving a security definition for a (new) cryptographic primitive, the main task is defining its security model. The security of all constructed schemes (protocols) for this primitive will be evaluated within this security model. That is, we do not consider whether an adversary could successfully break it or not outside its specified security model. Therefore, the security model should be strong enough to capture those potential attacks on this cryptographic primitive when it is applied to secure applications.

In general, we can start the definition of a security model with a very basic version. Then, we strengthen this security model in two ways.

- **Reinforce Input.** This direction allows the adversary to gain more information or control the choice of elements as input. For example, the adversary is allowed to query oracles for a polynomial number of times with any inputs instead of one query only.
- **Relax Output.** This approach lowers the difficulty of the attack for the adversary. Take public-key encryption as an example. The adversary is not asked to see the plaintext inside a given ciphertext but is relaxed to see which message has been encrypted inside a given ciphertext that encrypts either m_0 or m_1.

We will introduce how to propose security models for a cryptographic primitive in this chapter. Generally speaking, the final security model for a cryptographic primitive is stronger than real-world attacks. One reason is to simplify the modelling process. Take digital signatures as an example. When adversaries are allowed to access a signing oracle, the input messages for signature queries can be arbitrary messages. However, in the real world, a signer would only sign messages they consider meaningful.

Theoretically, we can give the strongest security definition by allowing the input to include everything except those elements/objects that would lead to trivial attacks. It is also important to note that a very strong security definition might not be necessary for specific applications. We must carefully strengthen security models because stronger security models make constructions harder, more complex, and less efficient for provable security.

7.3.7 Formulating Probability for Breaking

Overview

$$\text{Objects in Success Probability} = \begin{cases} \text{Input} \\ \text{Oracle} \\ \text{Output} \\ \text{Success Condition} \end{cases}$$

In this section, at the beginning, we introduced the framework of a security model, which consists of input, output, and success condition. Due to the characteristics of input, another term, oracle, has been introduced separately to represent part of the input from adversaries. Therefore, a security model comprises at least four components (input, oracle, output, and success condition) when defining the success probability $\Pr_{\mathcal{A}}$ of breaking it.

It can be somewhat complex or challenging for beginners to incorporate all these components into a probability formula to define the success probability $\Pr_{\mathcal{A}}$. We found that it is mainly due to three facts. Firstly, all objects must be presented with clear sources including those elements generated by cryptographic algorithms or chosen by the adversary. Secondly, all generated elements have some interconnected relations to oracles and hard to be presented independently. Lastly, where to place restrictions on queries is very tricky.

Take the framework of security model introduced in Section 7.3.5 as an example for formulating $\Pr_{\mathcal{A}}$. It can be presented in three ways as follows:

$$\Pr_{\mathcal{A}} = \Pr[x; y; y' \leftarrow \mathcal{A}^{\mathcal{O}}(x) : y' = y] \tag{7.1}$$

$$\Pr_{\mathcal{A}} = \Pr\begin{bmatrix} x \\ y \\ y' \leftarrow \mathcal{A}^{\mathcal{O}}(x) \end{bmatrix} : y' = y \end{bmatrix} \tag{7.2}$$

$$\Pr_{\mathcal{A}} = \Pr\begin{bmatrix} y' = y \;\Big|\; \begin{matrix} x \\ y \\ y' \leftarrow \mathcal{A}^{\mathcal{O}}(x) \end{matrix} \end{bmatrix} \tag{7.3}$$

7.3 Security Model, Revisited

These presentations convey the same meaning, all referring to the probability of the event $y' = y$ (where the adversary wins in the security model) in the experiment "$x; y; y' \leftarrow \mathcal{A}^{\mathcal{O}}(x)$". The second and third formulas include additional space for detailed descriptions of the experiment.

It is important to note that the above formulas are very simple and not complete. Nor can they cover all cases. We summarize shortcomings as follows.

- No source description for x and y in this probability formula.
- No description on queries to oracles from the adversaries. Security models for some cryptographic primitives must clearly state this part.
- No query restriction has been added inside this formula.

In the cryptology community, using external descriptions outside the probability formulation is a common approach to incorporating all components when defining success probability. We will introduce this approach and give examples when introducing ways for presenting security models in Section 7.5.12.

7.3.8 Security Property and Security Notion

We clarify the relationship between security definition (model) and security property (notion) in this section. In the first chapter, we introduced the cryptographic concept "$\mathcal{X}$-secure $\mathcal{Y}$". Now, it is clear that a syntax definition defines $\mathcal{Y}$, while a security definition defines $\mathcal{X}$. Given a scheme proposed for the cryptographic primitive $\mathcal{Y}$, we say the scheme is $\mathcal{X}$-secure if it satisfies the security definition for $\mathcal{X}$.

If no adversary can break a cryptographic primitive according to a security definition, we say the primitive possesses security properties (notions), which are named based on common characteristics derived from the security definition. In the cryptology community, there are many terms adopted to represent security properties of cryptographic primitives. For example, *chosen-message attacks, chosen-ciphertext attacks, unforgeable, adaptive, indistinguishable, semi-honest security,* and *malicious security*. These terms are commonly used to describe the security characteristics of many cryptographic primitives.

We emphasize that a security property only represents some characteristics of security models or security definitions. For example, chosen-ciphertext attacks mean that adversaries are allowed to access a decryption oracle in those security models for public-key encryption and its variant primitives. We will collect most popular security properties as exercises at the end of this chapter.

In cryptology, security properties are not the terms only used in security models but also on constructions (schemes and protocols). In particular, security properties are also used to name those characteristics related to security results of proposed schemes or protocols. For example, tight security, asymptotic security, and concrete security are related to security properties of constructed schemes or protocols. We clarify the differences between these security properties to prevent beginners from becoming confused or lost.

7.4 Defining Security for Non-Interactive Algorithms

In this section, we introduce how to define security for non-interactive algorithms. The security definition for interactive algorithms will be provided separately, as their security goals differ significantly. It is important to note that our introduction in this section is to show what a potential security model looks like for a cryptographic algorithm under each security concern. We are not yet ready to introduce the process of defining security models for a cryptographic primitive.

7.4.1 Algorithm Classifications

Overview

$$\text{Algorithms} = \begin{cases} \text{Keying Algorithms} & \begin{cases} \text{Public Keying Algorithms (Without Secret Key)} \\ \text{Secret Keying Algorithms (With Secret Key)} \end{cases} \\ \text{Combining Algorithms} & \begin{cases} \text{Public Combining Algorithms (Without Secret Key)} \\ \text{Secret Combining Algorithms (With Secret Key)} \end{cases} \\ \text{Seeing Algorithms} & \begin{cases} \text{Public Seeing Algorithms (Without Secret Key)} \\ \text{Secret Seeing Algorithms (With Secret Key)} \end{cases} \end{cases}$$

Previously, we have abstracted four categories of algorithms, and three of them are non-interactive. They are keying algorithms, combining algorithms, and seeing algorithms. Each of these can be further divided into two subcategories: algorithms that do not take a secret key as input (public algorithms) and those that do (secret algorithms). Several common security concerns arise when defining the security of these non-interactive algorithms. Therefore, we use two kinds of abstracted algorithms to analyze their security models.

- The first abstracted algorithm without secret key as input is:

$$Alg(x_1, x_2, x_3) \to (y_1, y_2),$$

where (x_1, x_2, x_3) is a tuple of inputs and (y_1, y_2) is a pair of corresponding outputs. These five elements $(x_1, x_2, x_3, y_1, y_2)$ do not have specific spaces.

- The second abstracted algorithm with secret key as input is:

$$Alg(x_1, x_2, sk) \to (y_1, y_2),$$

where (x_1, x_2) is a pair of inputs and (y_1, y_2) is a pair of corresponding outputs. Further, (pk, sk) is a key pair of public key and secret key. We assume the existence of such a key pair without considering where it comes from.

7.4 Defining Security for Non-Interactive Algorithms

The first abstracted algorithm represents the three categories of public algorithms, while the second represents the three categories of secret algorithms. This abstraction is not entirely general but is designed to be accessible for beginners learning about security models. This abstraction does not include algorithms with symmetric key as input, but their security models will be very similar to the models for the second abstracted algorithm.

7.4.2 Adversary and Security Goal

When a user runs the cryptographic algorithm $Alg()$ (as defined in the previous subsection) for security protections, there are two types of security concerns.

- On one hand, what the user has computed should be protected and secure against an external party treated as the adversary.
- On the other hand, the user should not be able to abuse this cryptographic algorithm to cheat the external party. In this case, the user is treated as the adversary.

That is, both the user and the external party can act as adversaries. It is important to note that who should be treated as adversaries depends on the application scenarios.

In cryptology, the most fundamental security concerns are confidentiality and integrity of elements. Confidentiality refers to the adversary wanting to find certain elements (after some computations), while integrity refers to the adversary wanting to change some elements meeting some conditions. Furthermore, the elements that the adversary wants to find or change can be either from algorithm output or algorithm input. Thus, security goals can be classified into four categories.

- **Output Confidentiality:** Adversaries cannot find output from input.
- **Input Confidentiality:** Adversaries cannot find input from output.
- **Output Integrity:** Adversaries cannot change output from a given input.
- **Input Integrity:** Adversaries cannot change input for a given output.

These four categories are mainly defined with hidden-target security but the input confidentiality could be defined with learn-nothing security.

Summary

$$\text{Security} = \begin{cases} \text{Confidentiality} \begin{cases} \text{Output Confidentiality} \\ \text{Input Confidentiality} \end{cases} \\ \text{Integrity} \begin{cases} \text{Output Integrity} \\ \text{Input Integrity} \end{cases} \end{cases}$$

Roughly speaking, for each algorithm, we can define four categories of security for it. However, the existing cryptographic primitives in the literature show that keying algorithms, combining algorithms, and seeing algorithms have their focuses and unique concerns. In the following six subsections, we will introduce security models for each abstracted algorithm.

7.4.3 Security Models for Public Keying Algorithms

Let $Key(x_1, x_2, x_3) \to (y_1, y_2)$ be the abstracted public keying algorithm. We introduce a security model for it.

Output Confidentiality

Input: (a_1, a_2, a_3, b_1)
Output: b_2 satisfying that

- (b_1, b_2) is a pair of output generated from $Key(a_1, a_2, a_3)$.

In this security model, given all inputs and the first half of the output, the adversary is tasked with finding the second half of the output. For example, the key generation algorithm $KeyGen(1^\kappa) \to (pk, sk)$ in public-key cryptography should be secure in this security model, where $\kappa = (a_1, a_2, a_3)$, $pk = b_1$, and $sk = b_2$. Otherwise, it means that an adversary can compute sk from pk and the security parameter.

It is important to note that no deterministic key generation algorithm can be secure in this security model because the adversary, knowing all input, can easily compute the full output by itself. Furthermore, this security model must have b_1 as the input; otherwise, it is easy to run the algorithm on input (a_1, a_2, a_3) to compute the pair (b_1, b_2).

7.4.4 Security Models for Secret Keying Algorithms

Let $Key(x_1, x_2, sk) \to (y_1, y_2)$ be the abstracted secret keying algorithm. We introduce two security models for this algorithm.

Output Confidentiality (1)

Input: (a_1, a_2, pk)
Output: (b_1, b_2) satisfying that

7.4 Defining Security for Non-Interactive Algorithms 175

- pk is the public key of sk, and
- (b_1, b_2) is a pair of output generated from $Key(a_1, a_2, sk)$.

The first security model is output confidentiality. In this security model, given the input (a_1, a_2, pk), the adversary is tasked with finding the output that is generated from $Key(a_1, a_2, sk)$. For example, the key generation algorithm $KeyGen(msk, ID) \to d_{ID}$ in IBE should be secure in this security model, where $ID = (a_1, a_2)$, $msk = sk$, and $d_{ID} = (b_1, b_2)$. Otherwise, it means that an adversary can compute d_{ID} for an identity ID by itself without knowing the master secret key msk.

Output Confidentiality (2)

Input: $(pk, \mathcal{O})$
Output: (a_1, a_2, b_1, b_2) satisfying that

- pk is the public key of sk,
- No query on (a_1, a_2) to the oracle, and
- (b_1, b_2) is a pair of output generated from $Key(a_1, a_2, sk)$.

Oracle $\mathcal{O}$: On input (x_1, x_2), it returns $(y_1, y_2) \leftarrow Key(x_1, x_2, sk)$.

The second security model is still output confidentiality. In the second security model for output confidentiality, given the input pk and an oracle that on input (x_1, x_2) returns $(y_1, y_2) \leftarrow Key(x_1, x_2, sk)$, the adversary is tasked with finding a tuple (a_1, a_2, b_1, b_2) satisfying $(b_1, b_2) \leftarrow Key(a_1, a_2, sk)$ and no query on (a_1, a_2). Compared to the first one, the adversary in this model is allowed to make freely queries and choose arbitrary (a_1, a_2). For example, the key generation algorithm in IBE should be secure in this model. Otherwise, it means that an adversary can compute a valid private key for an identity $ID = (a_1, a_2)$ by itself without knowing the master secret key msk after querying a set of private keys of other identities.

7.4.5 Security Models for Public Combining Algorithms

Let $Combine(x_1, x_2, x_3) \to (y_1, y_2)$ be the abstracted public combining algorithm. We introduce three types of security models for this algorithm.

Input Confidentiality

Input: (a_1, a_3, b_1, b_2)
Output: a_2 satisfying that

- (b_1, b_2) is a pair of output generated from $Combine(a_1, a_2, a_3)$.

The first security model is input confidentiality. In this security model, given part of the input and its full output, the adversary is tasked with finding the remaining unknown input a_2. For example, the encryption algorithm $Enc(pk, m) \to CT$ in public-key encryption should be secure in this security model, where $pk = (a_1, a_3)$, $m = a_2$, and $CT = (b_1, b_2)$. Otherwise, it means that an adversary given (CT, pk) can recover the encrypted message m. This will compromise the confidentiality.

Input Confidentiality (Decisional Variant)

Input: $(a_1, a_2^0, a_2^1, a_3, b_1, b_2)$
Output: c' satisfying that

- c is randomly chosen from $\{0, 1\}$,
- $c' = c$, and
- (b_1, b_2) is a pair of output generated from $Combine(a_1, a_2^c, a_3)$.

We can also define a decisional variant of input confidentiality, where a_2^c is randomly chosen from the two given elements (a_2^0, a_2^1) known by the adversary.

Output Integrity

Input: (a_1, a_2, b_1, b_2)
Output: (b_1', b_2') satisfying that

- $(b_1, b_2) \neq (b_1', b_2')$,
- (b_1, b_2) is a pair of output generated from $Combine(a_1, a_2, a_3)$, and
- (b_1', b_2') is another pair of output generated from $Combine(a_1, a_2, a_3)$.

The second security model is output integrity. In this security model, given part of input and its full output (b_1, b_2), the adversary is tasked with changing output into (b_1', b_2') that is also generated from $Combine(a_1, a_2, a_3)$. To prevent a trivial breaking, the adversary must not be given the full tuple (a_1, a_2, a_3). For example, the encryption algorithm $Enc(pk, m) \to CT$ in public-key encryption must be secure in this model. This ensures the public-key encryption can resist chosen-ciphertext attacks, where an adversary can query decryption. It guarantees

7.4 Defining Security for Non-Interactive Algorithms

that, given a ciphertext $Enc(pk, m) = (b_1, b_2)$ for finding its encrypted message, the adversary cannot create another valid ciphertext (b'_1, b'_2) equivalent to one generated by $Enc(pk, m)$. Here, $pk = (a_1, a_2)$ and $m = a_3$. Otherwise, the adversary would easily break it after knowing m from the decryption oracle's response.

Input Integrity

Input: $(a_1, a_2, a_3, b_1, b_2)$
Output: (a'_1, a'_2, a'_3) satisfying that

- $(a'_1, a'_2, a'_3) \neq (a_1, a_2, a_3)$,
- (b_1, b_2) is a pair of output generated from $Combine(a_1, a_2, a_3)$, and
- (b_1, b_2) is also a pair of output generated from $Combine(a'_1, a'_2, a'_3)$.

The third security model is input integrity. In this security model, given a tuple of input and its corresponding output, the adversary is tasked with changing input into (a'_1, a'_2, a'_3) such that $Combine(a_1, a_2, a_3) = Combine(a'_1, a'_2, a'_3)$. The cryptographic primitive called *Accumulator* [16] has defined an algorithm where multiple elements (namely a_1, a_2, a_3) are accumulated into a shorter representation (namely b_1, b_2). The security of an accumulator requires that no one, including its generator, can modify the aggregated elements, as specified in this security model.

7.4.6 Security Models for Secret Combining Algorithms

Let $Combine(x_1, x_2, sk) \to (y_1, y_2)$ be the abstracted secret combining algorithm. We introduce five security models for this algorithm.

Output Confidentiality (1)

Input: (a_1, a_2, pk)
Output: (b_1, b_2) satisfying that

- pk is the public key of sk, and
- (b_1, b_2) is a pair of output generated from $Combine(a_1, a_2, sk)$.

The first security model is output confidentiality. In the first security model, given (a_1, a_2, pk), the adversary is tasked with finding the output that is generated from $Combine(a_1, a_2, sk)$. For example, the signing algorithm $Sign(sk, m) \to \sigma_m$ in digital signatures should be secure in this security model, where $m = (a_1, a_2)$ and $\sigma_m = (b_1, b_2)$. Otherwise, it means that an adversary given (m, pk) can forge a signature on m. This will compromise the integrity.

Output Confidentiality (2)

Input: $(pk, \mathcal{O})$
Output: (a_1, a_2, b_1, b_2) satisfying that

- pk is the public key of sk,
- No query on (a_1, a_2) to the oracle $\mathcal{O}$, and
- (b_1, b_2) is a pair of output generated from $Combine(a_1, a_2, sk)$.

Oracle $\mathcal{O}$: On input (x_1, x_2), it returns $(y_1, y_2) \leftarrow Combine(x_1, x_2, sk)$.

The second security model is still output confidentiality. Compared to the first security model for output confidentiality, the adversary in this model is allowed to query an oracle that responds to (x_1, x_2) using sk. To prevent trivial attacks, the adversary is not allowed to query (a_1, a_2) to the oracle. Otherwise, the adversary can use the response from the oracle to obtain (b_1, b_2) directly. This security model can be seen as the prototype of the security model for digital signatures, where an adversary is allowed to know signatures on any queried messages before attempting to forge a signature on a new message $m = (a_1, a_2)$.

Input Confidentiality (1)

Input: $(a_1, a_2^0, a_2^1, pk, b_1, b_2)$
Output: $c' \in \{0, 1\}$ satisfying that

- $c' = c$,
- pk is the public key of sk,
- c is randomly chosen from $\{0, 1\}$, and
- (b_1, b_2) is a pair of output generated from $Combine(a_1, a_2^c, sk)$,

---

The third security model is input confidentiality. In this security model, given (a_1, a_2^0, a_2^1, pk) and full output (b_1, b_2), the adversary is tasked with finding which $a_2^c \in \{a_2^0, a_2^1\}$ has been used in computing (b_1, b_2). For example, the signcrypt algorithm $Signcrypt(pk_R, m, sk) \to \sigma_m$ in $Signcryption$ [45] requires a similar security model. Here, pk_R denotes the receiver's public key and sk is the sender's secret key. In this security model, given $pk_R = a_1$, pk, $(m_0, m_1) = (a_2^0, a_2^1)$, and $CT = (b_1, b_2)$, the adversary cannot determine whether $m_c = a_2^0$ or $m_c = a_2^1$.

Input Confidentiality (2)

Input: $(a_1, a_2, pk_0, pk_1, b_1, b_2)$
Output: $c' \in \{0, 1\}$ satisfying that

7.4 Defining Security for Non-Interactive Algorithms

- pk_i is the public key of sk_i ($i \in \{0, 1\}$),
- $c' = c$, c is randomly chosen from $\{0, 1\}$, and
- (b_1, b_2) is a pair of output generated from $Combine(a_1, a_2, sk_c)$.

The fourth security model is still input confidentiality. In the second security model for input confidentiality, given (a_1, a_2, pk_0, pk_1) and the full output (b_1, b_2), the adversary is tasked with finding which $sk_c \in \{sk_0, sk_1\}$ has been used in computing (b_1, b_2). For example, the proof algorithm in non-interactive zero-knowledge proof [18] requires a similar security model, where (a_1, a_2) is the statement and sk_c is the witness. The security requirement ensures that the proof (b_1, b_2) does not reveal which witness sk_c was used in its generation.

Output Integrity

Input: (a_1, a_2, pk, b_1, b_2)
Output: (b'_1, b'_2) satisfying that

- $(b_1, b_2) \neq (b'_1, b'_2)$,
- (b_1, b_2) is a pair of output generated from $Combine(a_1, a_2, sk)$, and
- (b'_1, b'_2) is another pair of output generated from $Combine(a_1, a_2, sk)$.

The fifth security model is output integrity. In this security model, given (a_1, a_2, b_1, b_2) and pk, the adversary is tasked with modifying the output into (b'_1, b'_2) while ensuring it remains a valid output of $Combine(a_1, a_2, sk)$. For example, the signing algorithm $Sign(sk, m) \to \sigma_m$ in digital signatures follows a similar security model, known as strong unforgeability, as defined in [9]. In this security model, given a signature $\sigma_m = (b_1, b_2)$ on $m = (a_1, a_2)$, the adversary cannot forge a valid signature $\sigma'_m = (b'_1, b'_2)$ different from σ_m.

7.4.7 Security Models for Public Seeing Algorithms

Let $See(x_1, x_2, x_3) \to (y_1, y_2)$ be the abstracted public seeing algorithm, which aims to "verify" input elements. We introduce three security models.

Input Confidentiality

Input: (a_1, a_3, b_1, b_2)
Output: a_2 satisfying that

- (b_1, b_2) is a pair of output generated from $See(a_1, a_2, a_3)$.

The first security model is input confidentiality. In this security model, given part of the input and its full output, the adversary is tasked with finding the remaining unknown input a_2. For example, the verifying algorithm $Verify(pk, m, \sigma_m)$ $\to 1/0$ in digital signatures should be secure in this security model. In particular, given $m = a_1$, $pk = a_3$, and $1 = (b_1, b_2)$, it should be hard for the adversary to find a valid signature $\sigma_m = a_2$ that can pass the validity check. In this security model for digital signatures, the condition $1 = (b_1, b_2)$ is necessary to prevent trivial attacks.

Learn-Nothing Confidentiality

Input: $(a_1, a_2, a_3, b_1, b_2)$
Output: s satisfying that

- $a_3 = pk$, and
- (b_1, b_2) is a pair of output generated from $See(a_1, a_2, a_3)$, and
- No PPT algorithm can compute s from pk.

The second security model is learn-nothing confidentiality. In this security model, the element s refers to any secret that cannot be computed from $a_3 = pk$ by any PPT adversary. This security model ensures that the adversary gains no additional information from the tuple (a_1, a_2, pk, b_1, b_2) beyond what can already be derived from pk. For example, the verification algorithm $Verify(\Sigma, pk) \to 1/0$ in non-interactive zero-knowledge proof (NIZKP) requires this security model. In particular, given proof $\Sigma = (a_1, a_2)$, statement $pk = a_3$, and $1 = (b_1, b_2)$, it is hard for the adversary to compute any s that cannot be computed from a_3. Notice that a random element set as Σ cannot pass the verification and it definitely cannot help the adversary learn something additional from $a_3 = pk$. Therefore, it is non-trivial to require $1 = (b_1, b_2)$ in this security model for NIZKP.

This is the first security model defining learn-nothing security. The security model is presented in a way like a computing problem that is friendly for beginners. The main challenge of this model lies in the uncertainty of output, which can refer to an infinite number of computational (search) problems. This contrasts with the clear success condition found in hidden-target security, and will therefore be revised later. The final security definition for learn-nothing security will be revised in Section 7.7 and become significantly different.

Input Integrity

Input: $(a_1, a_2, a_3, b_1, b_2)$
Output: (a_1', a_2') satisfying that

- $(a_1', a_2') \neq (a_1, a_2)$,
- (b_1, b_2) is a pair of output generated from $See(a_1, a_2, a_3)$, and
- (b_1, b_2) is also a pair of output generated from $See(a_1', a_2', a_3)$.

7.4 Defining Security for Non-Interactive Algorithms

The third security model is input integrity. In this security model, given a full tuple including all inputs and outputs, the adversary is tasked with changing input into (a_1', a_2') satisfying that $See(a_1, a_2, a_3) = See(a_1', a_2', a_3)$. For example, the verification algorithm $Verify(m, r, C_m) \to 1/0$ in the cryptographic primitive called *Commitment* [40] should be secure in this security model. In particular, given committed message $m = a_1$, random number $r = a_2$, commitment $C_m = a_3$, and $1 = (b_1, b_2)$, it is hard for the adversary who generated C_m to change the committed message into $m' = a_1'$ with $r' = a_2'$ satisfying $Verify(m', r', C_m) \to 1$. This security model also requires the condition $1 = (b_1, b_2)$ to prevent trivial attacks.

7.4.8 Security Models for Secret Seeing Algorithms

Let $See(x_1, x_2, sk) \to (y_1, y_2)$ be the abstracted secret combining algorithm which aims to "decrypt" input elements. We introduce two security models for this algorithm.

Output Confidentiality

Input: (a_1, a_2, pk)
Output: (b_1, b_2) satisfying that

- (b_1, b_2) is a pair of output generated from $See(a_1, a_2, sk)$.

The first security model is output confidentiality. In this security model for output confidentiality, given (a_1, a_2, pk), the adversary is tasked with finding the output (b_1, b_2) that is generated from $See(a_1, a_2, sk)$. For example, the decryption algorithm $Dec(CT, sk) \to m/\bot$ in public-key encryption should be secure in this security model. Specifically, given $CT = (a_1, a_2)$ and pk, it should be hard for the adversary to derive $m = (b_1, b_2)$ such that $Dec(CT, sk) \to m$. Notice that random elements set as CT will be rejected and returned a failure symbol by the decryption algorithm. Thus, it is non-trivial to require CT to be a valid ciphertext in this security model for public-key encryption.

Input Confidentiality

Input: (a_1, pk, b_1, b_2)
Output: a_2 satisfying that

- (b_1, b_2) is a pair of output generated from $See(a_1, a_2, sk)$.

The second security model is input confidentiality. In this security model, given part of the input and its full output, the adversary is tasked with finding its remaining input a_2. For example, the opening algorithm $Open(m, \sigma_m, sk) \to i$ in group signatures [8] should be secure in this security model. In this cryptographic primitive, a group signature σ_m on m can be generated by any group signing key gsk_i but can be verified using the same group public key pk. While sk can be used to open and see which group signing key has been used in generating σ_m. For group signatures, given $m = a_1$, pk, and $i = (b_1, b_2)$, it should be hard for the adversary to compute $\sigma_m = a_2$ satisfying $Open(m, \sigma_m, sk) \to i$. Otherwise, it means that an adversary could frame the i-th signer by forging σ_m such that $Open(m, \sigma_m, sk) \to i$.

7.5 Security Definition for a Cryptographic Primitive (Scheme)

In this section, we introduce how to define, select, or validate security models for a cryptographic primitive which is composed of multiple cryptographic algorithms. For beginners, it would be helpful to read some existing security models before reading the introduction in this section.

7.5.1 Challenges of Security Modelling

Defining security model(s) for a cryptographic primitive is similar to defining security model(s) for a cryptographic algorithm by clarifying

$$(x, \text{Oracle}, y, \text{Success Condition}),$$

where x and y denote the input and output in the framework of security model.

However, defining security model(s) for a cryptographic primitive is much more complicated than that for a cryptographic algorithm. There are two main reasons.

- Firstly, a cryptographic primitive is generally composed of multiple algorithms, and each algorithm has four types of security models to be considered. As a consequence, the number of security models is increased.
- Secondly, the security model for each algorithm has become complex. The adversary attempts to break an algorithm by leveraging other algorithms modelled as oracles. Oracles have made security models more complex, with numerous queries and responses that are not directly related to the studied algorithm.

Take functional IBE (Section 6.5.5) as an example. This cryptographic primitive is composed of algorithms $Setup(1^\kappa) \to (mpk, msk)$, $KeyGen(msk, ID, F) \to d_{ID,F}$, $Enc(mpk, ID, m) \to CT_{ID}$, and $Dec(mpk, CT_{ID}, d_{ID,F}) \to F(m)/\bot$. They consist of one public keying algorithm, one secret keying algorithm, one public combining algorithm, and one secret seeing algorithm. According to previous modelling for each algorithm, there will be at least eight security models in total. Regarding the second reason, when considering the input confidentiality of the encryption algorithm, the security model could include two oracles. The first oracle

7.5 Security Definition for a Cryptographic Primitive (Scheme)

allows the adversary (without knowing msk) to query private keys generated by the key generation algorithm using msk. The second oracle allows the adversary (without knowing $d_{ID,F}$) to query decryption results decrypted by the decryption algorithm using $d_{ID,F}$. Thus, defining the security of an algorithm must consider the influence of other algorithms modelled as oracles.

7.5.2 Overview of Security Modelling

As introduced in the above subsection, defining security models for a cryptographic primitive cannot simply follow the security models of individual algorithms due to the overall complexity. To address this challenge, we introduce a progressive approach to developing security model(s) for a cryptographic primitive in the following subsections.

This subsection provides an overview of the modelling process. It consists of 12 steps, divided into three phases.

- In the first phase, many basic security models will be proposed to define security requirements for each entity.
- In the second phase, security models will be selectively reinforced by modifying inputs, reducing the number of remaining security models.
- In the third phase, security models will be relaxed in terms of outputs and further reinforced in terms of inputs. The soundness of the security models will be verified before finalization.

The proposed modelling approach incorporates concepts such as security requirements, security attacks, element security, model implication, and user implication. They will be individually introduced before we present the modelling approach.

Security modelling is a highly complex process, primarily due to the uncertainty surrounding what needs to be protected and how it should be protected. When a new cryptographic primitive is introduced with a syntax definition, it is common to find that the security models proposed for this primitive by different researchers are usually not identical but only similar. We emphasize that the modelling approach presented in this book is not intended to teach beginners how to create fully correct security models for a given cryptographic primitive. Instead, it focuses on introducing methods to develop security models that address the essential security requirements of all entities and algorithms involved.

7.5.3 Security Requirements

Security requirements for a cryptographic primitive state that:
- Something (e.g., secret key) cannot be **extracted** by adversaries.

- Someone (e.g., signer or verifier) cannot be **framed** or **fooled** by adversaries.

Otherwise, adversaries will compromise confidentiality and/or integrity. These security requirements are general and high-level for all cryptographic primitives. It is important to note that any entity in a cryptographic primitive could act as an adversary unless it has nothing to extract, no one to frame, and no one to fool.

We provide examples to illustrate these two types of security requirements for cryptographic primitives in the initial stage, when each multi-user entity consists of a single user and each element type has only one instance. Each entity at this stage has already known some elements according to their role.

Example 1. In digital signatures, there are three entities: signer, verifier, and outsider. The verifier entity, who knows (pk, m, σ_m), cannot extract sk or forge a signature on a new message to frame the signer. The outsider entity, who knows (pk, m, σ_m), cannot extract sk or forge a signature on a new message to frame the signer and fool the verifier. The signer entity is not considered an adversary since the signer has nothing to extract, no one to frame, and no one to fool.

Example 2. In public-key encryption, there are three entities: receiver, sender, and outsider. The sender entity, who knows (pk, m, CT), cannot extract the receiver's secret sk. The outsider entity, who knows (pk, CT), cannot extract (sk, m). The receiver entity is not considered an adversary.

Example 3. In accountable IBE, there are four entities: PKG, receiver, sender, and outsider. The outsider entity, who knows (mpk, ID, CT_{ID}), cannot extract (msk, d_{ID}, m). The sender entity, who knows (mpk, ID, m, CT_{ID}), cannot extract (msk, d_{ID}). The receiver entity, who knows $(mpk, ID, d_{ID}, m, CT_{ID})$, cannot extract msk or change d_{ID} to a different d'_{ID} to frame the PKG entity. The PKG entity, who knows $(mpk, msk, ID, m, CT_{ID})$, cannot extract d_{ID} to frame the receiver entity.

Example 4. In escrow-free IBE, there are four entities: PKG, receiver, sender, and outsider. The outsider entity, who knows $(mpk, ID, pk, CT_{ID,pk})$, cannot extract (msk, d_{ID}, sk, m). The sender entity, who knows $(mpk, ID, pk, m, CT_{ID,pk})$, cannot extract (msk, d_{ID}, sk). The receiver entity, who knows $(mpk, ID, d_{ID}, pk, sk, m, CT_{ID,pk})$, cannot extract msk. The PKG entity, who knows $(mpk, msk, ID, d_{ID}, pk, CT_{ID,pk})$, cannot extract (sk, m).

Security requirements can be derived from the syntax definition. We introduce three aspects for exploring security requirements.

The first aspect lies in the correctness of the syntax definitions associated with seeing algorithms or forking algorithms. When entity A generates something for entity B to run a seeing algorithm, it requires that adversaries cannot extract secret belonging to B, frame entity A, or fool entity B. For example, in digital signatures, A generates a signature for B to verify. Adversaries cannot fool B or frame A by forging a valid signature on a new message. In public-key encryption, A generates a ciphertext for B to decrypt and see the plaintext. Adversaries cannot extract what B has secretly seen. Correctness serves as an indicator of the primary security requirements for each cryptographic primitive.

7.5 Security Definition for a Cryptographic Primitive (Scheme)

The second aspect is exploring security requirements for each cryptographic algorithm. Previously, we introduced four types of security models for cryptographic algorithms, namely output confidentiality, input confidentiality, output integrity, and input integrity. They have suggested how to extensively explore security requirements for each algorithm. In comparison with the first aspect, more security requirements could be explored from the second aspect. For example, take the encryption algorithm of IBE as an example. The encryption algorithm defines $Enc(mpk, ID, m) \to CT_{ID}$. The input confidentiality can also include the confidentiality of ID. That is, given (mpk, CT), an adversary cannot extract the receiver identity ID from this ciphertext. This kind of security is called anonymous IBE and has been defined in [24].

The third aspect is exploring security requirements for not only each cryptographic algorithm but also their interrelations. Take the encryption algorithm $Enc(mpk, ID, m) \to CT_{ID}$ in IBE as an example. An application scenario may require not only receiver anonymity from the perspective of a ciphertext but also the unlinkability of two ciphertexts. That is, given two ciphertexts, an adversary cannot extract the information whether these two ciphertexts have the same receiver. This kind of security has been defined in [15] for other cryptographic primitives.

This completes the introduction to where to explore security requirements. We emphasize that exploring detailed security requirements for a cryptographic primitive is rather complex. They should be carefully carried out by examining its application scenarios.

! **Attention**

Security requirements can be explored indefinitely. Instead of defining security at the highest possible level, we should tailor it to the specific needs of applications.

7.5.4 Security Attacks

In this book, security attacks refer to actions carried out by an adversary aiming to gain additional information to compromise security requirements. For example,

- The adversary uses passive attacks like eavesdropping to get elements like mpk, ID, CT_{ID} in IBE.
- The adversary uses active attacks like fooling the receiver ID to decrypt ciphertexts provided by the adversary to get their decryption results.

One might be confused about the distinction between security requirements and security attacks. We distinguish these two concepts as follows. When discussing a security requirement, we are primarily concerned with what adversaries cannot do from what they have been given. In contrast, when discussing a security attack, we primarily care what specific information adversaries can know through the attack.

We introduce the concept of security attacks because they can lead to the creation of new elements different from elements in syntax definition, which results in new security requirements. When an adversary frames or fools some other entities or users to do something, the victims may execute cryptographic algorithms using input elements (partially) provided by the adversary. These elements do not follow rules as defined in the syntax, and this results in new elements.

For example, in escrow-free IBE, a sender was fooled by an adversary to encrypt a sensitive message for receiver ID using a wrong public key pk^* provided by the adversary who knows its secret key sk^*. Then, security requirement requires that the adversary still cannot extract the encrypted sensitive message inside CT_{ID,pk^*}, which is a ciphertext different from $CT_{ID,pk}$ in its syntax definition.

> **! Attention**
>
> Security attacks allow adversaries to acquire additional information or knowledge before attempting to break it. The attacks could also generate new elements different from those elements appearing in the syntax definition. They could also lead to new security requirements.

7.5.5 Element Security

Overview

$$\left.\begin{array}{r}\text{Input Confidentiality}\\ \text{Output Confidentiality}\\ \text{Input Integrity}\\ \text{Output Integrity}\end{array}\right\} \rightarrow \text{Element Security} \rightarrow \left\{\begin{array}{l}\text{Finde } y \text{ outside } x\\ \\ \text{Change } z \in x \text{ into } y\end{array}\right.$$

In the previous section, we introduced four types of hidden-target security models for cryptographic algorithms. These fundamental security models are defined using input and output elements. We can abstract these fundamental security models into element security.

Let Δ be the set of all elements related to a cryptographic primitive. Element security asserts that, given a set of elements x as input, an adversary cannot compute element y. In the framework of the security model,

- x refers to a set of elements and is a subset of Δ.
- y refers to an element from Δ.

Otherwise, security will be compromised. We note that some security models involve guessing elements where y indicates which element has been used.

After taking security requirements into account, element security can be expanded into the following two questions:

7.5 Security Definition for a Cryptographic Primitive (Scheme)

> **? Questions**
>
> 1. On input x, will finding y outside x successfully attack another entity (user)?
> 2. On input x, will changing $z \in x$ into y successfully attack another entity (user)?

In the above two questions, it requires no trivial breaking or no way for computing y from x by running cryptographic algorithms. Generally speaking, only a subset of the elements in Δ need to be protected, but which elements need protection depends on the specific security application. If the answer to one of the two questions is positive according to security requirements, we should define (x, y) and its success condition into a security model.

The two questions above will play a key role in the proposed modelling approach. In the modelling process, all security models will be defined as either finding y outside x or changing $z \in x$ into y.

7.5.6 Model Implication

Let A and B be two security models presented as follows:

- Security Model A: On input x_A, output y_A.
- Security Model B: On input x_B, output y_B.

We say that security model A implies security model B (namely model implication) if a cryptographic primitive that is secure in security model A is also secure in security model B. In other words, if an adversary could break it in security model B, this adversary would also be able to break it in security model A. This implies that security model A is stronger than security model B. We write $x_A \Rightarrow y_A$ implies $x_B \Rightarrow y_B$ for short[2].

For two given security models A and B, we have security model A implies security model B if (1) $x_B \subseteq x_A$, and (2) y_B can be used to compute y_A. Take IBE as an example.

- $x_A = (mpk, ID, CT_{ID})$, $y_A = m$, where $CT_{ID} \leftarrow Enc(mpk, ID, m)$.
- $x_B = (mpk, ID)$, $y_B = d_{ID}$.

Suppose there exists an adversary $\mathcal{A}_{IBE}$ who can break IBE in the security model B. Given input x_A, we extract (mpk, ID) from x_A and provide it as input to the adversary $\mathcal{A}_{IBE}$, which should return $y_B = d_{ID}$. Then, we can use d_{ID} to decrypt CT_{ID} to get $y_A = m$. Therefore, we have security model A implies security model B. In general, model implication does not require $x_B \subseteq x_A$; instead, x_B must be computable from x_A under a reduction in complexity theory.

---

[2] The model implication means that it is easier for the adversary to break it in the security model $x_A \Rightarrow y_A$. It is harder to construct a secure scheme in the security model $x_A \Rightarrow y_A$. It is better for users to adopt a scheme secure in the security model $x_A \Rightarrow y_A$.

7.5.7 User Implication

Suppose there are only three entities, namely entity A, entity B, and entity C, attacking each other when modelling security for a cryptographic primitive. Furthermore, entity A is a multi-user entity, including users A_1 and A_2. When A_2 emulates A_1, they should have x_{A_1} and x_{A_2} with the same types of elements although they are not identical. For example, when A_2 emulates A_1 as a receiver in IBE, they both have private keys computed by the PKG, though their private keys correspond to different identities.

In this book, we introduce another unique concept called user implication, which is a generalization of model implication. On the condition that A_2 can emulate A_1, we have $x_{A_2} \Rightarrow y$ implying $x_{A_1} \Rightarrow y$ if y is the target at other entities (entity B or entity C). We use two examples to explain this concept.

- In IBE, the first sender knows $x_{S_1} = (mpk, ID, m_1, CT_{ID}^1)$ after generating CT_{ID}^1 on input (mpk, ID, m_1) and aims to find d_{ID}, which is the receiver's private key. The second sender emulates the first sender knowing $x_{S_2} = (mpk, ID, m_2, CT_{ID}^2)$ after generating CT_{ID}^2 on input (mpk, ID, m_2) and aiming to find d_{ID}. The user implication states that if the first sender can find the private key d_{ID}, then the second sender can also find d_{ID}.

- In IBE, the first receiver knows $x_{R_1} = (mpk, ID_1, d_{ID_1}, m_1, CT_{ID_1}^1)$ and aims to find msk, which is the PKG's master secret key. The second receiver emulates the first receiver knowing $x_{R_2} = (mpk, ID_2, d_{ID_2}, m_2, CT_{ID_2}^2)$ and aiming to find msk. Here, $CT_{ID_1}^1$ is a ciphertext for ID_1 on m_1 and $CT_{ID_2}^2$ is a ciphertext for ID_2 on m_2. The user implication states that if the first receiver can find msk, then the second receiver can also find msk.

For simplicity, we write $x_{E_2} \Rightarrow y$ implying $x_{E_1} \Rightarrow y$ to denote user implication, where x_{E_1} is the input of the first user of (multi-user) entity E and x_{E_2} is the input of the second user of entity E. It is important to note that user implication is only defined for attacking other entities. That is, computing y will compromise the security of users of other entities, not the i-th user E_i of the same entity for any i.

Model implication and user implication are important concepts in security modelling. With the help of these two concepts, we might be able to propose a strong model to replace many security models, as long as this strong security model implies all of these security models.

7.5.8 Security Modelling: First Phase

We now progressively introduce how security models are developed for a cryptographic primitive. In the first phase introduced in this subsection, many basic security models will be considered and developed to capture most security requirements.

7.5 Security Definition for a Cryptographic Primitive (Scheme)

Suppose that a cryptographic primitive with syntax definition is given along with potential security attacks and security requirements. The first phase of security modelling has four steps described as follows.

- **Step 1.** For each entity in this primitive, list the known elements according to the syntax definition and potential security attacks. We start with the very beginning stage when each multi-user entity has one user only and each type of element has one only. Then, we add new elements if security attacks would generate them. It is important to note that primitives like broadcast IBE must include n distinct receivers.
- **Step 2.** For each entity in this primitive, list the elements to be found or changed that will successfully attack other entities according to element security and security requirements. It is important to note that the finding lists and changing lists might not capture all security requirements. Those uncaptured security requirements should be noted and will be re-examined in the third phase.
- **Step 3.** Let $x \Rightarrow y$ denote that an entity having x aims to compute the element y. If $x_A \Rightarrow y_A$ implies $x_A \Rightarrow y'_A$, then remove y'_A from entity A's finding or changing list based on model implication. Apply this rule to all entities to reduce the number of elements in each entity's finding list and changing list.
- **Step 4.** If $x_A \Rightarrow y$ implies $x_B \Rightarrow y$, then remove y from entity B's finding or changing list due to model implication. Apply this rule to all entities to reduce redundancy of elements appearing in different entities' finding lists and changing lists.

For each remaining element y inside the finding list and changing list, there should be one security model $x \Rightarrow y$ for it. Generally speaking, a few security models should remain after Step 4.

In Step 1, we consider a known list with the minimum number of elements of the same type for efficient analysis. Take IBE as an example. It is not necessary for the sender entity to generate two ciphertexts CT^1_{ID}, CT^2_{ID} for the same identity ID if the outsider's goal is to extract the encrypted messages. This is because if the outsider can extract m_1 from (mpk, ID, CT^1_{ID}), it can also extract m_2 from (mpk, ID, CT^2_{ID}). They refer to the same computing problem but with different input instances.

We explain how Step 3 and Step 4 work for some selected primitives in Figure 7.2. We note that the explanation is based on lists created by the authors of this book, not the real lists according to security attacks and security requirements.

Example 1. In digital signatures, we have $x \Rightarrow (m^*, \sigma_{m^*})$ implies $x \Rightarrow sk$ in both the verifier's and the outsider's finding lists, and sk can be crossed out, denoted by $\cancel{sk}$. We also have that $x_V \Rightarrow (m^*, \sigma_{m^*})$ from the verifier implies $x_O \Rightarrow (m^*, \sigma_{m^*})$ from the outsider, and (m^*, σ_{m^*}) in the outsider's finding list can be crossed out, denoted by $\cancel{(m^*, \sigma_{m^*})}$. As a result, only one security model remains.

Example 2. In public-key encryption, we have $x_O \Rightarrow m$ implies $x_O \Rightarrow sk$ in the outsider's finding list, and sk can be crossed out. As a result, only only two security models remain.

Digital Signatures

Entities	Known List	Finding List	Changing List
Signer	–	–	–
Verifier	$\{pk, (m, \sigma_m)\}$	$\{~~sk~~, (m^*, \sigma_{m^*})\}$	–
Outsider	$\{pk, (m, \sigma_m)\}$	$\{~~sk~~, ~~(m^*, \sigma_{m^*})~~\}$	–

Public-Key Encryption

Entities	Known List	Finding List	Changing List
Receiver	–	–	–
Sender	$\{pk, m, CT\}$	$\{sk\}$	–
Outsider	$\{pk, CT\}$	$\{~~sk~~, m\}$	–

IBE

Entities	Known List	Finding List	Changing List
PKG	–	–	–
Sender	$\{mpk, ID, m, CT_{ID}\}$	$\{~~msk~~, d_{ID}\}$	–
Receiver	$\{mpk, ID, d_{ID}, m, CT_{ID}\}$	$\{msk\}$	–
Outsider	$\{mpk, ID, CT_{ID}\}$	$\{~~msk~~, ~~d_{ID}~~, m\}$	–

Functional IBE

Entities	Known List	Finding List	Changing List
PKG	–	–	–
Sender	$\{mpk, ID, F, m, CT_{ID}\}$	$\{~~msk~~, d_{ID,F}\}$	–
Receiver	$\{mpk, ID, F, d_{ID,F}, F(m), CT_{ID}\}$	$\{msk, m\}$	–
Outsider	$\{mpk, ID, F, CT_{ID}\}$	$\{~~msk~~, ~~d_{ID,F}~~, F(m), ~~m~~\}$	–

Accountable IBE

Entities	Known List	Finding List	Changing List
PKG	$\{mpk, msk, ID, m, CT_{ID}\}$	$\{d_{ID}\}$	–
Sender	$\{mpk, ID, m, CT_{ID}\}$	$\{~~msk~~, ~~d_{ID}~~, ~~d_{ID}~~\}$	–
Receiver	$\{mpk, ID, d_{ID}, m, CT_{ID}\}$	$\{msk\}$	$\{d_{ID}\}$
Outsider	$\{mpk, ID, CT_{ID}\}$	$\{~~msk~~, ~~d_{ID}~~, m\}$	–

Escrow-Free IBE

Entities	Known List	Finding List	Changing List
PKG	$\{mpk, msk, ID, d_{ID}, pk, CT_{ID,pk}\}$	$\{~~sk~~, m\}$	–
Sender	$\{mpk, ID, pk, m, CT_{ID,pk}\}$	$\{~~msk~~, d_{ID}, sk\}$	–
Receiver	$\{mpk, ID, d_{ID}, pk, sk, m, CT_{ID,pk}\}$	$\{msk\}$	–
Outsider	$\{mpk, ID, pk, CT_{ID,pk}\}$	$\{~~msk~~, ~~d_{ID}~~, sk, m\}$	–

Fig. 7.2 Examples of security modelling in the first phase

7.5 Security Definition for a Cryptographic Primitive (Scheme)

Example 3. In IBE, we have $x_O \Rightarrow m$ implies $x_O \Rightarrow d_{ID}$ and $x_O \Rightarrow msk$ in the outsider's list, and (msk, d_{ID}) can be crossed out. Similarly, in the sender's finding list, msk is also crossed out. Only three security models remain. We note that the current lists cannot be used to define security requirements for the unlinkability of receivers in different ciphertexts.

Example 4. In functional IBE, after Step 3, msk in the sender's and the outsider's finding lists are crossed out. The element $d_{ID,F}$ in the outsider's finding list is also crossed out. After Step 4, m in the outsider's finding list is crossed out because $x_R \Rightarrow m$ implies $x_O \Rightarrow m$. As a result, four security models remain.

Example 5. In accountable IBE, after Step 3, (msk, d_{ID}) in the outsider's finding list are crossed out due to implication by $x_O \Rightarrow m$. The element msk in the sender's finding list is crossed out because it is implied by $x_S \Rightarrow d_{ID}$. After Step 4, d_{ID} in the sender's finding list is crossed out because it is implied by $x_P \Rightarrow d_{ID}$. The receiver's changing list in this primitive is not empty, containing d_{ID}, and $x_R \Rightarrow d'_{ID}$ implies $x_S \Rightarrow d'_{ID}$, where $d'_{ID} \neq d_{ID}$ is another valid private key of ID. Then, d'_{ID} in the sender's finding list can be crossed out. As a result, four security models remain.

Example 6. In escrow-free IBE, after Step 3, msk in the sender's and the outsider's finding lists are crossed out. The element sk in the PKG's finding list is crossed out because $x_P \Rightarrow sk$ is implied by $x_P \Rightarrow m$. After Step 4, d_{ID} in the outsider's finding list is crossed out because $x_O \Rightarrow d_{ID}$ is implied by $x_S \Rightarrow d_{ID}$. The elements (sk, m) in the outsider's finding list are crossed out because they are implied by $x_P \Rightarrow (sk, m)$. As a result, four security models remain.

The introduced security modelling in this phase has the following disadvantages.

- The number of security models is still large although part of them have been removed using model implication. We aim to further reduce the number of security models in the next phase.
- These security models are not strong enough because what the adversary knows inside the input x is quite limited. Adversaries in the real-world could run security attacks to enlarge the input x.

Although security models developed in this phase are not perfect, they are useful for validation. Suppose there exists a security model claimed to encompass all security protections. We can validate this model by checking whether it implies all security models after Step 4 in this phase.

7.5.9 Security Modelling: Second Phase

The security modelling in the second phase aims to selectively strengthen certain security models by reinforcing their inputs, thereby allowing unselected security models to be removed through model implication or user implication.

There are four main changes in this phase. First, an entity is allowed to have multiple users if it is a multi-user entity. Second, the adversary aims to attack one of the entity users not an entity. Third, the adversary can impersonate another entity user if there is no trivial breaking. Here, impersonation is one kind of security attack. Lastly, we generalize part of the elements in the known list into oracles for formalization.

To provide a brief introduction to advancing security models in this phase, we assume there are three entities: adversary, multi-user entity A, and multi-user entity B. Notice that entities A and B are also adversaries (they are attacking each other) but we focus on the adversary entity. The second phase consists of four steps described as follows.

- **Step 5.** Let $x \Rightarrow y$ be one of security models defined for the adversary entity, and $x_A \Rightarrow y_A$ be one of security models defined for the first user of entity A. We should allow the adversary to impersonate another user of entity A to get x_{A_2} if $x \cup x_{A_2} \Rightarrow y$ implies $x_A \Rightarrow y_A$. Therefore, two security models $x \Rightarrow y$ and $x_A \Rightarrow y_A$ are reduced to one security model denoted by $x \cup x_{A_2} \Rightarrow y$. This approach should be applied to examine and reduce other security models.

- **Step 6.** Let $Alg(x_1, x_2, x_3) \to (y_1, y_2)$ be the abstracted public (keying, combining, seeing) algorithm. Let x be the input of the investigated security model. If $\{a_1, a_2, a_3, b_1, b_2\} \subseteq x$ satisfies $Alg(a_1, a_2, a_3) \to (b_1, b_2)$, all these five elements can be removed from x. This is because the adversary can run this algorithm by itself to generate these elements.

- **Step 7.** Let $Alg(x_1, x_2, sk) \to (y_1, y_2)$ be the abstracted secret (keying, combining, seeing) algorithm. Let x be the input of the investigated security model. If $\{a_1, a_2, b_1, b_2\} \subseteq x$ satisfies $Alg(a_1, a_2, sk) \to (b_1, b_2)$ and sk is unknown to the adversary, these four elements can be extracted from x and generalized into an oracle that on input (a_1, a_2), it returns (b_1, b_2).

- **Step 8.** For each element inside security model $x \Rightarrow y$, clarify the source of this element. At this stage, an element will be chosen by the adversary, randomly chosen from its space, or generated by cryptographic algorithms. For each oracle, restrictions should be clearly stated to avoid any trivial breaking.

Generally speaking, after Step 8, we should be able to obtain fewer but stronger security models that imply all security models produced in the first phase.

Step 5 is somewhat complex. We illustrate how it works in this phase using selected cryptographic primitives, as shown in Figure 7.3.

Example 1. In public-key encryption, the outsider impersonates the second sender knowing (pk, m_2, CT_2) which is generated using the same pk but a different message m_2. We have $x_O \cup x_{S_2} \Rightarrow m$ implies $x_O \cup x_{S_2} \Rightarrow sk$ which implies $x_S \Rightarrow sk$. Therefore, sk in the sender's finding list can be crossed out, denoted by $\cancel{sk}$. Only one security model remains. Roughly speaking, the security model says that an adversary who is given (pk, CT, m_2, CT_2) is tasked with finding the encrypted message m inside CT. The security model $x_O \cup x_{S_2} \Rightarrow m$ has implied the previous two security models $x_O \Rightarrow m$ and $x_S \Rightarrow sk$.

Example 2. In IBE, the outsider impersonates the second sender knowing $(mpk, ID, m_2, CT_{ID}^2)$ which is generated using the same (mpk, ID) but a different mes-

7.5 Security Definition for a Cryptographic Primitive (Scheme)

Public-Key Encryption

Entities	Known List	Finding List	Changing List
Receiver	–	–	–
Sender	$\{pk, m, CT\}$	$\{~~sk~~\}$	–
Outsider + Sender 2	$\{pk, CT\} + \{pk, m_2, CT_2\}$	$\{~~sk~~, m\}$	–

IBE

Entities	Known List	Finding List	Changing List
PKG	–	–	–
Sender	$\{mpk, ID, m, CT_{ID}\}$	$\{~~msk~~, ~~d_{ID}~~\}$	–
Receiver	$\{mpk, ID, d_{ID}, m, CT_{ID}\}$	$\{~~msk~~\}$	–
Outsider + Sender 2 + Receiver 2	$\{mpk, ID, CT_{ID}\} +$ $\{mpk, ID, m_2, CT_{ID}^2\} +$ $\{mpk, ID_2, d_{ID_2}, m_2, CT_{ID_2}^2\}$	$\{~~msk~~, ~~d_{ID}~~, m\}$	–

Functional IBE

Entities	Known List	Finding List	Changing List
PKG	–	–	–
Sender	$\{mpk, ID, F, m, CT_{ID}\}$	$\{~~msk~~, ~~d_{ID,F}~~\}$	–
Receiver	$\{mpk, ID, F, d_{ID,F}, F(m), CT_{ID}\}$	$\{~~msk~~, m\}$	–
Outsider + Sender 2 + Receiver 2	$\{mpk, ID, F, CT_{ID}\} +$ $\{mpk, ID, F, m_2, CT_{ID}^2\} +$ $\{mpk, ID_2, F, d_{ID_2,F}, F(m_2), CT_{ID_2}^2\}$	$\{~~msk~~, ~~d_{ID,F}~~,$ $F(m), ~~m~~\}$	–

Accountable IBE

Entities	Known List	Finding List	Changing List
PKG	$\{mpk, msk, ID, m, CT_{ID}\}$	$\{d_{ID}\}$	–
Sender	$\{mpk, ID, m, CT_{ID}\}$	$\{~~msk~~, ~~d_{ID}~~, d'_{ID}\}$	–
Receiver	$\{mpk, ID, d_{ID}, m, CT_{ID}\}$	$\{~~msk~~\}$	$\{d_{ID}\}$
Outsider + Receiver 2	$\{mpk, ID, CT_{ID}\} +$ $\{mpk, ID_2, d_{ID_2}, m_2, CT_{ID_2}^2\}$	$\{~~msk~~, ~~d_{ID}~~, m\}$	–

Escrow-Free IBE

Entities	Known List	Finding List	Changing List
PKG + Sender 2 + Receiver 3	$\{mpk, msk, ID, d_{ID}, pk, CT_{ID,pk}\} +$ $\{mpk, ID, pk, m_3, CT_{ID,pk}^3\} +$ $\{mpk, ID_3, d_{ID_3}, pk_3, sk_3,$ $m_3, CT_{ID_3,pk_3}\}$	$\{~~sk~~, m\}$	–
Sender + Receiver 2	$\{mpk, ID, pk, m, CT_{ID,pk}\} +$ $\{mpk, ID_2, d_{ID_2}, pk_2, sk_2,$ $m_2, CT_{ID_2,pk_2}\}$	$\{~~msk~~, d_{ID}, ~~sk~~\}$	–
Receiver	$\{mpk, ID, d_{ID}, pk, sk, m, CT_{ID,pk}\}$	$\{~~msk~~\}$	–
Outsider	$\{mpk, ID, pk, CT_{ID,pk}\}$	$\{~~msk~~, ~~d_{ID}~~, sk, ~~m~~\}$	–

Fig. 7.3 Examples of security modelling within Step 5

sage m_2. The outsider also impersonates the second receiver knowing $(mpk, ID_2, d_{ID_2}, m_2, CT^2_{ID_2})$ where (ID_2, d_{ID_2}) is generated by the PKG and $CT^2_{ID_2}$ is generated by the outsider itself for (ID_2, m_2). We have $x_O \cup x_{S_2} \cup x_{R_2} \Rightarrow m$ implies $x_S \Rightarrow d_{ID}$ and $x_R \Rightarrow msk$. Therefore, d_{ID} in the sender's finding list can be crossed out denoted by ~~d_{ID}~~, and msk in the receiver's finding list can be crossed out denoted by ~~msk~~. Only one security model remains. Roughly speaking, the security model says that an adversary who is given $(mpk, ID, CT_{ID}, m_2, CT^2_{ID}, ID_2, d_{ID_2}, CT^2_{ID_2})$ is tasked with finding the encrypted message m inside CT_{ID}. The security model $x_O \cup x_{S_2} \cup x_{R_2} \Rightarrow m$ has implied the previous three security models $x_O \Rightarrow m$, $x_S \Rightarrow d_{ID}$, and $x_R \Rightarrow msk$.

Example 3. In functional IBE, the outsider can impersonate the second sender and the second receiver such that the element $d_{ID,F}$ in the sender's finding list and msk in the receiver's finding list can be crossed out. The security model $x_O \cup x_{S_2} \cup x_{R_2} \Rightarrow F(m)$ has implied the previous three security models $x_O \Rightarrow F(m)$, $x_S \Rightarrow d_{ID,F}$, and $x_R \Rightarrow msk$. The target m in the receiver's finding list cannot be crossed out because $x_{R_2} \Rightarrow m_2$ does not imply $x_R \Rightarrow m$ (the outsider cannot impersonate the second receiver with unknown m but a different message m_2). Two security models remain and these are two essential security models for functional IBE, which cannot be further combined into one.

Example 4. In accountable IBE, the outsider can impersonate the second receiver such that the element msk in the receiver's finding list can be crossed out. That is, the new security model $x_O \cup x_{R_2} \Rightarrow m$ has implied the previous two security models $x_O \Rightarrow m$ and $x_R \Rightarrow msk$. Three security models remain. Two security models define that d_{ID} cannot be found by the PKG or changed by the receiver. The outsider cannot impersonate another user of PKG entity because this single-user entity has one user only.

Example 5. In escrow-free IBE, the sender can impersonate the second receiver such that the element msk in the receiver's finding list can be crossed out. That is, the new security model $x_S \cup x_{R_2} \Rightarrow d_{ID}$ has implied the previous two security models $x_S \Rightarrow d_{ID}$ and $x_R \Rightarrow msk$. The PKG can impersonate the third sender and the third receiver such that the target sk in the sender's finding list can be crossed out. That is, the new security model $x_P \cup x_{S_3} \cup x_{R_3} \Rightarrow m$ has implied the previous two security models $x_P \Rightarrow m$ and $x_S \cup x_{R_2} \Rightarrow sk$. Two security models are left.

We explain how Step 6, Step 7, and Step 8 work using IBE as an example. The security model $x_O \cup x_{S_2} \cup x_{R_2} \Rightarrow m$ after Step 5 will be revised into $x + \mathcal{O}_K \Rightarrow m$ after Step 8. The details are explained as follows.

- The elements $\{m_2, CT^2_{ID}\}$ in x_{S_2} and $\{m_2, CT^2_{ID_2}\}$ in x_{R_2} will be removed because they can be generated by the adversary itself by running the encryption algorithm.
- The elements $\{ID_2, d_{ID_2}\}$ in x_{R_2} will be generalized into an oracle $\mathcal{O}_K$ that on input an identity ID_i, it returns a private key $d_{ID_i} \leftarrow KeyGen(msk, ID_i)$.
- The input $x_O \cup x_{S_2} \cup x_{R_2}$ is updated with $x = (mpk, ID, CT_{ID})$, where (mpk, msk) is a master key pair generated by the setup algorithm, and CT_{ID} is generated from the encryption algorithm on input (mpk, ID, m) for randomly

7.5 Security Definition for a Cryptographic Primitive (Scheme)   195

chosen (ID, m). The adversary is not allowed to query ID to the oracle $\mathcal{O}_K$ due to trivial breaking.

Therefore, after Step 8, the security model becomes $x + \mathcal{O}_K \Rightarrow m$ and the success condition is that m is the encrypted message in CT_{ID}.

This completes the introduction to security modelling in the second phase. The security models after the second phase are fewer but stronger because the adversary can impersonate one of the users of other entities to enlarge x. After this phase, we should obtain security models showing what elements should be included in x, which oracles the adversary can access, and what its target y is.

7.5.10 Security Modelling: Third Phase

The security modelling in the third phase aims to further strength security models by relaxing and re-reinforcing and then finalize all security models. This phase has four steps.

- **Step 9.** Let $x + \mathcal{O} \Rightarrow y$ be a security model. Relax (x, y) into (x_r, y_r) such that $x_r + \mathcal{O} \Rightarrow y_r$ implies $x + \mathcal{O} \Rightarrow y$. In particular, we could allow the adversary to choose elements instead of being randomly chosen.
- **Step 10.** Generalize other oracles for the adversary to access as long as there is no trivial breaking. This will further reinforce what the adversary knows (can query) before breaking.
- **Step 11.** Check those uncaptured security requirements in Step 2. If they have been implied by security models after Step 10, there is no need to do anything additional. Otherwise, new security model should be proposed to define security for uncaptured security requirements.
- **Step 12.** Finalize security models including checking success condition to avoid trivial breaking and formulating advantage.

We might need to repeat the first three steps in this phase to adjust a security model until a satisfactory version has been developed. The first three steps are not very clear because they significantly depend on syntax definition, security attacks, and security requirements.

Take IBE as an example. So far, the security model is $x + \mathcal{O}_K \Rightarrow m$ where $x = (mpk, ID, CT_{ID})$ and $CT_{ID} \leftarrow Enc(mpk, ID, m)$.

- Within Step 9, we can allow the adversary to choose arbitrary ID instead of being randomly chosen. We can allow the adversary to set message space as small as having any two messages $\{m_0, m_1\}$. That is, the adversary is to guess $m \in \{m_0, m_1\}$ inside CT_{ID}, which is equivalent to guessing the bit (0 or 1) of chosen message.

- Within Step 10, another secret algorithm that has not yet been generalized into oracle is the decryption algorithm. We can also set this decryption algorithm as an oracle $\mathcal{O}_D$ that on input (ID_i, CT_{ID_i}), it returns decryption results by running the algorithm $Dec(mpk, d_{ID_i}, CT_{ID_i})$ where d_{ID_i} is generated by the algorithm $KeyGen(msk, ID_i)$. To avoid trivial breaking, no query on (ID, CT_{ID}) is allowed to this oracle.

We skip the explanation of Step 11. The Step 12 has been previously mentioned when introducing security models. We will introduce how to present finalized security models after Step 12 using IBE as an example at the end of this section.

7.5.11 Discussions on Modelling

Any change in syntax definition, security attacks, and security requirements for the cryptographic primitive could affect the known list, finding list, and changing list of each entity. For example, some cryptographic primitives have been considered security against side-channel attacks [4], which help the adversary eavesdrop some secrets related to secret keys. In the corresponding security model, the adversary is allowed to query a leakage function $f()$ to a leakage oracle that on input arbitrary function f satisfying some restrictions, it returns $f(sk)$.

We also found that some cryptographic primitives have ignored those non-critical abuses in the context of correctness to release security requirements and simplify modelling. For example, in searchable IBE, the adversary could generate a special ciphertext CT^* such that $Search(mpk, CT^*, T_{ID'}^{w'}) = 1$ for any ID' and w'. However, we have not yet found any security requirement or security definition addressing this type of security attack for this cryptographic primitive in the literature.

It is important to note that the cryptology community acknowledges the existence of variant security models for the same cryptographic primitive. This is because different factors have been considered in the modelling, including security attacks, security requirements, reinforcing approach, and relaxing approach. It also seems impossible to define the strongest security model for a cryptographic primitive. This is because researchers can always find new motivations (e.g., new attacks) to advance existing security models.

7.5.12 Ways of Presenting Security Models

Suppose the input, oracle, output, and success condition have been well-defined after security modelling. The next task is how to present the security model in a clear and user-friendly manner for a cryptographic primitive.

In this section, we take IBE as an example and introduce several methods of presenting a security model named as indistinguishability against adaptive identity and chosen-ciphertext attacks (IND-ID-CCA for short). In Section 7.3.7, we introduced

7.5 Security Definition for a Cryptographic Primitive (Scheme)

the formulation of the success probability for breaking it in a security model. In this subsection, security model presentations can be viewed as approaches to achieving a formal and comprehensive formulation of this success probability.

Overview

$$\text{Security Model Presentations} = \begin{cases} \text{Input-output Description} \\ \text{Game-based Description} \\ \text{Experiment-based Description} \\ \text{Probability-based Description} \end{cases}$$

The first way of presentation is using the input-output framework of the security model, as depicted in Figure 7.4. This kind of presentation is clear in terms of input and output, similar to defining a computing problem in complexity theory. However, this model presentation becomes complex when the security model involves multiple oracles with different restrictions (to exclude trivial breaking). Additionally, the input-output presentation becomes less effective when the relation between input and output is not clear or straightforward. While we use this approach as an entry point to introduce security model, we do not recommend it as the primary presentation for security models.

Input: $(mpk, \mathcal{O}_K, \mathcal{O}_E, \mathcal{O}_D)$
Output: $c' \in \{0, 1\}$ satisfying that

- (mpk, msk) is a key pair generated from the *Setup* algorithm,
- $c' = c$, c is randomly chosen from $\{0, 1\}$ by $\mathcal{O}_E$,
- No query on ID^* to $\mathcal{O}_K$, and
- No query on (ID^*, CT_{ID^*}) to $\mathcal{O}_D$.

Oracle $\mathcal{O}_K$: On input ID, it returns $d_{ID} \leftarrow KeyGen(msk, ID)$.

Oracle $\mathcal{O}_E$: On input (ID^*, m_0, m_1), it randomly chooses a bit $c \in \{0, 1\}$ and returns $CT_{ID^*} \leftarrow Enc(mpk, ID^*, m_c)$. This oracle can only be queried once.

Oracle $\mathcal{O}_D$: On input (ID, CT), it generates private key $d_{ID} \leftarrow KeyGen(msk, ID)$ and returns $m/\bot \leftarrow Dec(mpk, CT, d_{ID})$.

The advantage ϵ of the adversary in breaking IBE is defined as follows:

$$\epsilon = \left| \Pr\left[c' \leftarrow \mathcal{A}^{\mathcal{O}_K, \mathcal{O}_E, \mathcal{O}_D}(mpk) : c' = c \right] - \frac{1}{2} \right|.$$

Fig. 7.4 Input-output description

The second way of presentation is using a game played between an adversary and a challenger, as depicted in Figure 7.5. The game is divided into several phases, with each phase presented alongside a text description of the interactions. The challenger generates the inputs for the adversary and also serves as the entity (namely oracle) to answer queries from the adversary. This presentation is no longer like an input-output computing problem. However, what the adversary knows and aims to achieve are clearly explained in text. This presentation employs a game-based framework as an external description to define the success probability and is likely the most beginner-friendly approach.

Setup. The challenger runs the setup algorithm to generate (mpk, msk) and sends mpk to the adversary. The challenger keeps msk to respond to queries from the adversary.

Phase 1. The adversary makes private-key queries and decryption queries, where identities and ciphertexts are adaptively chosen by the adversary itself.

- For a private-key query on ID_i, the challenger runs the key generation algorithm on ID_i with the master secret key msk and then sends d_{ID_i} to the adversary.

- For a decryption query on (ID_i, CT_i), the challenger runs the decryption algorithm with the private key d_{ID_i} and then sends the decryption result to the adversary. The challenger should generate the private key first if it has not yet been computed.

Challenge. The adversary outputs two distinct messages m_0, m_1 from the same message space and an identity ID^* to be challenged, where m_0, m_1, ID^* are all adaptively chosen by the adversary itself. We require that the private key of ID^* has not been queried in Phase 1. The challenger randomly chooses $c \in \{0, 1\}$ and then computes a challenge ciphertext $CT_{ID^*} = Enc(mpk, ID^*, m_c)$, which is given to the adversary.

Phase 2. The challenger responds to private-key queries and decryption queries in the same way as in Phase 1 with the restriction that no private-key query is allowed on ID^* and no decryption query is allowed on (ID^*, CT_{ID^*}).

Guess. The adversary outputs a guess c' of c and wins the game if $c' = c$.

The advantage ϵ of the adversary in breaking IBE is defined as follows:

$$\epsilon = \Pr\left[c' = c\right] - \frac{1}{2}.$$

Fig. 7.5 Game-based description

The third way of presentation is using an experiment, as depicted in Figure 7.6. The experiment is performed or conducted by following the steps from the beginning to the end. All descriptions are formally presented with probabilities and algorithms. In this model, $\mathcal{K}$ and $\mathcal{D}$ are two sets defined to easily present success condition and query restrictions, which are placed after $c' = c$. This differs from the game-based description, where restrictions are distributed across the corresponding phases. This type of presentation uses experiment as the external description to define the success probability of breaking. It is not beginner-friendly but is much more compact and formal compared to the game-based description.

7.5 Security Definition for a Cryptographic Primitive (Scheme)

Experiment $\text{Exp}_{\mathcal{A}}^{\text{IND-ID-CCA}}(1^\kappa)$

1. $\mathcal{K} = \mathcal{D} = \emptyset$
2. $(mpk, msk) \leftarrow Setup(1^\kappa)$
3. $(ID^*, m_0, m_1) \leftarrow \mathcal{A}^{\mathcal{O}_K, \mathcal{O}_D}(mpk)$
4. $c \leftarrow \{0, 1\}, CT_{ID^*} \leftarrow Enc(mpk, ID^*, m_c)$
5. $c' \leftarrow \mathcal{A}^{\mathcal{O}_K, \mathcal{O}_D}(mpk, ID^*, m_0, m_1, CT_{ID^*})$
6. Output 1 if $c' = c$, $ID^* \notin \mathcal{K}$, and $(ID^*, CT_{ID^*}) \notin \mathcal{D}$; otherwise, output 0

$\mathcal{O}_K(ID)$

1. $\mathcal{K} = \mathcal{K} \cup \{ID\}$
2. $d_{ID} \leftarrow KeyGen(msk, ID)$
3. Return d_{ID}

$\mathcal{O}_D(ID, CT)$

1. $\mathcal{D} = \mathcal{D} \cup \{(ID, CT)\}$
2. $d_{ID} \leftarrow KeyGen(msk, ID)$
3. $R \leftarrow Dec(mpk, CT, d_{ID})$
4. Return R

The advantage ϵ of the adversary in breaking IBE is defined as follows:

$$\epsilon = \Pr\left[\text{Exp}_{\mathcal{A}}^{\text{IND-ID-CCA}}(1^\kappa) = 1\right] - \frac{1}{2}.$$

Fig. 7.6 Experiment-based description

The last way of presentation is using probability, as depicted in Figure 7.7. There is no space within the probability formula to hold the description of oracles and their query restrictions. The oracles and their query restrictions are described outside the formula using a text statement. This presentation is less formal but still acceptable by the cryptology community.

The advantage ϵ of the adversary in breaking IBE is defined as follows:

$$\epsilon = \Pr\left[\begin{array}{l}(mpk, msk) \leftarrow Setup(1^\kappa) \\ (ID^*, m_0, m_1) \leftarrow \mathcal{A}^{\mathcal{O}_K, \mathcal{O}_D}(mpk) \\ c \leftarrow \{0, 1\} \\ CT_{ID^*} \leftarrow Enc(mpk, ID^*, m_c) \\ c' \leftarrow \mathcal{A}^{\mathcal{O}_K, \mathcal{O}_D}(mpk, ID^*, m_0, m_1, CT_{ID^*})\end{array} : c' = c\right] - \frac{1}{2},$$

where $\mathcal{O}_K, \mathcal{O}_D$ are oracles for private key queries and decryption queries.

- On input any identity ID, the oracle $\mathcal{O}_K$ returns $d_{ID} \leftarrow KeyGen(msk, ID)$. A query on ID^* to this oracle is not allowed.
- On input (ID, CT), the oracle $\mathcal{O}_D$ generates private key $d_{ID} \leftarrow KeyGen(msk, ID)$ and returns $m/\bot \leftarrow Dec(mpk, CT, d_{ID})$. A query on (ID^*, CT^*) to this oracle is not allowed.

Fig. 7.7 Probability-based description

7.6 Defining Security for Interactive Algorithms

In this section, we introduce how to define security for interactive algorithms. The security goals can be either hidden-target security or learn-nothing security. We will discuss both of their security definitions.

7.6.1 Algorithm Abstraction

Previously, we introduced interactive algorithm where more than one party collaborates, with (or without) a secret as input, to compute some output. In the algorithm abstraction for this kind of interactive algorithms in this book, we focus on two-party interactive algorithm defined as follows:

$$Alg(x_1; x_2) \to (y_1, y_2),$$

where

- $x_i \in \{1, 2\}$ denotes the secret from party i,
- $y_i = f_i(x_1, x_2), i \in \{1, 2\}$, and
- f_1, f_2 are two deterministic functions defined inside the algorithm Alg.

Inside the abstracted algorithm, we use the symbol ";" to separate the inputs from each party.

It is important to note that f_1 and f_2 could represent two very general functions in this abstraction. For example, an interactive algorithm with integers as input is designed to compute the following result for the first party:

$$f_1(x_1, x_2) = \begin{cases} -1 & \text{if } \quad x_1 - x_2 < -10 \\ x_2 & \text{if } -10 \leq x_1 - x_2 \leq 10 \\ 1 & \text{if } \quad 10 < x_1 - x_2 \end{cases}.$$

That is, the first party, given input x_1, will receive -1, x_2, or 1 depending on the gap between x_1 and x_2. In short, these general functions may not protect secret inputs. This example actually has implied the core reason why security definition for protocols is different from that for schemes.

A specific case of the above abstracted algorithm is

$$Alg(x_1; x_2) \to (y, y),$$

where $y = f(x_1, x_2)$. We must highlight this case because the security requirements for this abstracted algorithm are not identical to those of $Alg(x_1; x_2) \to (y_1, y_2)$ when applied in real-world scenarios.

7.6 Defining Security for Interactive Algorithms   201

7.6.2 Adversary and Security Goal

The adversary against a two-party interactive algorithm could be one of the following three types of users:

- The first party who attempts to break the security protections for the second party.
- The second party who attempts to break the security protections for the first party.
- Any third party who attempts to break the security protections for both parties.

In some references outside this book, each party is not considered the adversary but rather a corrupted party that helps the third-party adversary break the security of the other party. These two descriptions of security are equivalent.

The security of interactive algorithms primarily focuses on confidentiality, encompassing both output confidentiality and input confidentiality. The security goals include hidden-target security and learn-nothing security, with the latter taking a more dominant role.

- For the abstracted algorithm $Alg(x_1; x_2) \to (y, y)$, one of the main applications is key exchange, where two parties can generate a shared secret key y for future cryptographic use. The security goal of this algorithm is to preserve the hidden target y against a third-party adversary. It is not essential to define learn-nothing security, especially when the learnt secret $F(y)$ related to y (for example, F being a cryptographic hash function) is useless for breaking secure communications using the secret key y. On the other hand, given y, no party (e.g., the first party) should be able to compute secrets related to the other party's input x_i (e.g., the second party) to compromise the security of that party.

- For the abstracted algorithm $Alg(x_1; x_2) \to (y_1, y_2)$, there is no specific application (like key exchange) for this and we need to consider the security in general. The security goal, therefore, is to prevent each party from learning more than the returned output. That is, the first party cannot learn more than (x_1, y_1), while the second party cannot learn more than (x_2, y_2). We note that it is not necessary to consider the security against any third party, as the security has been implicitly covered. If an algorithm is secure against the second party, it is certainly secure against a third party, who knows less than the second party.

Regarding integrity, input integrity means that the adversary cannot alter the input (x_1, x_2) for a given output (y_1, y_2), and output integrity means that the adversary cannot alter the output (y_1, y_2) for a given input. This book focuses on confidentiality because integrity is less studied in the cryptology community.

We have introduced who the adversary is and what the adversary is going to output in the above introduction. The next step is to introduce what the adversary knows for breaking security. We would like to highlight two commonly overlooked inputs in the frameworks of security models for interactive algorithms.

- We use ic_i to denote the internal coins (random numbers) chosen by party i when running the interactive algorithm with another party.

- We use IC to denote the intermediate communicated messages in all moves sent between the two parties and produced by the interactive algorithm.

That is, when defining a security model against party i as the adversary, we should assume that the adversary (party i) also knows ic_i and IC as part of the input when trying to break the security of this algorithm.

Summary

$$\left\{\begin{array}{l} \text{Adversary} \left\{\begin{array}{l} \text{First Party} \\ \text{Second Party} \\ \text{Any Third Party} \end{array}\right. \\ \text{Security Goal} \left\{\begin{array}{l} \text{Hidden-target Security for } Alg(x_1; x_2) \to (y, y) \\ \text{Learn-nothing Security for } Alg(x_1; x_2) \to (y_1, y_2) \end{array}\right. \\ \text{Easily-overlooked Input} \left\{\begin{array}{l} \text{Internal Coins (Random Number) } ic_i \\ \text{Communication Messages } IC \end{array}\right. \end{array}\right.$$

7.6.3 Hidden-Target Security for $Alg(x_1; x_2) \to (y, y)$

We first introduce a security model against a third party who is trying to compute the output without having input but communicated message only. The security model is presented as follows:

Output Confidentiality

Input: IC
Output: b satisfying that

- IC is the communication data by the algorithm for generating b, and
- (b, b) is a pair of output generated from $Alg(a_1; a_2)$.

In this security model, given IC, the adversary is to compute b. This is a very basic security model. For example, IC contains g^{a_1} sent from the first party to the second party and g^{a_2} sent from the second party to the first party, where $b = g^{a_1 \cdot a_2}$. Here, g is the generator of a cyclic group. This security model can also be relaxed into indistinguishability. More specifically, instead of computing b, the adversary is given another value R as input and is to decide whether $R = b$ or not.

Either party in a two-party setting could serve as an adversary aiming to learn the other's confidential input. A very basic security model can be defined as follows:

7.6 Defining Security for Interactive Algorithms

Input Confidentiality

Input: (a_i, b, ic_i, IC)
Output: a_{3-i} satisfying that

- ic_i is the internal coins chosen by party i,
- IC is the communication data by the algorithm for generating b, and
- (b, b) is a pair of output generated from $Alg(a_1; a_2)$.

In this security model, given all information from one party, the adversary is to compute the input belonging to another party. It is important to note that this security model implies two security definitions for two parties. In general, we need to prove these separately because the abstracted computing problems might be different for $i = 1$ and $i = 2$.

7.6.4 Learn-Nothing Security for $Alg(x_1; x_2) \to (y_1, y_2)$

We introduce the first security model where either party is trying to learn more secret than the total of input and output this party can gain. The first security model is presented as follows:

Learn-Nothing Confidentiality (1)

Input: (a_i, b_i, ic_i, IC)
Output: s satisfying that

- ic_i is the internal coins chosen by party i following the algorithm,
- IC is the communication messages by the algorithm,
- (b_1, b_2) is a pair of output generated from $Alg(a_1; a_2)$, and
- No PPT algorithm can compute s from (a_i, b_i).

In this model, given (a_i, b_i, ic_i, IC), the adversary is to compute any secret s that cannot be computed from (a_i, b_i). This learn-nothing confidentiality is passive because ic_i and IC are exactly generated by the interactive algorithm.

Next, we introduce the second security model where the adversary is given an oracle and therefore can freely interact with this oracle. For example, the adversary does not need to follow the algorithm when interacting with the oracle.

Learn-Nothing Confidentiality (2)

Input: $\mathcal{O}$ (one-time access)
Output: Any (a_i, b_i, s) satisfying that

- (b_1, b_2) is a pair of output generated from $Alg(a_1; a_2)$, and
- No PPT algorithm can compute s from (a_i, b_i).

Oracle $\mathcal{O}$: To interact with party i, it performs as party $j = 3 - i$ at running the interactive algorithm $Alg(x_1; x_2)$ with a_j as the input. The oracle will terminate once output has been returned or there is an error.

In this security model, given an oracle, the adversary is to compute any secret that cannot be computed from (a_i, b_i). Here, a_i is any input actively chosen by the adversary, and b_i is the output received from the oracle. Further, ic_i and other intermediate messages within IC can be generated by the adversary without following the interactive algorithm. We note that this model description is somewhat unclear or imprecise when there is an error and the oracle terminates without returning anything. This will be revisited and revised later.

In comparison with the first learn-nothing confidentiality, the second security model is stronger (i.e., easier for the adversary to break). If an interactive algorithm is secure in the second security model, it means that the adversary cannot learn any secret even if the adversary tampers with the right messages (generated by the interactive algorithm) sent from the adversary to the oracle during interactions. For example, during the interaction, when it is the adversary's turn to choose a random number r from $\mathbb{Z}_p$, the adversary always sets $r = 1$. In other words, the second security model implies both confidentiality (as in the first security model) and integrity (resistant to illegal changes or modifications by the adversary who did not follow the interactive algorithm).

7.6.5 Hidden-Target Security for $Alg(x_1; x_2) \to (y_1, y_2)$

The interactive algorithm $Alg(x_1; x_2) \to (y_1, y_2)$ can also be defined for hidden-target security. A proper security model is defined follows:

Output Confidentiality

Input: $\mathcal{O}$ (n-time access)
Output: Any (a_i, b_i) satisfying that

- (b_1, b_2) is a pair of output generated from $Alg(a_1; a_2)$, and

- No query on a_i to the oracle.

Oracle $\mathcal{O}$: It performs as party $j = 3-i$ at running the interactive algorithm $Alg(x_1; x_2)$ with a_j as the input.

In this security model, given an oracle with n-time access, the adversary is to compute a pair (a_i, b_i) for a new input a_i without being queried to the oracle. One primitive having this kind of security model is the interactive signing algorithm in blind signatures [41], where a_i is a message to be signed and b_i is a signature on a_i. The security model says that an adversary, after interacting with the signing process for receiving n signatures, cannot forge one more signature on a new message.

We have completed the introduction to security definitions for interactive algorithms. They provide a high-level view of what security models for protocols look like introduced in the next section.

7.7 Security Definition for a Cryptographic Primitive (Protocol)

Previously, we introduced the security models for interactive algorithms. Since a cryptographic protocol is primarily composed of one interactive algorithm, it seems that those security models can be applied to define the security of protocols. In this section, we explain why those security models are impractical and introduce how to revise the learn-nothing security definition for a cryptographic protocol into security definitions for cryptographic schemes.

7.7.1 Security Model, Revisited

In Section 7.6.4, we introduced two security models of learn-nothing confidentiality for the abstracted interactive algorithm $Alg(x_1; x_2) \to (y_1, y_2)$, as given in Figure 7.8. In the first security model, the input is $x = (a_i, b_i, ic_i, IC)$ and the output is $y = s$, where s can be any output as long as it cannot be computed by any PPT algorithm from (a_i, b_i). In other words, the security definition states that the algorithm $Alg(x_1; x_2) \to (y_1, y_2)$ is insecure if

- There exist s and a PPT algorithm such that this PPT algorithm can compute s from (a_i, b_i, ic_i, IC) with non-negligible probability, and
- Any PPT algorithm can only compute s from (a_i, b_i) with negligible probability.

This kind of learn-nothing security model is also equivalent to a computing problem, but there is no clear relation function R satisfying $R(x, y) = 1$ to link input and output. This kind of computing problem can be seen as composed of an infinite

---

Learn-Nothing Confidentiality (1)

Input: (a_i, b_i, ic_i, IC)
Output: s satisfying that

- ic_i is the internal coins chosen by party i following the algorithm,
- IC is the communication messages by the algorithm,
- (b_1, b_2) is a pair of output generated from $Alg(a_1; a_2)$, and
- No PPT algorithm can compute s from (a_i, b_i).

Learn-Nothing Confidentiality (2)

Input: $\mathcal{O}$ (one-time access)
Output: Any (a_i, b_i, s) satisfying that

- (b_1, b_2) is a pair of output generated from $Alg(a_1; a_2)$, and
- No PPT algorithm can compute s from (a_i, b_i).

Oracle $\mathcal{O}$:   It performs as party $j = 3 - i$ at running the interactive algorithm $Alg(x_1; x_2)$ with a_j as the input.

Fig. 7.8 Revisit of learn-nothing confidentiality

number of relation functions to represent the infinite cases of "any s" that can be learned from (a_i, b_i, ic_i, IC) but cannot be learned from (a_i, b_i). Although this security model is not wrong in definition, it is impractical and impossible to analyze the complexity of solving this computing problem by examining relation functions one by one due to its infinity. Therefore, the security model for a cryptographic protocol should be rebuilt in such a way that what the adversary is going to output is well-structured and related to input within one relation function.

7.7.2 Important Lemma

In the first security model of learn-nothing confidentiality, given (a_i, b_i, ic_i, IC), the adversary is to compute any s that cannot be computed from (a_i, b_i). To remove the infinite cases of s in the definition, the cryptology community has adopted the help of the important lemma as follows.

Lemma 7.1 (Learning Identical) *Let D_0, D_1 be two probability ensembles and x_0, x_1 be their sampled variables, respectively. If D_0 and D_1 are indistinguishable by all PPT adversaries (under some assumption), namely*

$$|\Pr[\mathcal{A}(D_0, D_1, \kappa, x_0) = 1] - \Pr[\mathcal{A}(D_0, D_1, \kappa, x_1) = 1]| \leq \epsilon(\kappa),$$

where $\epsilon(\kappa)$ is a negligible function in κ, we have what all PPT adversaries can learn from x_0 and from x_1 are identical except with negligible probability.

7.7 Security Definition for a Cryptographic Primitive (Protocol) 207

This learning-identical lemma is unique in this book. We propose it based on many references toward defining the security of cryptographic protocols and our personal understanding. It shows how to use indistinguishability to guarantee learn-nothing security without formally defining what learn-nothing security is. We stress that defining learn-nothing security (without mentioning any additional secret s) is rather challenging in the literature. This lemma can be seen as a very smart solution proposed by our academic colleagues. It is a claim, thesis, or assumption because it is still unknown (at least to the authors of this book) how to prove the correctness or incorrectness of this lemma.

Unfortunately, this lemma cannot be directly applied to revise the security model of learn-nothing confidentiality. This is because (a_i, b_i, ic_i, IC) and (a_i, b_i) are instances with different numbers of elements and therefore distinguishable. They cannot be directly set as variables from ensembles D_1, D_0, respectively. To solve the distinguishability issue, the cryptology community has invented "simulation" to mask the second ensemble generating (a_i, b_i) into a third ensemble, to be indistinguishable from the first ensemble (a_i, b_i, ic_i, IC).

7.7.3 Real-Ideal World Paradigm

The lemma introduced in the above subsection has brought "new" terms in the security definition for learn-nothing confidentiality, including ensembles and indistinguishability. To clarify the meaning of ensembles, the cryptology community has adopted the real-ideal world paradigm in its description.

An ideal world is used to emulate the ensemble or the algorithm that generates (a_i, b_i). In the ideal world, when two parties run the interactive algorithm $Alg(x_1; x_2)$ together, each party will securely send the input $x_i = a_i$ to a trusted third party (TTP, referred to as *Functionality* in most references). After receiving inputs from all parties, the TTP simply computes $b_1 = f_1(a_1, a_2)$ and $b_2 = f_2(a_1, a_2)$, and returns the results to all parties, respectively. In this ideal world, no matter which party is the adversary, it can only know the input a_i sent to the TTP and b_i sent by the TTP. Therefore, an interactive algorithm in this ideal world must be secure against adversaries who aim to learn more than (a_i, b_i).

A real world is used to emulate the ensemble or the algorithm that generates (a_i, b_i, ic_i, IC). In the real world, when two parties run the interactive algorithm $Alg(x_1; x_2)$ together, each party will interact with the other directly, namely without the help of a trusted third party. In this real world, each party needs to be involved in computing, including choosing internal coins ic_i and exchanging communicated messages IC. Therefore, an interactive algorithm in this real world allows the adversary to see (a_i, b_i, ic_i, IC), which is more than (a_i, b_i).

The learn-nothing security in the real-ideal paradigm aims to define that no PPT adversary can learn more knowledge from the real world than the ideal world.

7.7.4 Look-Real-but-Simulated-from-Ideal World

The real world and ideal world are distinguishable by the adversary. To obtain indistinguishable worlds for proving learn-nothing confidentiality, an intermediate world has been invented using simulation to be placed between the ideal world and the real world, which we call *look-real-but-simulated-from-ideal* world (short as simulated world). Informally speaking, a simulator is going to use an ideal world as input to generate a simulated world, which will be indistinguishable from a real world from the view of PPT adversaries.

To help beginners understand this simulated world, we use a simple example as follows. Let $(\mathbb{G}, g, p)$ be a cyclic group, where $\mathbb{G}$ is the set of group element, g is the group generator, and p is the group order.

- In the ideal world, the adversary will receive instance (g, g^a, g^b), where a, b are randomly chosen from $\mathbb{Z}_p$.
- In the real world, the adversary will receive instance (g, g^a, g^b, g^{ab}), where a, b are randomly chosen from $\mathbb{Z}_p$.
- In the simulated world, the adversary will receive instance generated by a simulator on input (g, g^a, g^b) from ideal world as follows.
  1. Choose a random integer c from $\mathbb{Z}_p$ and compute g^c.
  2. Return instance (g, g^a, g^b, g^c).

  We have (g, g^a, g^b, g^c) is an instance generated by a look-real-but-simulated-from-ideal world.

Given a world that is either a real world or a simulated world, the adversary cannot distinguish it (namely "look real") on the assumption that it is computationally hard to distinguish the tuple (g, g^a, g^b, g^{ab}) from the tuple (g, g^a, g^b, g^c).

As a result, we can claim that what the adversary can learn from the real world is the same as from the ideal world. The simulated world is generated from the ideal world such that what all PPT adversaries can learn from these two worlds is identical. Since the real world and the simulated world are (computationally) indistinguishable, all PPT adversaries will also learn identical knowledge from them except with negligible probability according to Lemma 7.1. Therefore, the claimed result holds. We have provided a relation overview in Figure 7.9.

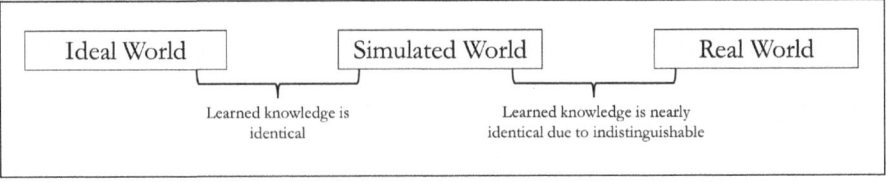

Fig. 7.9 Relations among three worlds

7.7 Security Definition for a Cryptographic Primitive (Protocol)

Back to the learn-nothing confidentiality of $Alg(x_1; x_2)$ using the ideal-real world paradigm, learn-nothing security is defined as ensuring that what the adversary can learn from these two worlds is "nearly" the same. The security holds if

- There exists a simulated world where the instance (a_i, b_i, ic'_i, IC') in this world can be simulated from (a_i, b_i) in the ideal world (meaning that what the adversary can learn from the simulated world and from the ideal world is identical), and
- The simulated instance (a_i, b_i, ic'_i, IC') is computationally indistinguishable from (a_i, b_i, ic_i, IC) generated in the real world (meaning that what the adversary can learn from the simulated world and from the real world is nearly identical due to indistinguishability).

It is important to note that our introduction to learn-nothing confidentiality up until now is rather informal, focusing on clarifying concepts. All knowledge will be put together into formal definitions introduced in the next subsection.

7.7.5 Semi-Honest Security

The framework of a security model has two main parts: what the adversary knows (can do), and what the adversary aims to break. In the cryptology community, the first attempt at defining the input component for learn-nothing security of an interactive algorithm (between two parties) is called the semi-honest assumption.

In the semi-honest setting, we assume that both parties have completed the interactive algorithm honestly, and one of the parties has later been corrupted, such that what this party has recorded and known, (a_i, b_i, ic_i, IC), is gained by the adversary. The adversary's goal is to analyze the view (a_i, b_i, ic_i, IC) and attempt to learn something more than (a_i, b_i), which it can only learn in the ideal world.

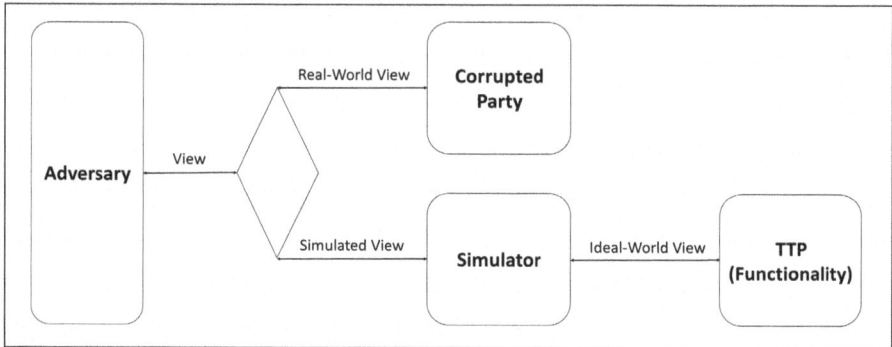

Fig. 7.10 Semi-honest security and view

In the security definition under the semi-honest setting, the core is the real-world view and the simulated-world view. A simulator uses the ideal-world view to simulate the real-world view. As long as the real-world view and the simulated-world view are indistinguishable by the adversary, learn-nothing security holds, as guaranteed by Lemma 7.1. In other words, given one view, PPT adversaries cannot distinguish whether it comes from the corrupted party in the real world or from a simulator (see Figure 7.10).

Now, we can present the security model for semi-honest security using the input-output framework without "any s" in definition.

Semi-Honest Security Model

Input: (a_i, b_i, ic_i^c, IC^c)
Output: $c' \in \{0, 1\}$ satisfying that

- $c' = c$, c is randomly chosen from $\{0, 1\}$,
- (a_i, b_i, ic_i^0, IC^0) is the real-world view (a_i, b_i, ic_i, IC), and
- (a_i, b_i, ic_i^1, IC^1) is a simulated view generated by a PPT simulator from ideal-world view (a_i, b_i).

This security model is still different from those security models for cryptographic schemes because it involves "a simulator". We emphasize that this simulator cannot be "any simulator" but "a simulator satisfying requirements". Otherwise, it is very easy for the adversary to distinguish. For example, a simulator simply sets $(a_i, b_i, ic_i^1, IC^1) = (a_i, b_i, 0, 0)$, which is distinguishable from (a_i, b_i, ic_i, IC). Therefore, semi-honest security in this book is defined as follows.

Definition 7.2 (Semi-Honest Security) Let $Alg(x_1; x_2) \to (y_1, y_2)$. We say that the algorithm is semi-honest secure if there exists a PPT simulator such that no PPT adversary has non-negligible advantage in correctly guessing c in the semi-honest security model, where the probability is taken over all internal coin tosses of related algorithms.

We present the above security definition to help beginners learn the security definitions for cryptographic protocols, building upon the knowledge of security definitions for cryptographic schemes. It is important to note that the cryptology community does not use Definition 7.2 with a separate security model to define semi-honest security. Instead, the security model is merged into the security definition, eliminating the need for a separate security model. In other words, the security definitions presented for protocols differ significantly from those for schemes. We attribute these differences to the diversity of researchers' preferences and the distinct characteristics between schemes and protocols. To follow a widely accepted definition of semi-honest security in the cryptology community, we recommend that beginners refer to the excellent tutorial [37] (Page 7).

7.7.6 Malicious Security

In the cryptology community, for learn-nothing security of an interactive algorithm (between two parties), the second approach, which reinforces the input component, is called the malicious assumption.

In this malicious setting, we assume that one of the parties has been corrupted before running the interactive algorithm with the other party. The adversary, on behalf of the corrupted party, will interact with the other party and may not follow the interactive algorithm. The adversary therefore controls and influences the interaction and aims to learn something more than what it can learn in the ideal world.

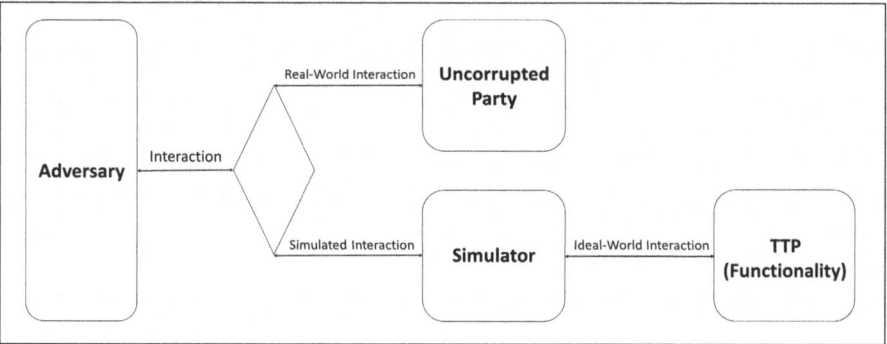

Fig. 7.11 Malicious security and interaction

In the security definition under the malicious setting, the core consists of the real-world interaction and the simulated-world interaction. A simulator uses interactions with the trusted third party (TTP) in the ideal world to simulate as the uncorrupted party interacting with the adversary (corrupted party) in the real world. As long as the real-world interaction and the simulated-world interaction are indistinguishable by the adversary, learn-nothing security holds, according to Lemma 7.1. That is, when a probabilistic polynomial-time (PPT) adversary interacts with uncorrupted party, it cannot distinguish whether it is interacting with uncorrupted party in the real world or the simulator (Figure 7.11). In comparison to the simulator in the semi-honest setting, this simulator acts as the uncorrupted party in front of the adversary and as the adversary (corrupted party) in front of the TTP in the ideal world (Figure 7.12).

Based on the above explanation, we can present the security model for malicious security using the input-output framework without "any s" in definition. The main difference compared to the previous model is using party $\mathcal{P}^c$ as the input instead of view (computational result).

Malicious Security Model

Input: $\mathcal{P}^c$
Output: $c' \in \{0, 1\}$ satisfying that

- $c' = c$, c is randomly chosen from $\{0, 1\}$,
- $\mathcal{P}^0$ is another uncorrupted party running $Alg(x_1; x_2)$ together, and
- $\mathcal{P}^1$ is the simulator who simulates as the another uncorrupted party interacting with the adversary, and also simulates as the adversary interacting with the TTP in the ideal world.

Similarly, the simulator cannot be any simulator but a simulator satisfying requirements. The malicious security is defined as follows:

Definition 7.3 (Malicious Security) Let $Alg(x_1; x_2) \rightarrow (y_1, y_2)$. We say that the algorithm is malicious secure if there exists a PPT simulator such that no PPT adversary has non-negligible advantage in correctly guessing c in the malicious security model, where the probability is taken over all internal coin tosses of related algorithms.

In comparison with semi-honest security, malicious security has an identical security definition except for the security model. Our introduction to malicious security can be seen as an introduction to understanding security definitions for protocols. Widely accepted definitions of malicious security without a security model and with more precise formulations can also be found in [37] (Page 34).

7.7.7 Comparison of Semi-Honest and Malicious

We compare the key differences between the definitions of semi-honest security and malicious security for two-party computation, abstracted as $Alg(x_1; x_2) \rightarrow (y_1, y_2)$, in Figure 7.12. Both security definitions involve a simulator.

- In semi-honest security, the simulator's input is what the corrupted party knows in the ideal world. The simulator will generate a final view such that the adversary cannot distinguish whether the view represents what the corrupted party knows in the real world or what the simulator has generated.
- In malicious security, the simulator has no input but can access the TTP functionality in the ideal world on behalf of the corrupted party. The simulator will interact with the adversary in such a way that the adversary cannot distinguish whether it is interacting with another uncorrupted party or with the simulator.

Both security definitions require the existence of such a simulator to achieve security. It is important to note that the simulator has no input in the malicious

7.7 Security Definition for a Cryptographic Primitive (Protocol)

security definition, yet it must send the adversary's input to the TTP in the ideal world. Otherwise, the simulator cannot simulate as the corrupted party (adversary) in the ideal world. Without receiving information from the TTP, the simulator will fail in simulating as the uncorrupted party in the real world. To satisfy the malicious security definition, the simulator must find a way to extract the adversary's input in the real world in order to interact with the TTP functionality in the ideal world on behalf of the corrupted party (see interactions in Figure 7.12).

	Semi-Honest Security	**Malicious Security**
Corruption Time	After Running protocol	Before running protocol
Simulation Party	Corrupted party	Uncorrupted party
Indistinguishable Object	Final View	Interaction
Simulator's Input	View of corrupted party in ideal world	Nothing but can access TTP functionality in ideal world

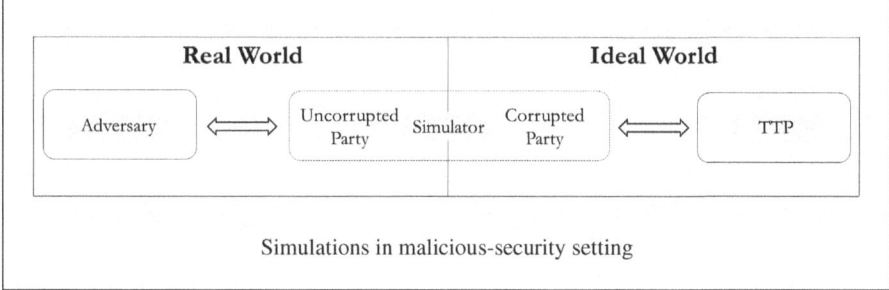

Fig. 7.12 Key difference between semi-honest security and malicious security

There exists a gap between semi-honest security and malicious security in practical applications. Consider a scenario where the adversary is a curious party who participates in an interactive algorithm with another party but honestly adheres to its protocol. This scenario differs from both the semi-honest and malicious settings. A security proof in the semi-honest setting is insufficient to guarantee protection against such an adversary, as this model only ensures the final view remains indistinguishable and does not allow the adversary to access intermediate processes or select internal coins. In contrast, a security proof in the malicious setting is unnecessary to ensure security against this type of adversary.

> **! Attention**
>
> This book might have addressed the most significant challenge in understanding security definitions for protocols. However, due to the authors' limited knowledge in this area, the introduction remains quite basic. The malicious security defined in academic papers is much more complex with a detailed ideal-world definition.

7.8 Practice Makes Perfect: Exercises

? Question 36

A security property can be seen as a shared characteristic of security models for different cryptographic primitives. We have collected part of security properties (notions) from the literature as follows.

1. Adaptive Security
2. Anonymous Security
3. Authenticity Secure
4. Binding Security
5. Chosen-Ciphertext Attacks
6. Chosen-Message Attacks
7. Chosen-Plaintext Attacks
8. Collision-Resistance Security
9. Computationally Secure
10. Concurrent Security
11. Confidentiality Secure
12. Dishonest-Majority Security
13. Forward Security
14. Hiding Security
15. Hidden-Target Security
16. Information-Theoretically secure
17. Indistinguishable Security
18. Integrity Secure
19. Key-Only Attacks
20. Leakage-Resistance Security
21. Learn-Nothing Security
22. Malicious Security
23. Multi-User Security
24. Non-Malleable Security
25. One-More Security
26. One-Way Security
27. Quantum Chosen-Message Attacks
28. Perfect Security
29. Selective Security
30. Selective-Opening Security
31. Semantic Security
32. Semi-Honest Security
33. Sequential Security
34. Simulation-Based Security
35. Soundness Security
36. Statistical Security
37. Subversion-Resilient Security

38. Unforgeable Security
39. Universal-Composability Security
40. Unlinkable Security

Understanding the above security properties is very beneficial for understanding security models. Therefore, for each property, you are asked to use external literature and readings to answer the following three questions

- Is this security property related to (1) adversary's computational model, (2) what the adversary knows or can query (namely the input in the framework of security model), or (3) what the adversary aims to do (namely the output in the framework of security model)?
- What are the characteristics of this security property inside security models?
- Which cryptographic primitive has been defined with this security property?

Take the first security property as an example. You are expected to give the following answers: *Adaptive security is a characteristic belonging to (2) where the adversary can choose what to query one by one after knowing some information (e.g., public key) in security models. The security definition for digital signatures have included this property allowing the adversary to adaptively choose messages for signature queries.*

? Question 37

Read the following security model for the abstracted secret keying algorithm.

Input Confidentiality (Variant)

Input: (a_1, a_2, pk, b_1, b_2)
Output: sk satisfying that

- pk is the public key of sk, and
- (b_1, b_2) is a pair of output generated from $Key(a_1, a_2, sk)$.

Prove that output confidentiality (2) implies this input confidentiality.

? Question 38

Define security for your proposed primitive *Lockable Identity-Based Encryption* in Section 6.9.

? Question 39

Define security for your proposed primitive *Relationship Identity-Based Encryption* in Section 6.9.

? Question 40

Define security for your proposed primitive *Registered Hierarchical Identity-Based Encryption* in Section 6.9.

? Question 41

Define security for your proposed primitive *Honeypot Identity-Based Encryption* in Section 6.9.

? Question 42

Define security for your proposed primitive *Partially Re-Encryptable Identity-Based Encryption* in Section 6.9.

? Question 43

Define security for your proposed primitive *Classifiable Identity-Based Encryption* in Section 6.9.

? Question 44

Define security for your proposed primitive *Order-Preserving Identity-Based Encryption* in Section 6.9.

Chapter 8
Other Readings

Abstract In this chapter, we provide supplementary readings that summarize and introduce related concepts (notations, syntax, and terms) discussed in previous chapters, which were difficult to incorporate elsewhere. These readings primarily reflect our thoughts and perspectives.

8.1 Definitions: Incomplete by Design

A definition is often the first step in understanding a concept. This initial step is usually incomplete by design for two main reasons.

We should start the first step with simplicity and clarity. Definitions are intended to be accessible by providing a clear foundation that allows people to build upon them without overloading with details. Simplicity ensures that complex ideas can be introduced and understood without being overwhelming. By focusing on clarity, a definition helps unify understanding, offering an initial framework that is comprehensible to everyone, regardless of background. For example, we often use syntax definitions to understand a cryptographic primitive without examining the intermediate operations within algorithms or constructions. This simplicity is not a flaw but a strategic choice to make the concept digestible and usable from the start. However, this simplicity and clarity can also cause misunderstandings if not supplemented with further explanation or background. For instance, a security definition may appear compact, but it often includes terms like PPT adversaries, negligible functions, and advantage that require separate learning.

We actually do not know the complete meaning of some concepts but understand their meaning within certain definitions. Many concepts are inherently complex or even partially unknown, so definitions often represent an approximation rather than a full picture. For example, the philosophical meanings of life, computational security, and learn-nothing security for protocols are three concepts hard to be completely and precisely defined. We use probabilistic polynomial-time to distinguish between legal users and adversaries in computing, but is this precisely accurate? Let us examine an example where $f_\mathcal{U}(\kappa)$ denotes the polynomial-time cost for users and $f_\mathcal{A}(\kappa)$ denotes the non-polynomial-time cost for adversaries in a scheme.

$$f_\mathcal{U}(\kappa) = \kappa^{1000000090000000000500000000000020000000000700000000},$$
$$f_\mathcal{A}(\kappa) = \frac{1}{2^{1000000090000000000500000000000020000000000700000000}} \cdot 2^\kappa.$$

When $\kappa = 128$, it is obvious to see that $f_\mathcal{U}(\kappa)$ is much larger than $f_\mathcal{A}(\kappa)$. Therefore, a proposed scheme meeting the computational efficiency requirements of the definition might be impractical in the real world. Nevertheless, a proper and formal definition provides a way to communicate concepts as they are currently understood, even if not capturing every case. Definitions can evolve over time, growing closer to an ideal form.

In summary, an incomplete yet simple definition helps us successfully start the journey of research. Our understanding and definitions evolve year by year, guiding the human toward the discovery of universal truths. At the current stage, cryptography and its security are defined by humans, for humans only. The definition excludes any hypothetical alien intelligences as adversaries, if they exist.

8.2 $\mathcal{P} = \mathcal{NP}$ and Cryptography

In the field of computational complexity, a complexity class is a set of computing problems that share common and well-defined characteristics. Researchers are concerned with the size of a defined complexity class. For example, is complexity class A a subset of complexity class B? A well-known example is the $\mathcal{P}$ vs. $\mathcal{NP}$ problem, which was defined in Section 4.4.1.

In cryptography, instead of focusing on the boundary of a complexity class, researchers are concerned with the set of algorithms that can solve a specific computing problem, and whether this set contains a probabilistic polynomial-time (PPT) algorithm. This is because the security of a cryptographic scheme generally requires that no PPT algorithm exists within this set.

Although the main concerns in complexity theory and cryptography are not identical, it is generally accepted that $\mathcal{P} \neq \mathcal{NP}$ is fundamental to the security of cryptography. That is, if $\mathcal{P} = \mathcal{NP}$, it would undermine cryptographic security. However, we clarify that while $\mathcal{P} = \mathcal{NP}$ would invalidate all known security definitions for cryptography, it would not immediately break cryptographic schemes. There are two additional steps required for breaking a cryptographic scheme.

- If $\mathcal{P} = \mathcal{NP}$, it implies the existence of PPT algorithms in the set capable of breaking a given scheme. However, to successfully break the scheme, one must find the appropriate PPT algorithm from this set, which contains an infinite number of algorithms.

- Furthermore, the identified PPT algorithm must remain efficient for the given security parameter that generates the scheme. Otherwise, it would still be impractical. For example, the only found polynomial-time algorithm with following time complexity

$$f_{\mathcal{A}}(\kappa) = \kappa^{9999999999959999999999999999999929999999999999999999979999999999}$$

would be highly inefficient to break a scheme generated with security parameter $\kappa = 128$.

Without completing these two steps, the given cryptographic scheme is still secure in the real-world applications, although its security is dead already from the view of security definition.

In summary, even if $\mathcal{P} = \mathcal{NP}$ were true, cryptographic schemes with computational security could still exist. However, cryptographic security would need to be rebuilt and redefined using entirely new foundations.

8.3 Clarifying Algorithmic Terms

Algorithms lie at the core of both computational complexity and cryptography. Terms such as polynomial time, non-polynomial time, secure, efficient, inefficient, easy, and hard are often used to describe these algorithms and constructions. We clarify the distinctions among these terms as follows:

- In the context of complexity, algorithms for solving computing problems are categorized as either polynomial-time or non-polynomial-time algorithms.
- In the context of computation, the operations within an algorithm are considered computationally efficient if its computational cost is polynomial-time. Conversely, it is deemed computationally inefficient if its computational cost is non-polynomial-time.
- In the context of security, breaking a cryptographic scheme is computationally hard or a cryptographic scheme is computationally secure if no polynomial-time attacking algorithm exists, meaning all attacking algorithms are non-polynomial-time. Conversely, breaking a cryptographic scheme would be computationally easy if a polynomial-time attacking algorithm existed.

In summary, while these terms have distinct meanings across subject areas, they revolve around the term "polynomial-time". Beginners should carefully select these terms with close attention to context and purpose: "efficient" and "inefficient" describe the feasibility of operations or computations; "easy" and "hard" refer specifically to the difficulty of breaking cryptographic schemes; "secure" refers to the result that no PPT algorithm can break schemes with non-negligible advantage.

8.4 Security Definition, Revisited

The security definition for a different cryptographic primitive is usually distinct. However, regardless of the specific security definition, it must include the selection of terms related to the following keywords.

Summary

$$\text{Security Definition} = \begin{cases} \text{Adversaries} \begin{cases} \text{Computational Models} \\ \text{Negligible Advantage} \end{cases} \\ \text{Security Model} \begin{cases} \text{Input \& Oracle} \\ \text{Output \& Success Condition} \end{cases} \end{cases}$$

Firstly, adversaries must be well-defined using a computational model. If they (security models) are too weak, we might have a proposed scheme that is secure according to the security definition but is actually insecure in the real world. If they are too powerful, we might have a proposed scheme that is insecure according to the security definition but is actually secure in the physical world. Probabilistic polynomial-time (PPT) algorithms are the most basic computational models in all cases, but they can be upgraded and replaced with non-uniform PPT algorithms or quantum polynomial-time (QPT) algorithms depending on the motivations. All security definitions require that any algorithm within the selected computational model can break it only with negligible advantage in a security model.

Secondly, a security model consists of input, oracle, output, and success condition, where all selected terms depend on the algorithms within the cryptographic primitive and its security requirements. A security model can be strengthened or enhanced by reinforcing input (oracles) or relaxing output. There can be many variants of security models for the same cryptographic primitive due to different applications and distinct security requirements. As long as the input, oracles, output, or success condition has been defined differently, it will result in a different security model. Compared to selecting adversaries, the process of defining a security model is much more complex than defining adversaries. If the defined syntax does not achieve a negligible advantage in a security model, either the syntax definition or the security model is incorrect.

After all terms related to adversaries and security models have been chosen, the remaining part of the security definition is the presentation. We emphasize again that the final presentation of a security definition may vary significantly, depending on the primitives (schemes or protocols) and also the authors' preferences.

8.5 Cryptographic Definition, Revisited

At the beginning of this book, we introduced the definition of digital signatures by separating syntax definition and security definition for several reasons. It is important to note that defining an $\mathcal{X}$-secure $\mathcal{Y}$ does not necessarily require a separation of syntax and security especially when both of them are compact in definitions. For example, zero-knowledge proofs can be defined by combining syntax and security definitions together including completeness, soundness, and zero-knowledge. Beginners should not feel lost when encountering a different presentation of a security definition.

We use one-way function as a detailed example to illustrate how syntax and security can be combined in a definition. The full name of a one-way function should be "one-way computationally-efficient function", where "computationally-efficient" represents the existence of an efficient algorithm in syntax and "one-way" represents the security property. The syntax definition and security definition are presented together as follows.

Definition 8.5.1 (One-Way Function). *A function* $f : \{0,1\}^* \to \{0,1\}^*$ *is called one-way function if:*

- *There exists a probabilistic polynomial-time algorithm such that on input x the algorithm outputs $f(x)$ in polynomial time in κ. Here we define $|x| = \kappa$.*
- *Every probabilistic polynomial-time algorithm $\mathcal{A}$ will invert $f(x)$ with negligible probability $\epsilon(\kappa)$.*

$$\Pr\left[x \leftarrow \{0,1\}^\kappa; x^* \leftarrow \mathcal{A}(f(x), \kappa) : f(x^*) = f(x)\right] = \epsilon(\kappa),$$

where the probability $\epsilon(\kappa)$ is taken over all random x and all internal coin tosses of related algorithms.

We deliberately close this book with the cryptographic definition for one-way function. We chose this concept because one-way function marks not the end, but the true beginning of research in modern cryptography.

May this definition and all the knowledge in this book serve as a stepping stone, guiding your cryptologic journey!

References

1. Abdalla, M., Bellare, M., Catalano, D., Kiltz, E., Kohno, T., Lange, T., Malone-Lee, J., Neven, G., Paillier, P., Shi, H.: Searchable encryption revisited: Consistency properties, relation to anonymous ibe, and extensions. In: V. Shoup (ed.) CRYPTO 2005, *Lecture Notes in Computer Science*, vol. 3621, pp. 205–222. Springer (2005). URL https://doi.org/10.1007/11535218_13
2. Abdalla, M., Dent, A.W., Malone-Lee, J., Neven, G., Phan, D.H., Smart, N.P.: Identity-based traitor tracing. In: T. Okamoto, X. Wang (eds.) PKC 2007, *Lecture Notes in Computer Science*, vol. 4450, pp. 361–376. Springer (2007). URL https://doi.org/10.1007/978-3-540-71677-8_24
3. Al-Riyami, S.S., Paterson, K.G.: Certificateless public key cryptography. In: C. Laih (ed.) ASIACRYPT 2003, *Lecture Notes in Computer Science*, vol. 2894, pp. 452–473. Springer (2003). URL https://doi.org/10.1007/978-3-540-40061-5_29
4. Alwen, J., Dodis, Y., Wichs, D.: Leakage-resilient public-key cryptography in the bounded-retrieval model. In: S. Halevi (ed.) CRYPTO 2009, *Lecture Notes in Computer Science*, vol. 5677, pp. 36–54. Springer (2009). URL https://doi.org/10.1007/978-3-642-03356-8_3
5. Asharov, G., Lindell, Y., Schneider, T., Zohner, M.: More efficient oblivious transfer extensions with security for malicious adversaries. In: E. Oswald, M. Fischlin (eds.) EUROCRYPT 2015, *Lecture Notes in Computer Science*, vol. 9056, pp. 673–701. Springer (2015). URL https://doi.org/10.1007/978-3-662-46800-5_26
6. Ateniese, G., Burns, R.C., Curtmola, R., Herring, J., Kissner, L., Peterson, Z.N.J., Song, D.X.: Provable data possession at untrusted stores. In: P. Ning, S.D.C. di Vimercati, P.F. Syverson (eds.) ACM CCS 200, pp. 598–609. ACM (2007). URL https://doi.org/10.1145/1315245.1315318
7. Baek, J., Zheng, Y.: Identity-based threshold decryption. In: F. Bao, R.H. Deng, J. Zhou (eds.) PKC 2004, *Lecture Notes in Computer Science*, vol. 2947, pp. 262–276. Springer (2004). URL https://doi.org/10.1007/978-3-540-24632-9_19
8. Bellare, M., Micciancio, D., Warinschi, B.: Foundations of group signatures: Formal definitions, simplified requirements, and a construction based on general assumptions. In: E. Biham (ed.) EUROCRYPT 2003, *Lecture Notes in Computer Science*, vol. 2656, pp. 614–629. Springer (2003). URL https://doi.org/10.1007/3-540-39200-9_38
9. Boneh, D., Boyen, X.: Short signatures without random oracles. In: C. Cachin, J. Camenisch (eds.) EUROCRYPT 2004, *Lecture Notes in Computer Science*, vol. 3027, pp. 56–73. Springer (2004). URL https://doi.org/10.1007/978-3-540-24676-3_4
10. Boneh, D., Boyen, X., Goh, E.: Hierarchical identity based encryption with constant size ciphertext. In: R. Cramer (ed.) EUROCRYPT 2005, *Lecture Notes in Computer Science*, vol. 3494, pp. 440–456. Springer (2005). URL https://doi.org/10.1007/11426639_26

11. Boneh, D., Franklin, M.K.: Identity-based encryption from the weil pairing. In: J. Kilian (ed.) CRYPTO 2001, *Lecture Notes in Computer Science*, vol. 2139, pp. 213–229. Springer (2001). URL https://doi.org/10.1007/3-540-44647-8_13
12. Boneh, D., Gentry, C., Lynn, B., Shacham, H.: Aggregate and verifiably encrypted signatures from bilinear maps. In: E. Biham (ed.) EUROCRYPT 2003, *Lecture Notes in Computer Science*, vol. 2656, pp. 416–432. Springer (2003). URL https://doi.org/10.1007/3-540-39200-9_26
13. Boneh, D., Lynn, B., Shacham, H.: Short signatures from the weil pairing. In: C. Boyd (ed.) ASIACRYPT 2001, *Lecture Notes in Computer Science*, vol. 2248, pp. 514–532. Springer (2001). URL https://doi.org/10.1007/3-540-45682-1_30
14. Boneh, D., Sahai, A., Waters, B.: Functional encryption: Definitions and challenges. In: Y. Ishai (ed.) TCC 2011, *Lecture Notes in Computer Science*, vol. 6597, pp. 253–273. Springer (2011). URL https://doi.org/10.1007/978-3-642-19571-6_16
15. Brzuska, C., Fischlin, M., Lehmann, A., Schröder, D.: Unlinkability of sanitizable signatures. In: P.Q. Nguyen, D. Pointcheval (eds.) PKC 2010, *Lecture Notes in Computer Science*, vol. 6056, pp. 444–461. Springer (2010). URL https://doi.org/10.1007/978-3-642-13013-7_26
16. Camenisch, J., Lysyanskaya, A.: Dynamic accumulators and application to efficient revocation of anonymous credentials. In: M. Yung (ed.) CRYPTO 2002, *Lecture Notes in Computer Science*, vol. 2442, pp. 61–76. Springer (2002). URL https://doi.org/10.1007/3-540-45708-9_5
17. Canetti, R.: Security and composition of multiparty cryptographic protocols. J. Cryptol. **13**(1), 143–202 (2000). URL https://doi.org/10.1007/s001459910006
18. Cramer, R., Damgård, I., Schoenmakers, B.: Proofs of partial knowledge and simplified design of witness hiding protocols. In: Y. Desmedt (ed.) CRYPTO 1994, *Lecture Notes in Computer Science*, vol. 839, pp. 174–187. Springer (1994). URL https://doi.org/10.1007/3-540-48658-5_19
19. Delerablée, C.: Identity-based broadcast encryption with constant size ciphertexts and private keys. In: K. Kurosawa (ed.) ASIACRYPT 2007, *Lecture Notes in Computer Science*, vol. 4833, pp. 200–215. Springer (2007). URL https://doi.org/10.1007/978-3-540-76900-2_12
20. Fiat, A., Shamir, A.: How to prove yourself: Practical solutions to identification and signature problems. In: A.M. Odlyzko (ed.) CRYPTO 1986, *Lecture Notes in Computer Science*, vol. 263, pp. 186–194. Springer (1986). URL https://doi.org/10.1007/3-540-47721-7_12
21. Fischlin, M.: Round-optimal composable blind signatures in the common reference string model. In: C. Dwork (ed.) CRYPTO 2006, *Lecture Notes in Computer Science*, vol. 4117, pp. 60–77. Springer (2006). URL https://doi.org/10.1007/11818175_4
22. Gamal, T.E.: A public key cryptosystem and a signature scheme based on discrete logarithms. IEEE Trans. Inf. Theory **31**(4), 469–472 (1985). URL https://doi.org/10.1109/TIT.1985.1057074
23. Garg, S., Hajiabadi, M., Mahmoody, M., Rahimi, A.: Registration-based encryption: Removing private-key generator from IBE. In: A. Beimel, S. Dziembowski (eds.) TCC 2018, *Lecture Notes in Computer Science*, vol. 11239, pp. 689–718. Springer (2018). URL https://doi.org/10.1007/978-3-030-03807-6_25
24. Gentry, C.: Practical identity-based encryption without random oracles. In: S. Vaudenay (ed.) EUROCRYPT 2006, *Lecture Notes in Computer Science*, vol. 4004, pp. 445–464. Springer (2006). URL https://doi.org/10.1007/11761679_27
25. Gentry, C., Sahai, A., Waters, B.: Homomorphic encryption from learning with errors: Conceptually-simpler, asymptotically-faster, attribute-based. In: R. Canetti, J.A. Garay (eds.) CRYPTO 2013, *Lecture Notes in Computer Science*, vol. 8042, pp. 75–92. Springer (2013). URL https://doi.org/10.1007/978-3-642-40041-4_5
26. Goldreich, O.: The Foundations of Cryptography - Volume 1: Basic Techniques. Cambridge University Press (2001). DOI 10.1017/CBO9780511546891. URL http://www.wisdom.weizmann.ac.il/%7Eoded/foc-vol1.html

27. Goyal, R., Vaikuntanathan, V.: Locally verifiable signature and key aggregation. In: Y. Dodis, T. Shrimpton (eds.) CRYPTO 2022, *Lecture Notes in Computer Science*, vol. 13508, pp. 761–791. Springer (2022). URL https://doi.org/10.1007/978-3-031-15979-4_26
28. Goyal, V.: Reducing trust in the PKG in identity based cryptosystems. In: A. Menezes (ed.) CRYPTO 2007, *Lecture Notes in Computer Science*, vol. 4622, pp. 430–447. Springer (2007). URL https://doi.org/10.1007/978-3-540-74143-5_24
29. Goyal, V., Pandey, O., Sahai, A., Waters, B.: Attribute-based encryption for fine-grained access control of encrypted data. In: A. Juels, R.N. Wright, S.D.C. di Vimercati (eds.) ACM CCS 2006, pp. 89–98. ACM (2006). URL https://doi.org/10.1145/1180405.1180418
30. Green, M., Ateniese, G.: Identity-based proxy re-encryption. In: J. Katz, M. Yung (eds.) ACNS 2007, *Lecture Notes in Computer Science*, vol. 4521, pp. 288–306. Springer (2007). URL https://doi.org/10.1007/978-3-540-72738-5_19
31. Guo, F., Mu, Y., Chen, Z.: Identity-based online/offline encryption. In: G. Tsudik (ed.) FC 2008, *Lecture Notes in Computer Science*, vol. 5143, pp. 247–261. Springer (2008). URL https://doi.org/10.1007/978-3-540-85230-8_22
32. Guo, F., Susilo, W.: Optimal tightness for chain-based unique signatures. In: O. Dunkelman, S. Dziembowski (eds.) EUROCRYPT 202, *Lecture Notes in Computer Science*, vol. 13276, pp. 553–583. Springer (2022). URL https://doi.org/10.1007/978-3-031-07085-3_19
33. Guo, F., Susilo, W., Chen, X., Jiang, P., Lai, J., Zhao, Z.: SoK: Research motivations of public-key cryptography. IACR Cryptol. ePrint Arch. p. 715 (2023). URL https://eprint.iacr.org/2023/715
34. Jager, T., Kiltz, E., Riepel, D., Schäge, S.: Tightly-secure authenticated key exchange, revisited. In: A. Canteaut, F. Standaert (eds.) EUROCRYPT 2021, *Lecture Notes in Computer Science*, vol. 12696, pp. 117–146. Springer (2021). URL https://doi.org/10.1007/978-3-030-77870-5_5
35. Lewko, A.B., Waters, B.: Decentralizing attribute-based encryption. In: K.G. Paterson (ed.) EUROCRYPT 2011, *Lecture Notes in Computer Science*, vol. 6632, pp. 568–588. Springer (2011). URL https://doi.org/10.1007/978-3-642-20465-4_31
36. Lindell, Y.: Composition of Secure Multi-Party Protocols, A Comprehensive Study, *Lecture Notes in Computer Science*, vol. 2815. Springer (2003). URL https://doi.org/10.1007/b13246
37. Lindell, Y.: How to simulate it - A tutorial on the simulation proof technique. IACR Cryptol. ePrint Arch. p. 46 (2016). URL http://eprint.iacr.org/2016/046
38. Liu, J.K., Chu, C., Zhou, J.: Identity-based server-aided decryption. In: U. Parampalli, P. Hawkes (eds.) ACISP 2011, vol. 6812, pp. 337–352. Springer (2011). URL https://doi.org/10.1007/978-3-642-22497-3_22
39. Ma, S.: Identity-based encryption with outsourced equality test in cloud computing. Inf. Sci. **328**, 389–402 (2016). URL https://doi.org/10.1016/j.ins.2015.08.053
40. Pedersen, T.P.: Non-interactive and information-theoretic secure verifiable secret sharing. In: J. Feigenbaum (ed.) CRYPTO 1991, *Lecture Notes in Computer Science*, vol. 576, pp. 129–140. Springer (1991). URL https://doi.org/10.1007/3-540-46766-1_9
41. Pointcheval, D.: Strengthened security for blind signatures. In: K. Nyberg (ed.) EUROCRYPT 1998, *Lecture Notes in Computer Science*, vol. 1403, pp. 391–405. Springer (1998). URL https://doi.org/10.1007/BFb0054141
42. Sahai, A., Waters, B.: Fuzzy identity-based encryption. In: R. Cramer (ed.) EUROCRYPT 2005, *Lecture Notes in Computer Science*, vol. 3494, pp. 457–473. Springer (2005). URL https://doi.org/10.1007/11426639_27
43. Seo, J.H., Emura, K.: Revocable identity-based encryption revisited: Security model and construction. In: K. Kurosawa, G. Hanaoka (eds.) PKC 2013, *Lecture Notes in Computer Science*, vol. 7778, pp. 216–234. Springer (2013). URL https://doi.org/10.1007/978-3-642-36362-7_14

44. Shin, J.S., Jo, M., Hwang, J.Y., Lee, J.: A verifier-based password-authenticated key exchange using tamper-proof hardware. Comput. J. **64**(8), 1293–1302 (2021). URL https://doi.org/10.1093/comjnl/bxaa178
45. Zheng, Y.: Digital signcryption or how to achieve cost(signature & encryption) << cost(signature) + cost(encryption). In: B.S.K. Jr. (ed.) CRYPTO 1997, *Lecture Notes in Computer Science*, vol. 1294, pp. 165–179. Springer (1997). URL https://doi.org/10.1007/BFb0052234

The manufacturer's authorised representative in the EU is Springer Nature Customer Service Centre GmbH, Europaplatz 3, 69115 Heidelberg, Germany. If you have any concerns regarding our products, please contact ProductSafety@springernature.com

Printed and bound by CPI Group (UK) Ltd, Croydon, CR0 4YY
26/03/2026
02078953-0006